JAMES L. PAYNE

LABOR AND POLITICS IN PERU

THE SYSTEM OF POLITICAL BARGAINING

JAMES L. PAYNE

LABOR AND POLITICS
IN PERU

THE SYSTEM OF POLITICAL BARGAINING

NEW HAVEN AND LONDON, YALE UNIVERSITY PRESS

TO MOM AND DAD

PREFACE

Underlying this study is a wholesome respect for the complexities of Peruvian politics. The Peruvian political system is,
from one point of view, more complicated than systems of many
"advanced" nations, for regularities are obscured by the wide
range over which behavior may vary. In order to grasp some of
these regularities we must circumscribe the subject matter of
analysis. Our response to complexity must be a subdivision of the
problem. I have followed this rule in my analysis and have
placed two general limits on the scope of concern.

First, I deal only with periods of what I shall term "free government." Such periods contrast with "authoritarian" or "dictatorial" regimes in that the freedoms to organize, speak, write,
demonstrate, and oppose the government are widely respected.
The period January 1961 to January 1962 during which research
for this study was undertaken formed part of the 1956–62 period of free government under Manuel Prado. The only other
recent free regime was that of Bustamante, 1945–48. I also make
some use of the more distant period of free government under
José Pardo, 1915–19.

The analysis has been confined to free governments simply
because the pattern of interaction in a dictatorship appears to be
substantially different. This is not to say that authoritarian regimes are unrelated to the free governments, for there are a
number of structural similarities. Also, the behavior of the participants during a period of free government is influenced by the
fact that dictatorship is a real possibility. But except for a few
brief comments in the historical account, dictatorship as an alternative pattern is not discussed in this study.

Secondly, as the title indicates, I shall be concerned with the politics of labor, actually organized labor. This restriction of focus makes it possible to study in detail one slice of political interaction in a free regime. It is a large slice, to be sure, and provides certain insights and general principles which apply beyond labor matters. Nevertheless there are many decision-making patterns which fall outside our view.

Turning now to what *has* been dealt with in this study, the subject matter requires a few words of introduction. I am concerned with two general areas which have, in the United States, two distinct academic backgrounds: labor politics and labor relations. The former falls under political science and concentrates on lawmaking, lobbying, and elections. The latter is claimed by labor economics and deals with collective bargaining, the strike, and related economic variables. In Peru it is not only possible but necessary to deal with both areas simultaneously. Labor politics and labor relations are the same thing and I make no distinction between the two.

However, the material of this book is independently relevant to these two areas of inquiry. That is, both the political scientist and the labor economist will find perspectives particularly directed toward his general body of theory.

In the political analysis I have discarded the model of constitutional democracy, something that few writers on Latin American politics have actually done. Analytically it is impractical to view Peruvian politics in a constitutional framework, for constitutionalism is not the modal pattern of interaction. To treat violence and the military coup as aberrations places one in the awkward position of insisting that practically all significant political events of the past half century have been "deviations." Demonstrations, clashes with the police, military takeovers: these are *normal* in a purely descriptive sense. They happen frequently and they are significant.

Consequently, I identify as a system for analysis the pattern of interaction characterized by violence and other extraconstitutional practices. In the same way that elections are central components of a constitutional democracy, the military coup is considered essential to the system in Peru. We cannot speak of "instability" of the system because we are not using a democratic model. The insecurity of the executive in the face of violence is as "normal" and "natural" as the insecurity of the American president at election time. Mass demonstrations and riots are fully a part of the Peruvian pattern, not merely distasteful, peripheral incidents—as they are considered in the United States. When we make violence the focal point of analysis the behavior of the participants becomes understandable and—over a certain range—predictable.

My perspective on labor relations is basically the same, discarding the American model. Instead of speaking in terms of a "developing" system of collective bargaining I construct a model based on the description of what actually happens. For purposes of identification I have employed the term *political bargaining* to describe this basic pattern. We shall see how political bargaining may be clearly distinguished from two other patterns: collective bargaining and legal enactment.

It appears that the general pattern of political bargaining is a common one throughout the world, although the variations are quite numerous. But until we have more detailed knowledge of these bargaining systems it seems unnecessary to subdivide political bargaining into more specific categories. Our present task is merely to establish and explain the existence of a pattern of labor relations which differs fundamentally from collective bargaining.

In expressing my appreciation to those who have assisted me in completing this work, I particularly want to thank Dr. Aaron Wildavsky. His criticisms, advice and moral support over the last four years have been of immense importance in making this book a reality. I also wish to thank Dr. George Lanyi who supported my research venture when encouragement was most needed. I express my sincere appreciation to Dr. Robert Alexander who provided me with much good advice and a bundle of letters of introduction to Peruvian labor leaders.

I am indebted to Benjamin Sowell, Labor Attaché at the

American Embassy in Lima, with whom I had many profitable discussions during my stay in Peru. I express deepest appreciation to Dr. Melvin K. Bers who shared with me his insights into the analysis of labor movements. Warm thanks are due Miss Suzanne Eisenberg who carried many of the heavy secretarial burdens connected with writing this book. Many people have read and criticized parts of the manuscript. For their helpful suggestions I am particularly indebted to Dr. John D. Lewis, Dr. William Glade, Dr. Kenneth Strand, Dr. Robert W. Anderson, Norman King, Oliver Woshinsky, Tony Lanyi, Andrew McFarland, Dr. Norman Bailey, and my father, Dr. William L. Payne.

Finally, I wish to express my gratitude to the many hundreds of Peruvian labor leaders and politicians who shared their time and knowledge with me.

CONTENTS

LIST OF TABLES

LIST OF FIGURES

1 THE LABOR MOVEMENT
IN ITS STRATEGIC ENVIRONMENT

1

THE BARGAINING FRAMEWORK

To understand the labor movement in Peru one must grasp the significance of violence. In the Peruvian context violence is not simply a peripheral phenomenon which can be explained in terms of carelessness, mental disorders, or climate. The individual who believes that riots, assaults, and clashes with the police are manifestations of a "hot-blooded Latin character" has been misled. In Peru violence is a political weapon, widely used by the coolest and most calculating politicians.

We are not speaking of criminal violence or personal feuds. Our concern is with acts of mass violence: demonstrations, parades, assaults on public officials or on government buildings, hunger strikes, sit-down strikes, particular or general strikes. All of these events are politically meaningful: they are usually directed against the executive by a group or groups with a specific purpose in mind.

It might at first appear inaccurate to call, let us say, an entirely peaceful parade an act of violence. And, indeed, if the event is considered separately, then it would not constitute political violence. But most events of this nature cannot be isolated from the context in which they occur. A protest parade has its antecedents and, much more important, it has its possible or probable consequences. Each event bears a relationship to the next,

so that we must speak of a pattern, of a process of political
violence. Perhaps the parade was uneventful, but the demonstration planned for the following evening may produce a bitter
clash with army troops. We cannot say that the parade was not
political violence any more than we can insist that a man is not
fishing unless there is a fish on his line. No participant knows
exactly when actual violence will break out. But all are acutely
sensitive to the relative probabilities of bloodshed at any moment,
and they behave largely on the basis of these probabilities.

Once blood has been spilled, the pattern of violence usually
intensifies: larger demonstrations, more aggressive parades, big-
ger newspaper headlines. Where does it all end? Sometimes it
just blows over. But it may terminate in a military coup against
the president, and all participants, especially the president,
clearly recognize this possibility. Political violence is an intelligible pattern of interaction the end product of which may be the
downfall of the chief executive. In order to explain this conclusion and relate it to the activity of the labor movement we must
analyze the elements of Peruvian politics.

During a period of free government[1] there are three major
political forces: the president and his supporters, the opposition
(including, usually, the left-extremists), and the armed forces.
Each of these participants, or groups of participants, plays a role
quite different from the roles played by their counterparts in
the United States.

The president has an extremely broad range of responsibility.
Placed in his hands are most of the decision-making functions
performed in the United States by Congress, the Supreme Court,
the regulatory agencies, state and local governments. In practice
he is capable of issuing a decree which has the force of law on
almost any conceivable subject. The president's behavior, however, while not curtailed by legal or formal restraints, is tightly
circumscribed by the actions of the opposition parties and their
allies.

The underlying drive for the Peruvian system, the mainspring

1. This term has been defined in the Introduction.

as it were, is the intensity of the conflict between the opposition and the president. Opposition forces do not view politics as a gentlemen's game played for moderate stakes in an atmosphere of restraint. They see it as a struggle of overwhelming significance. The intensity of conflict explains, in large part, the frequent use of violence. Opposition forces see the outcome of the struggle against the executive as more significant than constitutional norms, moral injunctions, or physical safety. We have in American history occasional examples of conflict so intense that it transcended the usual moral and constitutional norms— the Civil War, for example. But in Peru such intense conflict is not occasional; it is the permanent condition of political society.

We may briefly suggest certain conditions which seem to contribute to this high level of conflict intensity between opposition forces and the president.

1. The Peruvian government is, as pointed out above, highly centralized. At the apex of the system is the president. Local and regional governments, Congress, and the courts are in practice subordinate to him on practically all matters of political importance. The chief executive can and does issue authoritative decrees on a wide range of issues. As a consequence of this centralization of decision-making authority the president is considered omnicompetent and hence, omniresponsible. From the price of meat to the backwardness of agriculture; from holes in the streets of a provincial town to the profit rate in the mining industry; when anything goes wrong the executive is considered to have committed a sin of commission or omission. Needless to say, many things do go wrong, and the affected groups hold the incumbent president directly responsible. Whereas in the United States discontent is directed at diverse points in the various decision-making matrices, in Peru the president and his immediate subordinates, being the only decision-makers of consequence, receive its full impact.[2]

2. It is interesting to note that Alexis de Tocqueville, in discussing the causes of the French Revolution, noted a similar centralization under the *ancien régime*: "In times of dearth—and these were frequent in the eighteenth century—everyone expected the Intendant to come to the rescue as a matter

In addition to broadening the responsibility for policies, a dispersal of the decision-making processes also serves in countries like the United States to mitigate the opposition to the existing government. Because opposition forces have, in one way or another, a foothold in the existing system their hostility to it is never total. In the United States a Southerner may be opposed to the incumbent president, but he knows that he can make his views felt in the Senate as well as in local decision-making and administration. But in Peru a group excluded from the executive has no other arena in which to exercise influence. Consequently such a group finds its only practicable alternative is attempting to unseat the president.

2. The large amount of patronage the president dispenses is another factor which contributes to the isolation of the opposition. Whereas in a country like Sweden or Switzerland few posts go to political appointees, in Peru the civil service is based largely on the spoils system. Job hunters (and their friends and relatives) are numerous. In the above-named countries a change of government leaves public employees practically unaffected; in Peru it creates a horde of angered ex-officeholders who see the new president as directly responsible for their loss of employment.[3]

---

of course. For the government was held responsible for all the misfortunes befalling the community; even when these were 'acts of God' such as floods or droughts, the powers-that-be were blamed for them." *The Old Regime and the French Revolution* (New York, Doubleday, 1955), p. 71. In discussing the American system de Tocqueville praised the federal arrangement which insured that "political passion, instead of spreading over the land like a fire on the prairies, spends its strength against the interests and individual passions of every State." *Democracy in America* (New York, Mentor, 1956), p. 85.

3. Under some conditions patronage may not be a significant factor in party conflict, even when the spoils system prevails, since public jobs may not be very attractive. See Frank J. Sorauf, "Patronage and Party," *Midwest Journal of Political Science*, 3 (1959), 115–26, especially pp. 120–21. However, in Peru both the prestige value of public employment and the depressed state of the labor market do make government employment a coveted position. Merle Kling has, somewhat indirectly, pointed to the patronage problem in explaining violence and military coups in Latin America in "Toward a Theory of Power and Political Instability in Latin America," *Western Political Quarterly*, 9 (1956), 21–35.

3. Another condition which contributes to the intense conflict found in Peruvian society is the existence of exclusive, partisan communication patterns. Holders of different political views tend to locate themselves in the communication channel that reinforces their position. This phenomenon is most clearly seen in the case of the Aprista party organization. The Apristas have their own cafeteria and barber shop, their own medical assistance staff, soccer teams, and party newspaper, *La Tribuna*. In addition there are numerous functional groupings within the party: university students, workers, high school students, artists, lawyers, and so on. Hence an Aprista may live within the party's world and never have his loyalty weakened by contradictory communications. The other parties, to varying degrees, tend to provide their adherents with similar unified opinion environments.[4]

Two of the three major Lima newspapers, *La Prensa* and *El Comercio*, contribute to the partisan channels of communication. The former supported the government in the period 1959–62, the latter attacked it with skill and venom. Those individuals who sided with the opposition found in *El Comercio* a copious supply of criticism and invective which served to reinforce their dissatisfaction with the Prado government.[5]

Political conflict in Peru, then, is intense and bipolar: between the "Ins" and the "Outs." Those elements who are opposed to

4. The analysis here draws upon the general theory of cross-pressures and attitude formation. For specific reference to the problem of political conflict see: David B. Truman, *The Governmental Process* (New York, Knopf, 1951), pp. 157 ff., 507 ff.; Sigmund Neumann, *Modern Political Parties* (Chicago, University of Chicago Press, 1956), p. 404; Seymour Martin Lipset, *Political Man* (New York, Doubleday, 1963), pp. 74–79.

5. The third Lima paper, *La Cronica*, was more mass-consumption oriented and tended to avoid partisan political issues. The television stations were also relatively nonpolitical, again apparently because they were attempting to reach the largest possible audience and thereby realize the greatest possible return on their investment. One might expect that *El Comercio* and *La Prensa* may, in the future, be forced by economic necessity to "tone down" partisan politics. For an analysis of the relationships between political cleavage, economic changes and the mass media the reader should consult Otto Kirchheimer, "The Waning of Opposition in Parliamentary Regimes," *Social Research*, 24 (1956), 149–50.

the incumbent president are implacably opposed to the government which he represents. Centralization places in his hands enormous decision-making authority; consequently he is a significant target. Excluded from this pinpoint of decision-making responsibility the opposition forces have little to lose by his overthrow. Deprived of patronage and reinforced in their animosity by partisan channels of communication, opposition groups see the destruction of the president as a noble and patriotic task.

The visitor to Peru does not pass many days in the country before grasping the polarized nature of political society and the intensity of the opposition to the executive. A chat with a taxi driver, a newspaper headline—the American soon realizes that politics is a serious, even deadly business. The desire to destroy the incumbent president is of paramount significance. The intensity with which this objective is pursued results not only in the use of violence, as we have suggested, but also in the formation of seemingly incongruous alliances. For example, the Christian Democratic Party (in the opposition in 1961) had a peasant affairs bureau which worked closely with members of the Trotskyite and Rebel APRA parties who were attempting to foment a revolution through rural violence. That the Pope's sworn enemies should walk hand-in-hand with his disciples testifies to the overwhelming importance of the struggle against the executive in the eyes of these participants.

Groups which formed a permanent opposition during the Prado government (1956–62) included the Popular Action Party of Belaúnde, the Odría Party, the Christian Democratic Party, and all the left-extremist groups including Communists, two factions of the Trotskyite party, the APRA Rebelde, and the Progressive Socialists. Consistent with their position of isolation these groups maintained a posture of total opposition to the president.

The third major power in Peruvian politics is the armed forces. Ultimately it is the military which protects the president and upholds his government. Although the police force (*Guardia Civil*) bears the preliminary attacks against the president, it is the army which stands behind this force, ready to move in when violence reaches serious proportions. Given the task of maintaining the chief executive in office, the leaders of the armed forces are continually forced to question whether, indeed, the president deserves their support. Although the armed forces tend to establish broad limits to the actions of the president, they are characteristically uninterested in details of policy. What they are interested in is peace. It is incorrect to suppose that the military is the enemy of peaceful free government. Direct military intervention in politics has taken place only in times of acute crisis, in times when civilian political conflict threatened to lead to dangerous extremes. The military coup of July 1962 is a case in point. None of the three major presidential candidates—Odría, Haya de la Torre, and Belaúnde—obtained the requisite one third of the ballots for election. Belaúnde, seeing his position was weakest, adopted a menacing attitude and agitated for annulment of the election on the grounds of fraud. The other two candidates could not agree—until it was too late—on a coalition. After civilian politicians had struggled for nearly a month and produced only greater uncertainty, the armed forces stepped in and put an end to the chaotic scene.

The logic of the situation dictates that intervention should occur at such times of crisis. Composed of different factions holding differing political sympathies, the armed forces can act unanimously only if the civilian government has demonstrated its inability to keep order and to "represent the people." When things are going along smoothly an attempted coup by one faction would be opposed by neutral members and other factions which supported the president. A coup attempted in times of peace, when the armed forces are divided in their opinions, would be very dangerous. At best it could mean a court-martial for the losers; at worst, internecine war.

Consequently, as long as the executive manages to keep unrest at a minimum the military tends to support the existing government. But if armed forces are repeatedly engaged in clashes with agitated mobs and demonstrators, they will come to believe that the wisest course is to depose the object of civilian dissatisfaction, the president. Members of the armed forces are, after all, Peruvians. They do not derive great pleasure from being denounced by their friends and relatives as "tools of oppression." If it appears that the government has lost support from many sectors and if violence is incessant, then the armed forces tend to unite in their disapproval of the existing government and a coup can be quickly executed.

With these preliminary remarks we are in a position to understand the dynamic impulse given to the system by interest groups, particularly worker organizations. Three sets of actors with interrelated roles have been identified: the executive, the opposition, and the armed forces. But what sets these participants in motion? We have seen that political violence is not random but meaningfully patterned. A group of political party members cannot simply rush out onto the street and attack a policeman. The opposition parties require substantive issues of conflict on which to construct their attacks upon the government.

Worker organizations provide these issues. These groups, through their specific demands, provide opposition forces with a cause around which violence may be structured. In addition, labor groups provide a sizable supply of agitators to swell the ranks of opposition forces. Once a conflict has been initiated by worker organizations the opposition groups may swing into action with further demonstrations, denunciations, and parades. It follows, therefore, that if the workers are relatively quiet or if the president meets their demands rapidly with adequate concessions, violence will have little opportunity to build. The crucial "violence-initiating" position of worker organizations under a free government is the key to their success.

Labor unions, joined as they are in various alliances, present a potent threat to public order when they choose to challenge the government. In the highly charged political atmosphere a single clash with the army troops usually broadens and intensifies the conflict. One strike leads to solidarity strikes, one demonstration broken by the assault troops provokes a larger protest demonstration. The inevitable opposition to the president—opposition parties, hostile newspapers, and discontents of all varieties—is already sufficient to make his tenure uncertain. If the labor movement, or a sizable portion of it, leads these forces in persistent, intense attacks, the president's downfall is virtually assured.

Thus it is evident that the president, while all-responsible, is by no means all-powerful. With the ravenous opposition on one side and an ambivalent military on the other, he can be constantly alarmed by worker organizations threatening the use of violence. The executive must intervene in labor disputes to avert a dangerous chain reaction which might well end in a military coup. Short of dictatorial repression, the form of intervention which is most likely to prevent hostile worker organization activity is the imposition on the employer of settlements that tend to meet minimum worker demands. That is, the executive must and does order employers to grant specific concessions to workers.

These, then, are the basic features of the Peruvian pattern of labor relations, a pattern which I term "political bargaining": a highly centralized government deeply involved in the social and economic life of the nation; a high level of conflict intensity and an ambivalent military, rendering the executive of a free regime insecure in the face of violence; the use of violence as an effective worker organization tactic; and the direct settlement of labor–management disputes by the executive.

The labor movement in Peru, therefore, is politically oriented. This orientation is not primarily toward achieving favorable legislation through elected representatives and lobbying. Nor is it directed at the formation of a single labor party designed to gain control of the executive. The Peruvian labor movement employs primarily the method of political bargaining. This tactic has been chosen because it is successful.[6]

6. It is, of course, no revelation to assert that the labor movement in an underdeveloped country like Peru is "politically oriented." Many writers have noted this fact for both Latin America and underdeveloped countries in general. Of particular interest is the comprehensive account by Bruce H. Millen, *The Political Role of Labor in Developing Countries* (Washington, Brookings Institution, 1963). Here an attempt is being made to define and explain the

The Alternatives

It is important to realize that we are describing a bargaining system which differs in fundamental respects from other labor relations systems. There are two other general patterns, first identified by the Webbs in their great study of the English labor movement: the methods of collective bargaining and legal enactment.[7]

Collective bargaining is essentially a system based on economic coercion. The strike is effective as a concerted withdrawal of labor. The relative power of the employees is determined by many economic variables including condition of the labor market, size of firm, and industry structure. Decisions in this system are made independently of the government, at the firm or industry level.

Legal enactment is based upon political coercion, but through channels quite different from those employed in political bargaining. Legal enactment entails lobbying for laws which settle employer–employee conflicts. The activity of worker organizations is centered on elections, on votes, on influencing political parties —or the formation of a workers' party. Where this method is employed the government is usually quite secure. Violence is usually irrelevant to or even destructive of the workers' cause in that it does not threaten the government and may even result in the workers' losing electoral strength. The decision-making centers for legal enactment are the legislature, the courts, and the bureaucracy which administers the laws.

In order to fully understand the adoption of political bargaining by the Peruvian labor movement it is helpful to explain why these other methods—collective bargaining and legal enactment —have been substantially rejected.

---

precise nature of this political orientation, to set up a model of interaction which separates causes from effects and which distinguishes basic variables from superficial conditions.

7. Sidney and Beatrice Webb, *Industrial Democracy* (London, Longmans, Green, 1919). A third method which the Webbs described, "mutual insurance," has apparently fallen into disuse today.

Collective Bargaining. To the uninitiated observer what transpires in Peruvian labor disputes often looks like collective bargaining. The union presents demands, the leaders sit down at a table with the employer representatives and discuss the matter, and sometimes they sign a contract without a strike. But missing in this picture is what is in the minds of the participants, what forces would operate if agreement had not been reached. The workers would have gone on strike, but not in the same sense as American workers strike. They would not walk *off,* they would walk *into,* into streets and squares, into rallies and demonstrations, laying the groundwork for violence and executive imposition of a satisfactory solution. It is what the workers do or threaten to do while on strike that makes the method of political bargaining so different from collective bargaining.

If Peruvian workers were to stay home during a strike or quietly walk picket lines, they would—except in unusual circumstances—lose the strike. To account for the inefficacy of the economic strike (the simple withdrawal of labor), the difference between the American and Peruvian environments must be examined.

To explain why the American labor movement chose collective bargaining rather than political action, a reasonable hypothesis is that the relative scarcity of labor in the United States enabled the economic strike to be successful. Because strikers were difficult to replace, an economic strike was relatively coercive upon the employer. If the employer could find few workers to replace strikers, then he would be forced to deal with the union.[8] This

8. The relative scarcity of skilled labor in the United States during the nineteenth century has been discussed by Lloyd Ulman in *The Rise of the National Trade Union* (Cambridge, Harvard University Press, 1955), p. 7 ff., and also in "The Development of Trades and Labor Unions" in Seymour E. Harris, ed., *American Economic History* (New York, McGraw-Hill, 1961), pp. 367–68. The analysis of the effectiveness of the economic strike as determined by labor supply and replacement variables was presented to me by my former teacher and colleague, Melvin K. Bers. Unfortunately there is not space to present more than a partial outline of his approach. Scholars who have noted labor supply and replacement variables as affecting the success of collective bargaining include: J. B. Clark, "The Theory of Collective Bargain-

hypothesis is consistent with the fact that skilled workers, who were in shortest supply, were most successful in trade union activity. It is also consistent with the observed failure of economic unionism during periods of depression in the United States.[9] Because during depressions the labor supply was swelled by unemployed workers, strikes were undermined by those workers. It was in times of prosperity, when few replacements were available, that the economic strike was an effective weapon.

Applying this hypothesis to Peru it is evident why collective bargaining, based on the strike as a withdrawal of labor, would be ineffective. The relative abundance of labor in Peru makes the replacement of strikers a comparatively simple task. For every worker who goes on strike at a particular establishment there will be dozens eager to take his place.

To be sure, there is a scarcity of certain types of skilled workers in Peru. These workers can in effect stage a coercive economic strike, given the difficulty which their employers would experience in attempting to replace them. Examples of such groups are aviation mechanics and radio operators. Insofar as they rely on organized activity, these groups may successfully employ collective bargaining. But such groups of workers are very much the exception in Peru. The modal pattern of labor relations is determined by the method which most workers, who can be easily replaced, have been forced to adopt.

The relative abundance of labor in Peru can be accounted for

---

ing" in American Economic Association, *Papers and Discussions*, series 3, Vol. 10 (1909), pp. 24–39; Milton Friedman, "Some Comments on the Significance of Labor Unions for Economic Policy" in David McCord Wright, *The Impact of the Union* (New York, Harcourt Brace, 1951), p. 204; Lloyd Ulman, *The Rise of the National Trade Union*, pp. 305–18.

9. See John R. Commons and Associates, *History of Labor in the United States* (4 vols. New York, Macmillan, 1918), *1*, 10–11 and passim. Recent economic and institutional changes have altered certain variables so that some modifications must be introduced into the analysis to deal with present-day conditions. Specifically, the Wagner Act combined with the growth of firms to enormous size produced large working forces with relatively high solidarity so that to replace the entire labor force at one time was a difficult task for the employer.

partly by the nature of the source of manpower. Although Peru has one of the highest annual rates of population growth—about 2.7 per cent—the greatest increase in the industrial labor force comes not from natural population growth but from internal migration. Peru may be divided into three regions: the coast, the mountainous *sierra,* and the jungle (see map). The sierra region is inhabited by Indians, most of whom lead a semicivilized life in small communities and villages. As transportation improved, as the land grew more crowded, and as news of opportunity reached these Indians, they began to migrate. A large portion of this migration has been to the industrial towns and cities on the coast, particularly Lima, larger than any other city in Peru by a factor of ten and the center of industrial activity.

Lima is today surrounded by *barriadas*—slums—where perhaps 200,000 recent arrivals from the sierra live in extreme poverty. For the student of social welfare the barriadas are a tragedy. For the political scientist they are, contrary to popular belief, of little importance because the highly disorganized state of these migrants precludes sustained, concerted political activity. But to the labor economist these slums are significant as an abundant source of low-cost labor, labor which would undermine a strictly economic strike overnight.

One may also point to the demand side to explain the depressed state of the labor market. Certainly if Peru experienced a prolonged period of vigorous industrial expansion, the unemployment problem would tend to disappear. But although Peru has had occasional booms in certain industries (guano, nonferrous metals, natural rubber, and fishmeal), these have not been sufficient to induce and maintain a high rate of economic development. A combination of factors—the small internal market and capital shortage among others—has prevented economic expansion of a magnitude sufficient to absorb the nation's surplus labor.

The presence of excess labor, in addition to facilitating replacement of striking workers, weakens collective bargaining in another way. In Peru industrial jobs are precious. The oversupply of labor has depressed "competitive" wages to extremely low

Talara
Piura
Trujillo
Chimbote
Huanuco
Cerro de Pasco
La Oroya
Callao
Lima
Huancayo
Pisco
Ica
Nazca
Cuzco
Puno
Arequipa
Mollendo
Iquitos
Amazon River
Marañon River
Ucayali River
Pucallpa
Tingo Maria

PACIFIC OCEAN

PERU

Major Roads —————
Division of basic regions —·—
Railroads ++++++++++++++++

scale :
0   50   100   200   300 miles

16

levels, perhaps five or ten sols a day. But wages in industrial firms, maintained by trade union activity, are many times higher, varying between 40 and 80 sols per day. Even to assume that a discharged worker could gain employment at all is, given the fierce competition for jobs, extravagant.

The value of the job to the worker is significant in determining the solidarity of a strike. If the worker values his job as he does his life he will be reluctant to join a strike and anxious to return to work as soon as there is any indication that the strike will fail. Always in the forefront of his mind is the fear that he will be replaced. The economic strike requires, however, that a walk-off be nearly complete and that the strikers stay off the job even when the danger of partial replacement arises. If solidarity is low, as it is in Peru for the reason given above, an economic strike has less chance of success.

For Peruvian workers success lies in the method of political bargaining. Using this tactic the problems of solidarity and replacement become practically irrelevant. The strike does not need to be complete because it is not the firm which is being coerced but the executive. In the United States an employer weakens the bargaining power of the union by hiring defectors and replacements. But in Peru this practice is likely to strengthen the union by encouraging greater violence on the part of the strikers and, hence, greater executive concessions.

Legal Enactment. As a means for achieving worker organization objectives legal enactment is also a relatively ineffective weapon. Successful use of this method requires two conditions: (1) a stabilized, representative electoral system; (2) an efficient, far-flung national bureaucracy. Peru has lacked both.

The electoral system in Peru is disorganized—a result of intense political conflict and turbulent political history. In this century there have not been two successive elections which determined the transfer of power. Instead military intervention and congressional selection have marked all but a few elections widely separated in time. Consequently it has not been possible for the labor movement to exercise its electoral strength in a meaningful fashion. It has not had the opportunity to learn whom to back and whom to oppose. The policy of rewarding friends and punishing enemies is possible only if it is known who the friends and enemies are.

And since periods of free government have been preceded by at least moderately repressive regimes, worker organizations have found it difficult to select and back candidates. Communication, decision-making, and electioneering have been stifled by dictatorial governments.

Legal enactment also requires a bureaucracy to enforce the laws which are passed. It does little good to pass a minimum wage law, for example, if violations cannot be detected and punished. If the resources of the administration are scarce—and they are scarce indeed in Peru—then a law remains a piece of paper. Hence the method of legal enactment, neat and civilized a tactic as it may seem, is of relatively little use to the Peruvian labor movement.[10]

Political bargaining, then, is the basic trade union method in Peru. It has been chosen because the workers find it much more effective than other strategies. The political and economic environment is such that with this method the rate of return per unit of worker effort greatly exceeds the rate of return for other strategies. Violence and violence-related activities cannot, therefore, be considered foolish or temperamental; they are rational tactics.

Trade Union Method as a Tool of Analysis

The implications of political bargaining as the prevailing worker organization strategy are many and far-reaching. In the United States the existence of collective bargaining and, more recently, legal enactment as the basic trade union methods has

10. It must be pointed out that this is a discussion of the modal pattern of labor relations in Peru. Legal enactment has been employed on occasion with success, as will be shown in Chapter 4.

a profound effect on many facets of the labor movement, from the local unions to the AFL–CIO and beyond. In Peru we should expect to find numerous contrasts with the American labor scene, arising from the fundamental differences in bargaining strategy. By way of introducing the reader to the salient characteristics of the Peruvian pattern of labor relations, we shall review the findings of this study on the subjects of wage differentials and inflation, political party activities, and labor movement structure.

Under political bargaining the concessions made to any group of workers will tend to be proportional to the degree to which that group threatens the security of the executive. Consequently, any analysis of wage differentials existing between two groups of workers must take into account the "violence potential" of the different worker organizations. Among the factors that determine this violence potential are: size and cohesion of the worker organization; the proximity (both ideological and psychological) of the worker organization to other organizations (particularly federations and the national confederation) which might initiate solidarity strikes; the geographical location of the workers; and the prominence of the workers in the public eye.

When all these variables are favorable, we may expect to find a premium wage rate prevailing. Because the requisites for success are different under political bargaining than with collective bargaining, we find that in Peru printing workers (the traditional American "aristocrats of labor"), for example, are poorly paid. But textile workers, who in the United States have experienced great difficulty in raising their wages, are among the best paid blue-collar workers in Peru.

A statistical picture of wage differentials and wage trends is found in Tables 1, 2, and 3. Table 1 shows that real wages of industrial workers, after suffering a decline during World War II, about doubled in the period 1945–59. Table 2 indicates that from 1959 to 1961 real wages continued to climb, the *obreros* (blue-collar workers) making more substantial gains than *empleados* (white-collar workers). Although the figures are far from

TABLE 1

Real and Money Wages of Workers (Obreros) in the Four
Major Industries, 1938–1959*

	Year	MANUFACTURING		TRANSPORTATION AND COMMUNICATION		MINING AND PETROLEUM		AGRICULTURE AND FISHING	
		Real	Money	Real	Money	Real	Money	Real	Money
	1938	26.2	3.11						
	1939	29.3	3.42			24.2	2.82		
Prado	1940	29.5	3.70			24.5	3.07		
(first term)	1941	27.8	3.77			19.4	2.64		
	1942	25.2	3.85			18.2	2.97		
	1943	23.8	4.00			19.9	3.33		
	1944	21.3	4.19	27.1	5.21	19.4	3.73	9.7	1.89
	1945	25.0	5.36	27.8	5.98	21.7	4.66	10.0	2.14
Bustamante	1946	27.1	6.37	24.2	5.66	25.3	5.96	14.5	3.41
	1947	35.5	9.74	33.7	9.24	22.4	6.15	12.8	3.50
	1948	32.3	12.50	28.8	11.20	20.3	8.06	13.4	5.35
	1949	35.3	16.14	30.1	13.66	22.7	10.16	14.2	6.44
	1950	39.0	19.97	32.7	16.66	27.3	13.87	15.3	7.85
Odría	1951	39.0	21.96	30.3	17.02	30.5	17.15	14.3	8.07
	1952	40.5	24.35	35.1	21.05	32.2	19.35	17.5	10.15
	1953	41.0	26.78	35.2	23.15	33.0	21.60	20.9	13.65
	1954	40.5	28.05	34.6	23.38	35.0	24.47	20.0	13.80
	1955	41.2	29.87	34.5	25.00	na	na	19.0	13.82
	1956	43.2	33.00	43.0	32.87	36.0	27.58	22.2	16.87
Prado	1957	42.6	35.20	41.5	34.00	37.2	30.55	24.0	19.67
(second	1958	46.2	41.15	50.9	46.00	39.0	34.50	28.2	25.00
term)	1959	51.0	51.0	53.89	53.89	36.65	36.65	26.40	26.40

* All figures are in average daily earnings (assuming 5½ days in the work week) in sols. Real income is expressed in constant sols, 1959 = 100.

Sources: The figures for money wages have been taken from unpublished records of the Department of Statistics of the Ministry of Finance. These figures have never been cited publicly as proving or disproving anything. Hence, we have no reason to suspect that the data have been tampered with for political reasons. The figures may be criticized on technical grounds: their scope is limited (especially for the earlier years) and the methods employed for data gathering and processing are unrefined. However, assuming that the same aberrations appear from year to year, these figures may be considered as a useful long-term index of changes in money wages.

The cost-of-living index used to prepare this table is also compiled by the Department of Statistics of the Ministry of Finance. As one would expect, the index is frequently attacked by labor leaders, housewives, extremists, and opposition parties. I spent several days following the procedures and investigating possible sources of error and concluded, that while minor shortcomings may be noted, the index gives a reliable picture of the changes in the cost of living to the typical obrero consumer. It is significant to note that when a monthly rise in the cost-of-living index is unusually high, opposition forces do not hesitate to cite the figure as proof of the government's failure. It must be noted that the index is prepared for the Lima–Callao area only. Consequently it is somewhat misleading to use the index to calculate real wages of miners and agricultural workers since those workers do not purchase in the Lima–Callao area.

complete, they provide a strong refutation to the allegation frequently heard in Peru that workers are becoming progressively
impoverished.

A rough comparison of the relative standard of living of workers in Peru and the United States can be made from the data
given in Table 2. With the exchange rate at 26.80 sols/dollar in

TABLE 2

Changes in Money and Real Wages of Workers in the Manufacturing
Industry in the Lima–Callao Area, 1959–1961 (in sols)[a]

	OBREROS (M NUAL)			EMPLEADOS (WHITE-COLLAR)		
Year	Money wages	Real wages[b]	Change in real wages	Money wages	Real wages	Change in real wages
1959	36.5	41.5		2,620	2,990	
1960	42.5	44.5	7.2%	2,870	3,010	.7%
1961	46.5	46.5	4.5%	3,130	3,130	4%

a. These figures were compiled from the monthly averages collected by the statistical service of the Ministry of Labor which includes about 45,000 obreros and
18,000 empleados in manufacturing in the Lima–Callao area. Because the figures
for the last half of 1961 were not available when this table was composed, only the
figures for the first half of each year were used.

The figures in Table 2 cannot be compared with those of Table 1. In addition to
differences in scope and data collecting, the figures in Table 2 treat every day as an
earning day; those of Table 1 give average wages for working days only.

b. Real wages have been computed on the basis of the Ministry of Finance cost-
of-living index: 1959 = 88, 1960 = 95, 1961 = 100. Price index figures for the entire
years have been used.

Wages for obreros are in sols per day, assuming seven days in the work week.
The weekly wage for obreros would be seven times the figures appearing above.
Empleado wages are in monthly earnings in sols.

Source: Ministerio de Trabajo, *Estadísticas de Trabajo* (Lima, Bulletins for 1959,
1960, 1961).

1961 we can calculate the weekly wage of the Lima obrero:
7 × 46.5 ÷ 26.80 = $12.10. Since the purchasing power of the
dollar in Peru was about twice that in the United States (for
the items purchased by the obrero family) the average Lima blue-
collar worker's earnings in United States terms came to about

23 to 26 dollars.[11] For groups of workers with strategic power positions—textile workers, Lima bus workers—the average wage was 40 to 80 per cent higher.

Table 3 gives a comparison between workers in related industries where worker organization activity has apparently made a significant difference in wage levels. Both the textile and beverage industries are highly organized, while workers in the foodstuffs and garment industries are practically unorganized. Workers in the unorganized industries received higher wages than the comparable groups in 1939 when the Benavides dictatorship ended, but by 1959 workers in the organized industries were earning 45 to 85 per cent more. Although differing marginal productivities of labor in the different industries (as well as shortcomings of the statistics themselves) may account for some of this variation, we would suspect that the greater violence potential of the workers in the organized industries accounts for part of the difference.

The real wage, however, is constantly being eroded by inflation. The cost-of-living index has been rising steadily in recent years at the rate of about 8 per cent yearly (see Table 4). The downward pressure on real wages is one factor which affects the nature of industrial conflict in Peru. Because the cost of living is constantly rising worker organizations must make wage demands yearly. Two- or five-year agreements are out of the question. Nor can workers forego demanding a wage increase in any one year to concentrate on other gains, gains which might enhance organization security, for example.

There is reason to believe that inflation, at least in part, is

11. Retail price comparisons compiled for the upper middle class for March 1958 gave the relative cost of living in Lima compared to New York City (100) an index number of 73 at the prevailing exchange rate. It would seem that these figures, compiled on the basis of expenditure habits of United Nations employees, must be corrected downward for obreros, who have extremely low housing costs and who do not purchase expensive imported items such as American cigarettes, washing machines, automobiles, refrigerators, etc. See *Retail Price Comparisons for International Salary Determination*, United Nations Statistical Papers (New York, 1959), Series M, No. 14, Add 2.

TABLE 3

Trends in Real Worker Wages in Related Industries With
and Without Extensive Organization of the Workers,
1939–1959

Year	TEXTILE INDUSTRY (organized)	GARMENT INDUSTRY (unorganized)	BEVERAGE INDUSTRY (organized)	FOODSTUFFS INDUSTRY (unorganized)
1939	28.6	30.5	34.0	41.8
1940	30.1	26.5	29.7	39.6
1941	28.4	25.2	30.6	38.2
1942	26.7	22.8	28.7	33.0
1943	25.9	24.0	27.0	35.0
1944	25.0	23.8	29.4	32.0
1945	27.0	27.7	27.6	27.2
1946	32.3	28.0	21.7	30.0
1947	47.5	29.6	34.0	26.0
1948	44.0	24.6	28.0	23.0
1949	46.0	23.5	33.0	21.7
1950	49.1	30.3	37.6	31.1
1951	45.7	28.5	41.0	34.4
1952	49.9	29.5	39.6	32.0
1953	50.0	33.8	43.6	29.0
1954	47.2	32.0	47.4	30.5
1955	53.0	36.1	49.0	29.8
1956	50.9	34.0	52.5	34.0
1957	60.8	36.5	52.0	30.3
1958	58.8	36.2	54.0	42.5
1959	60.3	35.0	54.3	na

Source: Department of Statistics, Ministry of Finance (*Hacienda*); Elaboration of real income by the author using the Ministry of Finance cost-of-living index, 1959 = 100. All wages in sols per working day, yearly average.

the product of the political bargaining system. The executive tends to see a decreed wage increase as the best, and perhaps only, way to avoid a military coup. Even though the Peruvian president fears inflation because it may eventually lead to a dangerous political climate as worker organizations protest against their declining real wage, he fears more the immediate danger which resides in the actual use of violence. Of course, if it appears that violence is less likely to have disastrous consequences, then the executive will withstand, to a degree, worker organiza-

TABLE 4

Cost-of-Living Index, 1936–1961

Year	Cost-of-Living Index Number	Per cent Change with Respect to Preceding Year
1936	100	
1937	111	11%
1938	112	1
1939	110	−2
1940	119	8
1941	129	8
1942	144	12
1943	159	10
1944	181	14
1945	202	12
1946	221	10
1947	259	17
1948	374	45
1949	429	15
1950	481	12
1951	530	10
1952	567	7
1953	618	9
1954	652	6
1955	683	5
1956	720	5
1957	773	7
1958	835	8
1959	941	13
1960	1022	9
1961	1070*	5

* Includes estimates for November and December.

Source: Ministry of Finance, Bulletin of the Department of Statistics (Lima, 1961), p. 3.

tion demands. We should expect, then, that inflation is likely to be most severe when the executive feels most insecure, that is, when he has little or no civilian support and a military coup is imminent. A comparison of the increases in the cost of living index under Bustamante (1945–48) and Prado (1956–62) would seem to support this hypothesis. Bustamante, as will be pointed out in the next chapter, was by 1947 opposed by all major political parties. Manuel Prado retained the support of the APRA party throughout his term.

The political bargaining system also has important implications for the relationship of political parties to the labor movement. Because worker organizations offer a potential for violence directed against the incumbent president, labor leaders who are members or sympathizers with political parties are greatly tempted to shape their strike policy to favor their party. In the United States this temptation seldom exists for labor leaders, since a strike does not usually affect the tenure of elected officials.

Peruvian labor leaders who ally with opposition groups wish to attack the government and thereby cause a military coup. Consequently they make their demands excessive and prolong strikes. Solidarity strikes are more readily sought and acts of violence more energetically attempted by these leaders. Government-supporting leaders (APRA labor leaders in 1961) attempt to minimize violence. They will, in order to gain rank and file objectives, work toward a pattern of violent activity, but their intention is to maximize the use of threats rather than engage in actual violence.

Labor leaders of both opposition and government-supporting parties face rank and file constraints. The former are too aggressive for the rank and file, the latter too moderate. Workers are reluctant to lose wages in a solidarity strike which brings them no benefit, but, on the other hand, they are anxious to fight when the issue concerns them directly. This tension between rank and file and politically oriented leadership explains, in part, the high rate of leadership turnover, the decentralization of labor movement structure, and the transitory existence of many secondary organizations and alliances. The rank and file is repeatedly resisting partisan policies by voting out leaders, by refusing to obey secondary organization decisions, and by withdrawing individually or collectively from one organization and joining another.

The structure of the Peruvian labor movement is oriented not toward labor and product markets as it is in the United States but toward the "political market." Craft divisions, based on differentiated labor markets, are practically unknown. Instead the workers in one work center are grouped together so that their numbers may be fully exploited in demonstrations and similar activities. These work center organizations (which in this study are termed "unions") are drawn into secondary organizations (federations) of industries and regions as well as informal alliances. The pressure to affiliate is great in Peru because the bargaining power of a union depends significantly on the number and size of the organizations which will support it in actions of solidarity.

Knowledge of the basic trade union method, as we have attempted to show in the preceding paragraphs, provides an important tool for analyzing the different features of a labor relations system. Once a model of the bargaining framework has been constructed, one may derive hypotheses which explain, at least in part, the existence and persistence of a wide range of phenomena. In the next chapter we shall discuss the historical development of the Peruvian labor movement. One of our concerns will be to explain why the labor movement emerged when it did and why certain groups of workers formed permanent organizations before others. In seeking to answer these questions we shall look to the model of political bargaining to provide some basic hypotheses.

2

THE HISTORICAL DEVELOPMENT

OF THE LABOR MOVEMENT IN PERU

The emergence and development of the Peruvian labor movement bears an interesting contrast to the history of the labor movements in the United States and Great Britain, where worker organizations can trace their beginnings to the advent of a market economy and the subsequent competition between producers. Essentially the market economy led to a differentiation of economic functions so that two groups with conflicting interests arose: employers and employees. Through the impact of competition independent artisans were transformed into either owners of large shops or propertyless workers. Finding themselves with a common cause against the employer, the workers united into trade unions to defend their special interests. In this way Sidney and Beatrice Webb and John R. Commons have explained how the labor movements in Great Britain and the United States, respectively, emerged many decades before industrialization took place.[1]

In Peru it does not seem that the development of a market

1. Sidney and Beatrice Webb, *The History of Trade Unionism* (London, Longmans, Green, 1920), Chapter 1; John R. Commons and Associates, *History of Labor in the United States, 1*, 10, 134–37.

economy led to the formation of trade unions. Rather it was industrialization which gave rise to the labor movement. Because the economic strike was of little utility in Peru—the supply of labor being so copious—small groups of skilled workers, such as would have been found in workshops of the preindustrial period, were not successful in coercing employers. Nor could the government be coerced by these groups of craftsmen since they were so small that they presented no serious political threat. Larger groups (over 30 or 40 workers), because they could generate a significant political impact, tended to be more successful, and hence survived. It was not until the advent of industrial forms of production, however, that large numbers of workers were brought together.

It is significant to note, as a demonstration of the above hypothesis, that the first permanent organizations were not formed of construction workers, printers, and other skilled workers as occurred in the United States. The first workers to organize permanently in Peru were textile workers, longshoremen, sugar workers, and miners. The small groups of skilled workers could not form viable organizations because they could not employ the political strike successfully in defense of their members.

In the United States the skilled workers were first to organize because they had an effective economic weapon based on the relative scarcity of skilled labor. Given the feasibility of the economic approach, the small size of these crafts worked to their advantage in simplifying control of the labor market. Unskilled workers in the United States, on the other hand, have not until more recently been able to effectively use the strike because the supply of unskilled labor was sufficient to facilitate replacement of strikers. Without either an economic strike or—except in rare cases—a political strike, American organizations of unskilled workers were destroyed or disappeared as quickly as they were formed.

The only exception to the above generalizations is the organization of bakery workers, *Federación de Panaderos Estrella del Perú*, the oldest labor organization in Peru and the only analogue

of the American craft union. Founded in 1887, two decades before labor began to organize on a significant scale, this organization has managed to survive as a social center and informal hiring
service. With its members scattered in small bakery shops all over
Lima the organization had—and has—little political or economic
potential. In a strike in 1919, for example, three decades after
its formation, accounts showed that it could not cut off the supply of bread to the city.[2]

The indispensable position of industry as the base for the
Peruvian labor movement is clearly seen in an examination of
the situation in the jungle region of Peru. There the population
is scattered in tiny villages or in farming colonies. One occasionally encounters a tiny union formed by the workers in a soft
drink plant or a saw mill, both new industries in this region made
possible by the opening of roads and the growth of towns. Truck
drivers have organizations of 15 or 20 members in the towns
along the highways, but their small size precludes effective political activity.

In the jungle port of Iquitos (pop. 55,696), there is a more
vigorous labor union life. The four movie houses have provided
a nucleus for the formation of one union, the city transportation
company another, the dock services, large construction projects,
and the central market, others. Table 5 gives a picture of the
relationship between centralization and worker organization
membership. The reader will note how the *proportion* of organized workers increases from small towns to cities.

To understand why labor unions appeared in Peru when they
did, we must take a brief look at the history of this country's
economic development. Peru, like the United States, developed
in two overlapping but broadly distinguishable steps. The first
corresponds to the unfolding of international trade; the second, to
the development of a national market large enough to encourage
industrialization. However, Peru lagged almost a full century
behind the United States in experiencing both of these stages.

2. *El Comercio* (Lima, January 2–15, 1919).

TABLE 5

Relationship Between City Size and Proportion of Organized Workers

City[a]	Population, 1961[b]	Number of organized workers in city, 1961	Proportion of organized workers to total city population
Huánuco	24,721	200	.8%
Iquitos	55,696	1,900	3.4%
Arequipa	149,406	11,000	7.4%
Greater Lima (including Callao)	1,849,736	197,000	10.6%

a. These cities have been selected as typical for their size. Obviously it would be misleading to use mining encampments or the towns formed around a sugar hacienda.

b. The figures for total population are preliminary releases of the 1961 census. Figures for number of organized workers were gathered by me.

For Peru, the first stage corresponded roughly to the period 1840–1915. One product, guano, provided the impetus for an enormous expansion in trade with Europe. Before 1840, while the United States had been sending large quantities of agricultural and forest products to Europe, Peru's only international trade had been shipments of gold, silver, or quinine. The guano boom, which reached its height in the 1860s, opened Peru to the world—and to itself. According to one of Peru's economic historians, Emilio Romero,

The greatest steps taken on the road to progress from 1850 to the end of the last century must be attributed to its [guano's] effect on the national economy. With its income the great railroads were built, steamship navigation and South American commerce were intensified, the telegraph system was built, the negro slaves were freed, and great companies were formed.[3]

3. Emilio Romero, *Historia Económica del Perú* (Buenos Aires, Editorial Sudamericana, 1949), p. 358.

Later sugar, wool, cotton, copper, and rubber swelled and diversified the export trade. Table 6 gives a statistical picture of the expansion of trade in this period.

TABLE 6

Increase in Maritime Commerce Seen in Number of Ships
Leaving Callao (the Lima Seaport), 1838–1879

Year	Number of ships leaving Callao
1838	32
1841–1860 (yearly average)	186
1861–1867 (yearly average)	319
1868	438
1870	507
1870–1879 (yearly average)	937

Source: Emilio Romero, *Historia Económica del Perú* (Buenos Aires, Editorial Sudamericana, 1949), p. 346.

The existence of a world demand for raw materials such as copper and wool necessitated the development of internal communication. Centers of supply and distribution, roads and railroads, were the result of participation in the world economy. As in the development of international trade, Peru was many decades behind the United States in establishing internal communication. For example, all major railroads were constructed after 1870,[4] and major highways were not built until after 1920.[5]

With communications established, the population of cities, especially Lima, increased; with foreign markets, foreign know-how, and foreign capital brought into the country, Peru was ready after the turn of the century for the development of a semi-modern economy. Beginning with the textile, shoe, food, beverage, and mass transportation industries, and later including glass,

4. C. Reginald Enock, *Peru* (London, T. Fisher Unwin, 1908), p. 209.
5. Romero, p. 424.

paper, electrical goods, and light metal fabrication, a partial industrial economy came into being.

Rather than enter upon a detailed description of this second period, only the statistical profile will be presented—Tables 7 to 10 —leaving the reader to construct the relationships between industrial growth and the formation of labor unions. The increase in copper production has an obvious relationship with miners' and metallurgical workers' organizations, city growth with transporta-

TABLE 7

Copper Production in Peru, 1903–1958
(in metric tons)

1903	9,497
1906	13,474
1958	56,324

Sources: C. Reginald Enock, *Peru* (London, T. Fisher Unwin, 1908), p. 255; *Anuario de la Industria Minera del Perú* (Lima, Ministerio de Fomento y Obras Públicas, 1959), Boletín No. 22.

TABLE 8

Cotton Production in Peru, 1900–1959
(in metric tons)

1900	8,000
1916	24,000
1936	84,000
1945	70,000
1959	125,000

Sources: Enock, p. 224; Romero, p. 415; Banco de Crédito del Perú, *Anuario*, 1960.

TABLE 9

Sugar Production in Peru, 1900–1960
(in metric tons)

1900	112,220
1905	161,850
1943	455,000
1959	700,000
1960	800,000 (est.)

Sources: Enock, p. 224; Romero, p. 414; Banco de Crédito del Perú, *Anuario*, 1960.

TABLE 10

Population Growth of Lima (excluding Callao),
1876–1961

1876	155,486
1940	661,508
1961	1,729,892

Sources: *Anuario Estadístico del Perú, 1958,* (Lima, Ministerio de Hacienda, 1959), Censo Nacional, 1961, preliminary release.

tion, chain store, and bank workers' unions, and so on. Figure 2 shows the growth of United States investment in Peru during this second period. Since most Peruvian development has been effected by foreign capital, and since after 1920 this was predominantly North American, this graph provides a useful picture of industrial growth.

FIGURE 2.

United States Private Investment in Peru in Selected Years

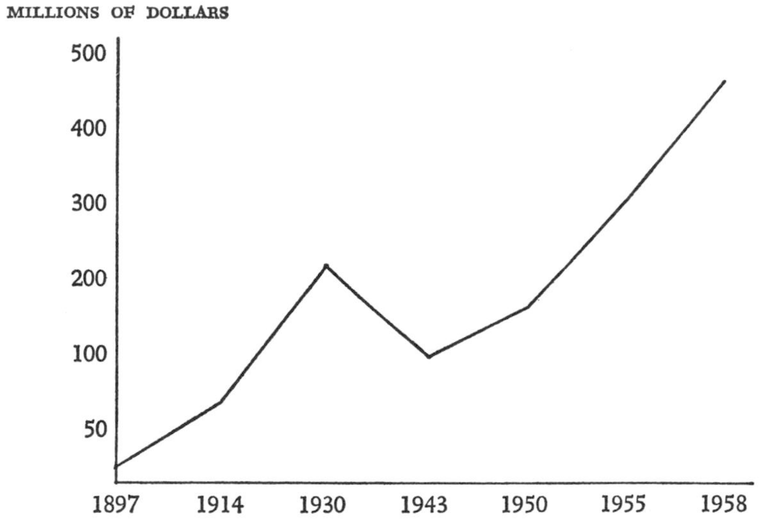

MILLIONS OF DOLLARS

Source: *United States Business and Labor in Latin America,* Study Prepared for the Committee on Foreign Relations, United States Senate by the University of Chicago Research Center in Economic Development and Cultural Change. (Washington, Government Printing Office, 1960), p. 2.

FIGURE 3.

Years of Formation of Fifty-nine Labor Organizations, by Decades, 1910–1950

Source: *Guía Obrera del Perú*, comp. Nicolás Mendoza (Lima, 1951). These 59 organizations selected from over 100, appearing in the *Guía*, include all those for which the date of formation was given as additional data, and therefore may be considered a representative cross-section of worker organizations existing in 1951.

Understanding that modern industrial development began to take place in Peru during the first decades of this century, we would expect to find the first signs of a labor movement in this same period, for the economic prerequisite for labor unions in the Peruvian context was not present before this time. One by one, unions began to appear: longshoremen of Callao and Chicama in the first decade of this century,[6] textile workers of Vitarte and Santa Catalina No. 1, both in 1911. But it was not until the latter part of the second decade that such union formation could be called a movement. Figure 3 shows the rate of formation of

6. Luis Felipe Barrientos C., *Los Tres Sindicalismos* (Lima, Ediciones Continente, 1958), p. 148.

these organizations. What this table does not show is the rapid increase in the number of worker organizations since 1956, the date which marks the end of the Odría dictatorship and the organization of new centers of industrial activity: chain stores, aviation, metal fabrication, the fishmeal industry, as well as further development in mining, agriculture, foodstuffs, and other established industries.

To trace the physical development more clearly, we may note a few of the most indicative changes. The Federation of Textile Workers was founded in 1919 with eight member unions and a total membership of about 1,200.[7] In 1950, the Federation had 60 member unions.[8] In 1961 there were 82 member unions and a total membership of about 21,000 workers.[9]

The Federation of Hotel and Restaurant Workers was founded in 1941. In 1950 it had 12 member unions and a total membership of 2,000.[10] In 1961 there were 25 unions with an approximate total of 5,000 workers.

The Federation of Metallurgical Workers was founded in 1957 with five unions. In 1960 it had 21 member unions and in 1961, 23. The total membership in 1961 was about 3,000. Indicative of the youth of the metal fabrication industry, of the 21 member organizations in 1960, only two had been founded before 1954.[11]

The growth of the national centers gives another view of the same phenomenon. In 1918 the first center (although including only the workers in the Lima area, it may be considered national because of the overwhelming concentration of organized workers in that city), the *Federación Obrera Local*, was founded with a

7. *Obrero Textil* (organ of the Federation of Textile Workers) (Lima, February, 1961), p. 16. I am assuming an average membership of 150 men in each union.

8. *Guía Obrera del Perú*, comp. Nicholas Mendoza (Lima, 1951).

9. Unless otherwise noted, the figures given for size have been calculated from diverse sources: union and other publications, leadership estimates, management estimates, and personal observation.

10. Mendoza, *Guía Obrera del Perú*.

11. *Norte Sindical* (Lima, September, 1960), p. 14.

total membership of about 3,200 workers.[12] The second national center, the *Confederación General de Trabajadores del Perú*, founded in 1929, was estimated to have a membership of 18,000 in 1930.[13] In 1961 the *Confederación de Trabajadores del Perú* counted a total membership of about 240,000.[14]

The growth in importance of white-collar workers, empleados, in the labor movement is a phenomenon of the last fifteen years. Although there were organizations of empleados existing in the early decades of this century, their small size, dispersed nature, and mild ideology limited their impact on the labor movement.[15] However, in 1955, with the organization of the *Central Sindical de Empleados Particulares del Perú*, white-collar workers gained a position at the forefront of the labor movement. The growth of that organization since 1955 has been meteoric. For example, in September 1960, it had 67 member organizations, and in August 1961, the number was 85. In September of the same year the number had climbed to 92.[16]

The Emergence of Political Bargaining

Antedating the labor movement by many years were mutual assistance and artisan societies. The former were, and still are, quite distinct from labor unions. Grouping workers from many occupations, the mutual assistance societies fulfilled certain social and cultural needs of the members, as well as their primary function, social security. The oldest of these organizations still in existence is perhaps the "Philanthropic-Democratic" in Callao, founded in 1854. A confederation of mutual societies (*Asamblea de Sociedades Unidas*) was founded in 1901 and had, in 1961,

12. Calculated on the basis of 21 member organizations (given in Luis Felipe Barrientos C., p. 149) assuming an average membership of 150 men.
13. Moises Poblete Troncoso, *El Movimiento Obrero Latinoamericano* (Mexico, Fondo de Cultura Económica, 1946), p. 244.
14. See page 167 infra.
15. See pages 179–81 infra.
16. *Central Sindical* (Organ of the Confederation of White-Collar Workers) (Lima, September 1960), p. 4, and (September 15, 1961), p. 8.

65 member organizations.[17] Because of the wide diversity of the interests and attitudes of their members (carpenters, policemen, school teachers, store owners, etc.) mutual societies have always confined their scope of action to providing personal services for their members, remaining apart from major political battles.

Artisan organizations, or guilds, more closely resembled labor unions, but with important differences. Although grouping workers in only one trade, their size was relatively small and the scope of activity was confined to social activities and partial attempts to order a competitive market. A guild, however, had nothing to gain by a strike or violence. Its interests coincided with domestic peace and the maintenance of the established order. The guilds more nearly resembled producers' organizations than labor unions—a natural result of the ownership position of most of their members.

These organizations existed before Peru's independence from Spain, but as the cities, especially Lima, grew, their importance increased. In 1884 a confederation of guilds (*Confederación de Artesanos Unión Universal*) was founded and grouped organizations of shoemakers, tailors, painters, plasterers, and others. Highly conservative, "it did not accept doctrines in conflict with the state [e.g. anarchism] nor those who did not abide by the laws of the Republic." In 1905 this confederation began to receive a subsidy from the government.[18]

Labor-government relations were tranquil at the turn of the century. The guilds and mutual assistance societies fitted smoothly into the postcolonial rhythm of Lima and the smaller cities. But different forms of economic organization—industrial forms—soon gave rise to a new force: large groups of workers who could make concerted attacks on the employer and the state. When strikes were called the employers simply continued production with those who stayed on the job and proceeded to fill the vacant positions from the surrounding abundance of

17. Interview with officers of the *Asamblea de Sociedades Unidas* in Lima on June 6, 1961.
18. Poblete Troncoso, p. 244.

labor. The strikers, deprived of their livelihood, resorted to violence: mass demonstrations and assaults on the factory or the owner's house, smashing of machinery, attacks on strikebreakers, and, in some instances, mass thefts of provisions to replenish the dwindling food supply. The government was naturally drawn in to protect life and property and maintain public order. Bitter clashes broke out between police forces and masses of agitated workers on strike. One of the first such clashes occurred in 1906; others followed in 1908, 1912, 1913, and 1914.[19]

Initially these incidents resembled the many episodes which marked the early history of the American and British labor movements. Workers on strike, seeing their jobs falling into the hands of replacements, turned to violence out of desperation. The police power of the government was used to maintain order and, in effect, to break the strike. But as time went on, the Peruvian government, in order to quiet the violence which was threatening its existence, relinquished the role of passive guardian of order and began to intervene directly by dictating settlements. The labor problem had spilled over into a political problem.

In 1913 an office was set up in the Ministry of Interior (police) to deal with labor conflicts.[20] Through this office police officers were instructed to dictate settlements when violence grew excessive. Since the workers could not be coerced by the police— except by mass murder—the government settlements had to meet minimum worker demands. The employers had no alternative but to acquiesce. The December 1914 strike of the Vitarte textile workers was one of the first examples of government settlement in favor of the workers after violence had occurred, in this case after one worker was killed in a clash with the police.[21]

The system of political bargaining which was emerging in the second decade of the twentieth century blossomed forth in the January 1919 general strike for the eight-hour day. Begun on

19. Luis Felipe Barrientos C., pp. 148–49.
20. Guillermo Gonzales Rosales, *Administración de la Legislación del Trabajo* (Lima, Dirección General de Trabajo, 1953), p. 15.
21. Demetrio Flores Gonzales, *Medio Siglo de Vida Sindical en Vitarte* (Lima, 1957), pp. 25–27.

January 10, 1919, this first general strike demonstrated clearly that the workers had the power to shake the government. With the support of the university students and other opposition forces the workers alarmed President José Pardo into decreeing, on January 15, the legal establishment of the eight-hour day.

Several months later, in May 1919, a second general strike took place. This time, however, the leaders were jailed and the strike suppressed. This event foreshadowed the eclipse of the system of political bargaining through dictatorship. Repression was and still is an alternative to political bargaining in a free environment.

On July 4, 1919, Augusto Leguía took power in a popularly supported coup. At first Leguía appeared to be anxious to include worker demands in his program. He released the union leaders arrested in connection with the general strike of May 28–31,[22] and enlarged the office of worker affairs.[23] However by 1922 the Leguía regime had grown hostile to organized labor. It became both desirable and possible to take repressive action against worker organizations preparing violence. It was desirable because, from Leguía's point of view, worker violence endangered his tenure in office. It was possible because the labor movement was small and poorly organized and because opposition to Leguía was, at the time, quite moderate; consequently the repercussions of repression were feeble.

In contrast to the previous government of José Pardo which had intervened in labor matters only when violence had broken out, Leguía began to restrict worker organization activity itself. He apparently realized that mass movements of dangerous proportions required considerable time and organization to effect, and that such activity could be stopped in the early stages— given the disorganization of the labor movement at that time— by a few well-calculated arrests. The general strike of May 28– 31, 1919, for example, was preceded by the formation of a strike

22. Ricardo Martinez de la Torre, *El Movimiento Obrero en 1919* (Lima, Amauta, 1928), p. 38.
23. Gonzales Rosales, p. 15.

committee two months before, three protests to the government, and three demonstrations.[24]

There were attempts to create mass movements of protest, but generally they were cut short by arrest. For example, in 1922 the Committee for the Reduction in the Cost of Living[25]—the nucleus which had organized the May 28–31, 1919, general strike—began once again to raise demands before the government. This time the Committee was outlawed and the leaders jailed.[26]

The ideological emphasis had shifted in this period (1920–29) from an anarchist to a Marxist sentiment. The latter, in direct contrast to the former, looked at the job of destroying the capitalist state as a long and difficult process requiring discipline and organization. It would not be, as the anarchists believed, the result of one glorious moment of spontaneous mob action. Another important difference was that the Marxists were thinking not in terms of an absence of recognized government, but of their "dictatorship of the proletariat."

The Marxists talked of developing a class consciousness and rational tactics. They also spoke—as did the anarchists—of a glorious future. As José Carlos Mariátegui, a leading ideologist of the time, put it, "A proletariat without a larger ideal than the reduction of working hours and wage increases of a few pennies will never be capable of a great, historic achievement." [27] This statement indicates the irrational content of the Marxism of that day. A proletarian revolution (the "historic achievement") was held to be an end in itself, working conditions, wages, and hours being only secondary, if important at all. Today the Marxist-extremists are more pragmatic; a revolution is presented to the workers as the means for bettering their material condition.

During the period 1910–29 the guilds had been under extreme

24. Martinez de la Torre, pp. 14–24.
25. Comité pro-Abaratamiento de las Subsistencias.
26. Barrientos C., p. 164.
27. José Carlos Mariátegui, "Mensaje al Congreso Obrero (1927)" in Ensayos Escojidos, ed. Aníbal Quijano (Lima, Patronato del Libro Peruano, 1956), p. 59.

strain. Their conservatism put these organizations totally at odds with the labor movement. During the second general strike of 1919, for example, when workers were engaging in armed clashes with the army, the Confederation of Guilds presented the government with the mild request that it release the union leaders and listen to their demands. Many labor leaders were disgusted with the Confederation's conservative behavior. In the confusion of Leguía's coup on July 4, 1919, they demonstrated their annoyance by breaking into headquarters of the Confederation of Guilds, destroying property, and keeping the building for their own use.[28]

From 1919 on guilds began to disappear. The decline of the hand craftsman, the growth in importance of the labor unions, and the entrance of revolutionary doctrines into their own organizations finally drove them into near oblivion. The membership drifted to the mutual assistance societies or to labor unions. Today, one finds only traces of these organizations in Lima. In the provincial cities they are phantom organizations used by the leaders of regional federations to swell voting strength in their favor. It should not be supposed, then, that in Peru the labor movement grew out of either guilds or mutual assistance societies. It has been distinct from these ever since its beginning.

In the decade of the 1930s a new force came into the labor movement: political parties. Before this time the labor leaders had confined their hopes for violent change to the labor movement. If a revolution were to come about, they apparently believed, the workers themselves would effect it. The ideology in the period 1920–29 was a nebulous, primitive Marxism, without organized parties or formal divisions.

But for several reasons—the weakness of organized labor, the intransigence of management, and the hostility and repression of the Leguía regime—it appeared to many labor leaders that the workers would not advance unless a new political party came to power and used government force to defend the worker. Hence it became the party which had to be defended first in

28. Martinez de la Torre, pp. 30,37.

order that the workers receive their rewards second. The parties, for their part, recognized the violence potential of worker organizations and energetically sought to control them.

The two parties which had and still have the greatest influence in the labor movement are the Communist and APRA organizations. Both parties had their roots in the diffuse Marxist sentiment of the twenties. By the early thirties, both had emerged as distinct ideologies. The Communist party began in 1928 as a tiny, uncommitted Marxist–socialist party, the *Partido Socialist del Perú*. Two years later it changed its name to *Partido Comunista* and applied for full affiliation to the Comintern.[29] The national labor center, the *Confederación General de Trabajadores del Perú* (CGTP), founded with difficulty in 1929[30] (the latter part of the Leguía dictatorship), was frankly communist by 1930.[31]

The APRA (*Alianza Popular Revolucionaria Americana*—Popular American Revolutionary Alliance) was formally founded in Mexico by an exiled Peruvian, Victor Raúl Haya de la Torre, in 1924,[32] but it did not arrive in Peru until the fall of Leguía in 1930. In essence, the Aprista movement was one of reform. When it arrived in Peru, the country had just come out of an eleven-year period of dictatorship characterized by inaction, repression, and, most sources agree, corruption. At the same time, educated Peruvians had become increasingly aware of accepted democratic principles and practices in other countries. The Russian revolution, distant as it was, had provided them with a new perspective on political change. The urban population— manual and white-collar workers, school teachers, and university

29. Robert J. Alexander, *Communism in Latin America* (New Brunswick, N.J., 1957), pp. 222, 224. The Communist Party in Peru today considers 1928 as the founding date. See *Unidad* (organ of the Communist Party of Peru) (Lima, October 11, 1961), p. 1.

30. Ricardo Martinez de la Torre, *Apuntes para una Interpretación Marxista de Historia Social del Perú* (4 vols. Lima, Empresa Editoria Peruana, 1947), 3, 6–7. Other sources claim the CGTP was founded in 1927. See: Luis Felipe Barrientos C., p. 173.

31. See *El Trabajador* (organ of the CGTP) (Lima, October 17, 1930, and December 8, 1931).

32. Luis Felipe Barrientos C., p. 171.

students—had been growing steadily during this period, and when the dictatorship collapsed in 1930, this large group of indignant, idealistic citizens was to demand, in one form or another, reforms and progress. It was from this sentiment for reform that the APRA party was built.

Unfortunately for both the Apristas and Peru, APRA did not become a party with pragmatic, rational goals. Instead, it quickly developed a near-religious doctrine, completely self-contained and almost entirely out of contact with political reality. The first APRA platform, approved by a congress of the party in 1931, is perhaps the finest example of an unrealistic political program ever to be put forward in the history of Latin America. Many demands were, in the 1931 Peruvian context, frightfully extravagant; most were dangerously specific.[33]

In short, hard-hitting sentences the Apristas called for: (1) separation of church and state (when the Catholic church had been a constitutional part of the government since independence); (2) Latin American citizenship (at a time when most Latin American countries, including Peru, were engaged in serious border disputes); (3) specific measures to punish corruption in government (when only a tiny fraction of the public administration—based on the patronage system—could consider themselves unblemished); (4) control of both the export of capital and foreign investment (which, in the light of the Aprista claim to being Marxist, implied violent upheaval of the entire economic system); (5) removing the armed forces from politics (a proposal which, in view of the intensity of the party's opposition to the army, could only be interpreted as the intention to destroy the existing army, and create an APRA-controlled military in its place).

These five points constitute only a small segment of the scores of demands which the party made. Before they had finished construction of their image of the ideal state, the Apristas had

33. See "Programa Mínimo, approbado en el Primer Congreso Nacional del Partido, Lima, 1931" in Victor Raúl Haya de la Torre, *Política Aprista* (Lima, Editorial Cooperativa Atahualpa, 1933), pp. 10–16.

alienated almost every center of power in the country, including the military, the church, foreign and local business, landowners, and the existing government. Buried in the avalanche of demands were many proposals that were realistic: a social security system (which was created in 1936—by a dictator); the establishment of a Ministry of Labor and Industry (dictator Odría created the Ministry of Labor in 1949); the lowering of the voting age to 18; increased attention to the Indian population of Peru.

Since 1931, the Apristas have learned a great deal. Specifically: (1) they have dropped the proposal for the separation of church and state discovering, incidentally, that as attitudes change and new forces enter the political system the importance of the church diminishes, even while not formally separated from the state; (2) they have sublimated their desire for political unity of Latin America into occasional support for the Latin American common market; (3) they have realized, after taking part in the government themselves, that corruption is not simple either to define or eliminate, and while encouraging movement toward a more responsible civil service, they no longer speak of apocalyptic punishment for "evil doers"; (4) they have accepted the existing economic system as an adequate base on which gradual, carefully-thought-out improvements may be made; (5) they have realized that the best way to keep the army out of politics is not to attack it.

The APRA doctrine, it should be pointed out, had been constructed on a contradiction: while the party agitated for total reform and held an exclusivistic conception of politics (the APRA slogan was "Only Aprismo will save Peru"),[34] it advocated the establishment of a genuine democratic system—a system which cannot function with absolute doctrines of total change. It certainly seemed in the early years of the party that the Apristas

34. Harry Kantor, *The Ideology and Program of the Peruvian Aprista Movement* (Berkeley, University of California Press, 1953), p. 58. It is interesting to note that by 1961, obviously by conscious party decision, this slogan had been dropped to make the party appear less absolutist.

were so convinced of the wisdom of their proposals and the justice of their program that, if they had come to power, they would have silenced those who dared suggest that a measure was unsound or unfair. Consequently, in addition to alienating most of the vested interests in the country, APRA was a source of concern to those individuals who were simply interested in political and personal freedom.

Although APRA accepted certain principles of Marxism, it broke sharply with the Communists in rejecting the Soviet Union as either the example or leader of the revolutionary transformation to be performed in Latin America, Peru in particular. Because the APRA party represented a highly organized popular force—a new phenomenon on the Peruvian political scene—the Communists rightly held it to be a serious threat to their importance. Attacks and counterattacks have characterized Communist–APRA relations since 1930 with the exception of a lull during World War II.

In the short space of time between Leguía's resignation (August 25, 1930) and the day Sánchez Cerro took office (October 11, 1931), Haya de la Torre and his doctrine had radically affected both the political texture of the country and the labor movement. Zealous and highly organized, the Apristas gained control of many unions. Although APRA doctrine was not as revolutionary as that of the Communists, the Apristas managed, by presenting a staggering program of precise demands, to fully terrorize the upper class and parts of the middle class. The Aprista popular strength presented an even more important source of worry.

The period of freedom 1930–31 also gave worker organizations an opportunity to reach a high level of activity once again. The first general strike since 1919 was executed on May 11–14, 1931, by the CGTP.[35]

Sánchez Cerro began labor union repression on January 7, 1932, with a decree of national emergency (*Ley de Emergencia*)

35. Martinez de la Torre, *Apuntes para etc.*, 1, 161–87.

which outlawed the CGTP.[36] From that date on both the CGTP
and the *Central Sindical de Trabajadores Peruanos* (the APRA
national center) led a clandestine half-life, gradually fading into
obscurity.[37] When Sánchez Cerro was assassinated in 1933 (apparently by an Aprista), control of the government was delivered
by Congress to General Oscar R. Benavides, who ruled the
country with a firm hand until 1939. Influential Apristas, many
of whom were labor leaders, were sought out and imprisoned or
exiled.

Benavides' innovations in labor union repression tactics included a system of informers who attended union meetings to
report on preparations for overt activity and "undesirable" leadership. He also expanded and controlled the process of official
recognition of worker organizations. The very small number of
organizations recognized in this period (see Figure 4) reflects
Benavides' attitude toward organized labor. On the other hand,
Benavides, although anti-APRA, and consequently anti-union, was
not oblivious to the needs of the workers. He created the social
security system, began worker housing projects, and dictated a
number of laws and resolutions on working conditions and wages
favorable to the workers.[38]

In the elections of 1939, the APRA party was still outlawed.
The Communists, representing an anti-APRA force, fared better.
For example, Juan P. Luna, one of the top Communist leaders
of that time, was permitted to run for a deputy seat.[39] The government of Manuel Prado (1939–45) was less repressive than
that of Benavides, but his firm hand on the labor movement in-

36. Martinez de la Torre, *Apuntes para etc.*, 3, 466.

37. John J. Crowley, *Labor and Political Parties in Latin America—Three
Examples* (mimeographed paper) (Madison, Wisconsin, 1960). The importance of the CSTP was considerably less than that of the CGTP; even many
Aprista labor leaders active during that period could not, in 1961, recollect its
existence. As late as May 1, 1934, an issue of the CGTP organ, *El Trabajador*,
appeared, attempting to deny that the CGTP had gone out of existence, but
the anonymity of the publication is mute testimony to the shadowy existence
which the organization was leading.

38. Luis Felipe Barrientos C., p. 204.

39. Alexander, *Communism in Latin America*, p. 230.

FIGURE 4.

Recognition of Worker Organizations[a] by the Government, 1936–1960

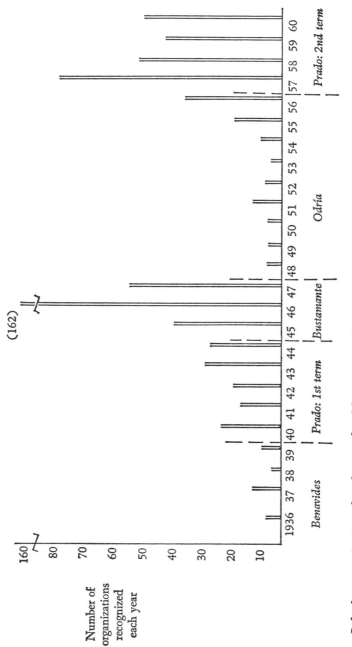

a. Only those organizations of workers employed by private establishments are included.

Source: Ministry of Labor, *Estadísticas de Trabajo* (Lima, Bulletin for the First Quarter, 1960).

dicated that Peruvian conservatives still had doubts about the intentions of the Aprista labor leaders. Although it seems true that the conservative government reached understandings with the Communists, these agreements included nonactivity of the Communists in the labor movement. During the Second World War, such an agreement was in accord with the party line: a productive Peru contributed to the defense of Russia.

As Prado's term came to a close he relaxed the control of the labor movement and legalized the Aprista party. APRA mobilized for the 1945 elections and succeeded in placing a large number of their candidates in congressional posts. The National Democratic Front candidate for president, José Luis Bustamante y Rivero, supported by APRA, also won. During the next three years (1945–48) Peru experienced freedom for the first time in fifteen years. Labor unions were given a free atmosphere in which to operate. The astounding number of organizations recognized in 1946 (162) is one indication of the changed climate. Many new unions were formed during this period, and a great deal of consolidation took place. A new national center, the *Confederación de Trabajadores del Perú* (CTP) was founded in 1944, toward the end of the Prado government. At first the CTP was in extremist hands but soon passed into Aprista control in the environment of freedom that followed the 1945 elections.[40]

Politically, the situation was far from smooth. APRA, with a long history of frustrated expectations, presented plan after plan for the revolutionary transformation of the country. APRA's inability to temper its demands to the political and economic realities, as well as intense anti-APRA feelings were perhaps the chief reasons for the political immobilization which reached a climax in 1948.

Both houses of Congress, boycotted by anti-APRA forces, did not meet after the middle of 1947 and President Bustamante ruled by decree. A number of instances of violence marked the period, and while an assassination, for example, might have been quickly forgotten in another context, in the highly polarized

40. Ibid., p. 231.

Peruvian environment such acts took on great significance: whether true or not, the anti-Apristas held most of the acts of violence to be the work of the APRA party.

Soon after Bustamante was elected, it became clear that the coalition was a failure. The Apristas claimed that Bustamante had been impeding reform and had allied himself with the anti-APRA conservatives. The anti-APRA forces held that APRA had attempted to gain totalitarian control of the country, and, in the process, had been driving the nation toward chaos. Whatever the difficulty, the government was left without the popular support of the APRA party.

With its position of influence in the labor movement, APRA harassed the government by causing strikes and other disturbances.[41] The strike of the APRA-controlled Lima Regional Federation (*Unión Sindical de Trabajadores de Lima*) in August 1947 seriously disturbed life in Lima and was broken by arrests and governmental suspension of personal guarantees.[42] Ex-President Bustamante, in his book *Tres Años de Lucha por la Democracia en el Perú*, gives an extensive—perhaps exaggerated—account of Aprista agitation in worker organizations designed to weaken the government.[43]

The pressure built to a climax in 1948. A cabinet composed entirely of military officers was appointed on February 28, 1948. On June 17 all members resigned, apparently because President Bustamante refused to comply with their demand that the APRA party be outlawed.[44] There was one revolt of anti-APRA military at Juliaca early in July, another revolt of apparently pro-APRA naval forces at Callao on October 3, and finally, on October 28, 1948, the army, headed by General Manuel A. Odría, took control of the country.

41. Publicly Apristas today deny this but a few APRA labor leaders have informed me that the party did use unions for the political purpose of harassing the government.

42. Kantor, *Ideology*, p. 19.

43. José Luis Bustamante y Rivero, *Tres Años de Lucha por la Democracia en el Perú* (Buenos Aires, 1949), pp. 150–57.

44. Kantor, p. 19.

In retrospect, it does not appear that the free government could
have survived under the existing circumstances. Ex-President
Bustamante, writing from exile in 1949, summed it up:

> [The government], deprived of an organized force of its
> own, devoid of a party which would back up its actions,
> found itself situated between two irreconcilable forces and
> vigorously opposed by both: APRA, intent on the total cap-
> ture of power, and the extreme right, highly dissatisfied be-
> cause I would not order the repression [of the APRA party].[45]

Facing opposition from practically all sides, buffeted by repeated
acts of violence, Bustamante could not survive; his removal by
the military was a foregone conclusion.

Once again the labor movement suffered for its political connections. The APRA party was, in the eyes of many, the most
dangerous enemy of domestic peace. Odría, for one, saw it that
way. Party members were searched out and jailed or exiled; once
again, they were frequently labor leaders. Odría also arranged
matters so that key organizations were in the hands of collaborators who agreed to make no trouble in return for protection of
the dictator. Sometimes the arrest of the APRA leaders of an organization was sufficient to deliver it into the hands of Odría's
men. In the Lima Union of Taxi Drivers and the National
Federation of Taxi Drivers, extremist collaborators gained full
control after the arrest of APRA leaders. In the Lima Union of
Bus Workers (SUTA), a five man team of extremist collaborators
was given full control for the entire eight years of Odría's rule.
For the cooperation he received from the leaders of the Lima
Union of Construction Workers, Odría gave them the most
luxurious headquarters building ever seen in Peru, before or
since.

Odría took no chances with larger, more dangerous worker organizations. Both the APRA-controlled national center, the CTP,
and the Lima Regional Federation were quickly destroyed and
not permitted to function even with collaborators in the leader-

45. Bustamante, p. 86.

ship positions. In other organizations where Odría had few sympathizers, he relied on informers and arrests to keep activities at a minimum. Going to prison under Odría was apparently quite common. But to be fair, it appears that being released was almost equally as common. Despite the repression, there were strikes by APRA-led organizations. Both the National Union of Bank Clerks and the Federation of Textile Workers, in APRA hands at the time, were surprisingly active.

Odría, like Benavides, was antiunion but not antiworker. While on one hand he gave employers what amounted to complete liberty to destroy the unions in their shops, he would give startling wage and social benefits to the workers. He decreed, for example, seven blanket wage increases while in power. Although a study of real earnings during his rule (see Tables 11–12) shows that real wage gains paralleled, at best, those of the previous government, Odría did leave power with many people convinced that he had done more for the worker than anyone in the history of Peru. Odría's labor policy was, in an elephantine manner, paternalistic. Smashing or incapacitating worker organizations, but using government power to make employers deliver his presents to the workers, he practically destroyed what little existed in the way of conflict-resolving processes.

On balance, then, the eight years of Odría's rule marked another setback for the labor movement. He rescued the country from a chaotic political situation, and there was certain economic progress during this period. But he left the labor movement in shambles, or in the hands of extremists. Odría did provide for the orderly, just transfer to democratic government. It is true that the APRA party was legally not allowed to run its own candidates, but in view of the acute conflict the party would have generated, perhaps it was the best way to insure stable, free government at the time. In retrospect, it seems that the choice to make APRA work through less partisan candidates was a wise one, for the particular configuration of power resulting from the 1956 elections gave Peru an unprecedented period of freedom and stability.

The winner of the 1956 elections was not the Odría-supported candidate, but Manuel Prado (the same man who ruled the country from 1939–45), who won with Aprista support. The circumstances, with APRA supporting a non-APRA president, were basically the same as they had been in 1945, but this time APRA demonstrated a remarkable degree of patience and foresight. The party continued to support the government to preserve the free system, even though it meant the temporary sacrifice of much of the APRA program.

Peru's longest period of constitutional free government in this century came to an end on July 18, 1962. Elections for a new president were held on June 10, 1962, as scheduled, but failed to provide any candidate with the constitutionally required one third of the ballots. The three major contenders, Haya de La Torre (APRA), Belaúnde (*Acción Popular*), and Odría (*Unión Nacional Odriista*), each with a substantial portion of the votes, remained unreconciled for several weeks following the election. Belaúnde and his supporters, realizing that Acción Popular would be excluded from a majority coalition (since neither of the other groups would consent to back him) claimed that the elections were fraudulent. Certain members of the armed forces, bitterly opposed to Haya de La Torre and fearful that he might gain the presidency if Congress chose the president—as it would under the constitution in such a situation—also insisted that the elections be annulled.[46]

The intense rivalry between the three forces, the menacing attitude taken by Belaúnde, and the ambiguity of future political relationships created an atmosphere conducive to military takeover. APRA did come to an understanding with Odría one day before the coup, agreeing to back him in the congressional election of a president. But the tardiness of this agreement as well as the improbability of its successful implementation for a six-year period rendered it ineffective in preventing the military coup.

46. For an account of this period see Richard W. Patch, "The Peruvian Elections of 1962 and Their Annulment," *American Universities Field Staff, West Coast South America Series*, Vol. 9, No. 6 (1962).

APRA, acting through the Confederation of Peruvian Workers (CTP) which it controlled, ordered a general strike in an attempt to coerce the military into turning the government back to civilians. Called for July 23, 1962, the strike was a failure. The military junta had a considerable amount of support including extremists and Acción Popular, and rank and file worker sentiment for the strike was not sufficiently aroused.

This entire event illustrates—if the point needed further illustration—that free government in Peru is a risky undertaking. The body politic is divided into hostile forces, each struggling to gain control of the executive. And in struggling these forces jeopardize the very existence of constitutional government. But it is this fact, that free, constitutional government is risky, that gives meaning to the behavior of worker organizations. Tactics, the role of political parties, structure, power distribution: these things become intelligible when viewed in the light of the insecurity of a constitutional executive.

As we have seen, an environment of freedom in which political bargaining could take place has been an infrequent phenomenon in Peru. Although the eclipse of freedom has not prevented the reemergence of political bargaining, the long interludes of repression have had a profound effect in retarding the institutionalization and stabilization of this system.

In the first section of this chapter we noted that the labor movement in Peru was young. Even with unimpeded growth, we should expect to find it far behind similar movements in the United States or European countries. But what should be clear from the preceding exposition is that it has not grown freely. In 42 years of existence (1919–61), the labor movement has experienced 21 years of intense repression, eleven years of moderate repression, and only nine years of freedom (see Figure 5). Worker organizations in Peru have been rather like plants growing under a box, receiving sunlight only occasionally.

There are two facets to a labor movement: organizing and sophisticating. In an atmosphere of continuous freedom the two bear a fixed relationship to each other. But in an environment

FIGURE 5.

Political Leadership of Peru and Worker Organization Repression, 1919–1961

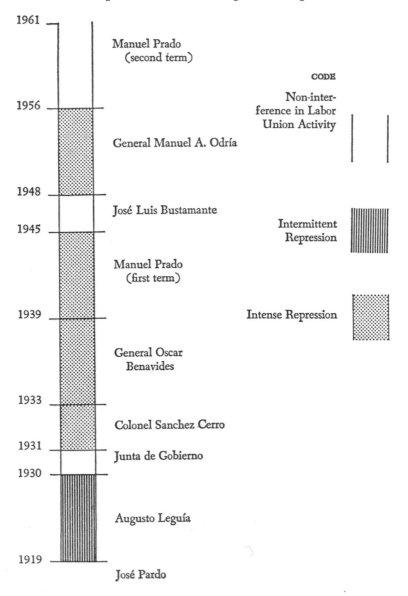

where freedom is only occasional, the organizing outruns the sophisticating. It takes only a few weeks or months to form a union but many decades of unimpeded activity to develop satisfactory processes of decision-making, sound finances, cohesion, productive political attitudes, and mechanisms for dealing with and influencing centers of power. The situation existing today is one of many worker organizations but relatively little labor union experience.

One example of the lag in the sophistication of the Peruvian labor movement is the small number of national congresses held by regional, industrial, and national worker organizations. These congresses are important for shaping policy, informing the members, unifying the organization, and developing and encouraging new leadership. During the present period of freedom, labor leaders have found it convenient to hold such congresses every two or three years.

Ideally then, most organizations should have had in 1961 the experience of ten or fifteen such reunions. But as a result of the past history of repression, there are few organizations which in 1955 had held even one congress. The Federation of Printing Workers, founded in 1919, held its first congress in 1955. The Federation of Textile Workers, also founded in 1919, held its first congress in 1958. The very important National Union of Primary School Teachers, established in 1936, did not hold a congress until 1956. The Lima Regional Federation was founded in 1940 and held its first congress in 1959. The dates for other organizations are similar. Youthfulness, then, characterizes the labor movement in Peru. An understanding of this fact will give the reader a useful perspective from which to evaluate Peruvian worker organizations today.

3

WORKER ORGANIZATIONS AND THE EXECUTIVE

Political bargaining, as already defined in this study, is the settlement of labor conflicts by the executive who has been coerced through the use of violence. As explained in the first chapter, this pattern is essentially the product of a political system which renders the president insecure in the face of civilian opposition and violence. When worker organization attacks combine with opposition party agitation, the armed forces are increasingly tempted to remove the president in a coup. Consequently, the executive must intervene in labor disputes to survive. This chapter will describe the mechanisms of intervention and analyze the different forces which determine the when, where, and how much of executive decision-making.

Violence, however, cannot be considered the only element of coercion. It will be shown how economic sanctions, as applied to either the individual firm or to the organizations of employers, may affect certain outcomes. In addition, there are resources of an interpersonal nature such as friendship, trust, and obligation. Finally, as will be pointed out in the next chapter, legal enactment (lobbying before the legislature for laws) is also employed by the workers on certain occasions. Thus the pattern of political bargaining does not exist in pure, uncontaminated form in Peru.

Nevertheless, the basic dimensions of the system are un-equivocally those of political bargaining. The workers employ tactics directed toward agitation and violence. The executive is their target. And he responds in terms of this threat to his survival. Economic, legal, or personal influences are secondary; they operate within the limits set by the measures necessary for executive survival. In Peru labor's primary weapon is neither votes nor economic pressure. It is its ability to threaten an insecure executive with extinction.

The branch of the government which deals with labor–management disputes has undergone considerable development since this decision-making function was institutionalized in 1913. It began as a subdepartment in the Ministry of Interior (government and police) "for the responsibilities which that Ministry has with respect to the maintenance of public order." [1] Later, in 1920, it was transferred to the Ministry of Health and Public Welfare, gaining the status of a department in 1936. In 1942 the department was placed in the Ministry of Justice and in 1949 the Ministry of Labor and Indigenous Affairs was created by Odría.

The Ministry of Labor is fully established to deal with the legal, technical, and political aspects of workers employed by private companies. It is the smallest of the twelve ministries, having received 37,000,000 sols (1.4 million dollars) in the fiscal year 1961. This amount was about one third the budget of the Ministry of Foreign Affairs and about 0.4 per cent of the national budget of 9.8 billion sols (360 million dollars). In essence, the Ministry of Labor is the president's agency for settling labor conflicts quickly, before the political potential of these issues builds to a dangerous level. There is not time to allow a strike to have serious effects on the employer, nor may these issues be ventilated for weeks or months in the legislature. The survival of the government and the tranquility of the nation depend on a swift decision.

1. Guillermo Gonzales R., *Administración de la Legislación del Trabajo,* p. 16.

Whether the issue be the wage level for all Lima construction workers, the length of the working day, or the rehiring of a discharged worker, if important organizations are on strike, the executive cannot permit other bodies to handle the issue. Legislative, judicial, and managerial functions must be usurped. Allowing matters to take a supposed "natural course," without executive intervention, would be suicidal.

Although the basic element of ministerial intervention is quite simple, the actions and reactions of the different parties are diverse and complicated. As a starting point it should be pointed out that the dispositions concerning intervention state that except in the case of a violation of law, workers must first deal with management before going to the Ministry of Labor. The reasoning behind this norm seems to be that with direct employer–employee bargaining an accord—if reached—will enhance productivity by contributing toward harmonious worker–management relations. In addition, the ministry prefers to avoid as much direct responsibility as possible. If workers and employers can settle their conflicts peaceably and privately, the ministry is indeed happy to let them do so.

Such private conciliation is the process by which the vast majority of labor conflicts are settled. Labor Ministry officials believed that the number of independent solutions had been increasing in the period 1956–61, but no statistics are available to verify this view. However, it must be remembered that the larger, more important issues are the ones which usually come before the ministry. In addition, those conflicts which are settled independently are threatened by the shadow of ministerial intervention if the workers fail to receive a satisfactory bargain.

If labor and management do not reach an agreement, then the issue is brought before the conciliation section of the ministry's department of labor conflicts. In separate meetings with labor and management, the conciliator tries to discover the real positions of each, the maximum and minimum which management and labor respectively are willing to accept. If the two interests cannot be brought together to a common solution, a departmental (*subdirectoral* in Peruvian terminology) resolution is issued which the workers may or may not accept. If the departmental resolution is not accepted then, after an unspecified time a ministerial resolution (*directoral*) identical to the first or more favorable to the workers is put forth. The ministry may review it, but usually upholds this second decision.

On issues of a legal nature the process is somewhat different, conciliation not being included in the process and there being three steps of appeal. There is considerable coordination within the ministry so that the various resolutions, their timing and content, could be thought of as being controlled by one man, the minister. But these two variables, content and timing, are subject to many forces and considerations. It is inaccurate to suppose that the minister imposes a solution on the basis of personal whim. First, let us examine the forces the workers bring to bear. From the discussion above, the reader may imagine the general questions which relate to a labor organization's political power: Can it strike? For how long? How much violence is it prepared to use? How many members does it have? What is its strategic position in the public eye? What are the possibilities for sympathy strikes or strikes of higher labor organizations to which the group in question belongs? The last two points are especially important. If an organization has a strategic position, that is, if the public will immediately feel the effect of its striking, then the ministry will act much more quickly to give the workers what they want. Organizations of bus workers, trolley car operators, and telephone workers are examples of strategically located organizations.

The ability of an organization to engage other labor groups in sympathy strikes greatly affects its power. Although in rare cases a regional federation may call a sympathy strike in support of a striking member organization, it is usually the industrial federations and the national center, the Confederation of Peruvian Workers (CTP), which present the most important threats. When a textile workers' or metallurgical workers' union calls a strike, the political effect is small. But if the federation to which the union belongs threatens to strike or actually does so, then ministry officials take notice. Of course, in order to gain the support of secondary organizations, the group on strike must convince both leadership and rank and file of the federation that their cause is just and that they have suffered. Therefore, all available publicity means are employed in an attempt to make the conflict known and to gain popular sympathy. Press releases, public demonstrations, handbills, and occasionally hunger strikes are used.

If a union wishes to gain popular support for its strike, it must also demonstrate that it has attempted to work through the accepted channels. Even the extremists recognize this necessity. As one communist leader put it: "In order that the workers decide to go out on strike, it is important that they arrive, from their own experience, at the conclusion that they can no longer obtain any gains by peaceful methods or bureaucratic procedures." [2] Extremists themselves must go through the motions of presenting a demand and discussing it. If they do not, the success of their own strike is endangered and sympathy strikes are unlikely.

Within the secondary organizations a union leader presents his case many times, even before his own strike materializes, so that officers and delegates of the secondary body might feel disposed to support his organization. Although support is not usually forthcoming at once, after 15 or 20 days of the union's strike, the federation may decide to call a general strike—especially if the cause of the conflict has been a scandalous abuse of an accepted norm.

One quite common practice of the unions is to call upon leaders of secondary organizations to participate in the discussions with officials of the Labor Ministry. In this way the officials become aware that the higher organization is taking a position on the issue, and the federation leaders themselves, knowing the problem and having taken a certain responsibility for solving it, will be more energetic in urging their secondary organization to begin a solidarity strike.

2. Jorge del Prado, *Cursillo—Manual de Sindicalismo* (Lima, 1961), p. 180.

In order to get satisfactory results an organization must maintain its threat. Decisions highly favorable to the workers are not imposed automatically. There are many forces and circumstances that oppose extravagant solutions. First, the ministry officials are aware of the economic concepts of inflation, cost of production, capital needs, and investment climate. Although they are willing to accede to worker demands to a limited extent, they realize that excessive generosity could have undesirable effects.

The problem of inflation is a particularly critical one for the ministry. The inflation resulting from decreed wage increases does provide a temporary solution to a dangerous political situation. But the solution is only temporary. Inflation leads to further wage demands and agitation as well as protests from many quarters against rapid increases in the cost of living. There is a real dilemma here and no simple solution exists. In its most extreme form the problem is posed between death now, or death later, for the government. Quite reasonably, the president and his Labor Minister will seek to postpone the day of reckoning. We may then offer the following hypothesis: as executive insecurity increases—other things being equal—inflation will tend to increase.

During the period under study the Prado government was not faced with the inflation-or-death dilemma in its most terrifying proportions. The relatively secure position of the executive (made so particularly through the support of the APRA party) enabled the government to offer fairly stiff opposition to worker organization demands. The ability of the government to withstand inflation without seriously endangering its survival was increased by its refusal after 1959 to grant blanket wage increases. Practiced extensively by Odría and the Prado government until 1959, such wage decrees automatically increased all wages, usually by 4 to 8 per cent. The practice after Pedro Beltran became Minister of Finance was to grant increases only to those workers who actually posed a political threat. This procedure permitted the government to insure its survival by dealing generously with powerful worker organizations, while not excessively increasing the price level. Of course the policy somewhat prejudiced groups of weak or unorganized workers. The selective concession policy, combined with the relative security of the government, enabled it to restrain inflation in 1961 to a five per cent increase in the cost-of-living index—a substantial achievement in Peru (see Table 4).

A second general force resisting worker demands is the collection of employer organizations that voices management's position before the ministry. The *Sociedad Nacional de Industrias* (National Society of Industrial Producers) is the most important of these ownership organizations. It is composed of committees from many different industries such as textile manufacturers and footwear producers. In addition there are several organizations of commercial establishments and other associations of mineral, fishmeal, and sugar producers. These organizations have considerable access in the government; their officers occasionally lunch with the Labor Minister and the Prime Minister. In their many battles over tariffs, taxes, and prices, the producer organizations have become thoroughly familiar with the governmental process. Contrary to what labor leaders believe, these groups often present a case far more convincing than the workers'. Today Peru is committed to an economy based on private enterprise. The executive realizes that there are certain conditions of freedom employers should have if the system is to function productively. Contact which producer organizations have with the Ministry of Labor serves to keep abuse of management to the minimum possible within the political context.

In connection with management access, it is worth considering the possibility of corruption. It is customary to assume that all Latin American bureaucracies are corrupt. Though perhaps true for certain other branches of the Peruvian government, such an assumption does not seem to apply to the Ministry of Labor. Both the function and the results of ministry activity are incompatible with the idea that management bribes labor officials. Decisions which the ministry issues on both individual and collective conflicts are by no means always favorable to management, and they cannot be. The ministry engages with real political forces, in the raw; it cannot sell itself to the highest bidder. Personal interviews with both present and past labor officials have corroborated my conclusion that corruption, although it may occur in some cases, is a peripheral phenomenon in the Ministry of Labor.

Ownership associations are by no means permanent, intransigent opponents of labor. In certain cases they may actually support the workers' position. There are occasions when the industrial ownership organization may urge a solution favorable to the workers in one factory in order to avoid the shutdown of the entire industry by the industrial federation in a sympathy strike. The ownership organization is especially likely to support the workers if the one firm where the problem has arisen has precipitated the conflict by violating accepted norms which the other producers respect. The other producers wish to avoid both the shutdown of their own plants and the competitive advantage which one firm would obtain by paying less than an established minimum wage, for example.

The existence of an association of hotel operators, for instance, gives the Federation of Hotel Workers more power than it would have otherwise. A strike of the workers in this industry is highly inconvenient for operators of luxury tourist hotels in Lima; guests check out and threaten never to come back. It seems quite certain that this organization's influence was instrumental in the speedy solution to the strike that the Federation of Hotel Workers called on July 22, 1961, in support of the union at the Savoy Hotel which had been on strike for two weeks to obtain the reemployment of a discharged officer. The matter was settled satisfactorily for the workers after two days of the industry-wide walkout. In another case, when the Federation of Metallurgical Workers was on strike in defense of four workers who had been discharged while attempting to form a union in their own factory, the other producers agreed to hire these men in their own shops to put an end to the strike which had paralyzed the entire industry.[3]

The ministry, then, performs its role of conflict resolution in a complicated framework of conflicting interests and considerations and continuously changing circumstances. The configuration of forces may change from day to day. A strike in one small factory may be permitted to continue without any resolution at all. Then, as the strike progresses and the industrial federation considers a solidarity strike, a departmental resolution may be issued which the minister knows the workers will not accept. When the solidarity strike materializes, when political parties begin agitating, and the union resorts to violence, the second resolution is issued and the minister hopes the workers will accept. If, however, the strike continues, the producers' organizations suggest that a settlement must be made, the CTP holds an assembly to discuss a national strike, demonstrators are arrested by the police, and some deputies are drawing up a motion to censure the Labor Minister, the minister will review the second disposition and make the offer even more generous.

Of course, these would be the ideal conditions for worker success. On the other hand, circumstances may be very unfavorable. The union may be unable to sustain the 25 to 40 days of strike necessary for full exploitation of the political potential of the issue. The federation to which it belongs may not feel itself obligated to undertake a sympathy strike. Or management may view the issue as a matter of principle and offer rigid opposition to the workers. Ownership associations may take an uncompromising stand in defense of the producer member.

For example, the strike of the workers at the Bata–Rimac shoe factory in Callao beginning on June 28, 1961, was a case where the workers were on the losing end from the beginning. The irresponsible extremist leadership of the union had provoked the conflict by presenting a wage demand in advance of the date stipulated by the existing contract as well as demanding that

3. Interview with Luis Gutierrez, past secretary-general of the Federation of Metallurgical Workers, Lima, June 26, 1961

management discharge one of the supervisors. They thus violated two accepted norms of worker–management relations.

The company obtained the full support of both the committee of footwear manufacturers and the National Society of Industrial Producers.[4] The extremist-led Callao Regional Federation, much as its leaders may have wanted to call a strike, was so weak and disorganized that this was out of the question. The leaders of the Federation of Footwear Workers were not convinced that the union deserved support, and the relatively low cohesion of their organization would have made it dangerous to press the issue. Moderate leaders in general were disgusted with the behavior of the union leaders, and the small sector of the public which knew of the conflict sided with management; consequently a sympathy strike of either moderate or extremist forces was out of the question. Left alone, the union received no ministerial resolution and after two months of strike patched up its differences with the management.

Of course, the Labor Minister's decrees are invariably unpopular with management. The settlements are basically gauged to meet the violence potential of the particular conflict and may have no relation to the needs of the firm. Consequently the employer is often aghast at the contents of the decree, and may initially refuse to comply. To make management yield, persuasion is first applied. The same channels of access used by management to influence the government are now used in reverse to pressure management. The Minister of Labor, the president of the National Society of Industrial Producers, even the Prime Minister discuss the matter privately with the management of the firm in question. Perhaps the Minister of War drops in for a chat. Foreign firms can always be threatened with adverse publicity and even nationalization. All companies can be pressured with lower tariffs and higher taxes.

If management holds firm, the issue may be passed to the Ministry of Interior which can employ police to enforce the

4. *Comunicado* of the *Comité de Fabricantes de Calzado de la Sociedad Nacional de Industrias,* printed in *La Tribuna* (Lima, August 9, 1961).

decision. This occurred twice in 1961. The first instance concerned the Lima bus companies. In order to avoid a short but crippling bus strike, the ministry decreed a wage increase which the companies refused to pay on the grounds that fares would not cover any additional labor costs. The government refused to raise fares in a pre-election year so the workers were left without the raise. To avoid another strike, the Ministry of Interior sent officials to collect and count all fares received by the conductors. In the meantime, the government began paying the wage increase from its own treasury. Later, auditors were appointed to determine the truth of the companies' claim.

The second case concerns the Santa María textile company, which in September suddenly discharged 13 workers, among them eight officers of the union. Labor interpreted this as an attempt to destroy the union and immediately demanded that the ministry order the workers replaced. Since the issue was of such importance, the ministry lost no time in ratifying a former resolution which protected labor leaders from discharge and ordered the reinstatement of the workers. However, the company refused to comply. The Federation of Textile Workers began a solidarity strike just as the Ministry of Interior ordered compliance. After two days of the solidarity strike the workers were back on the job with a police escort.

There is nothing either the Ministry of Labor or the police can do directly to force workers to comply with a disposition. The strike may be declared illegal and the minister can refuse to consider the matter. If public sentiment is neutral or even against the labor organization so it is left without the hope of further support, the strike may continue for a time, creating an uncomfortable situation for the management of the firm involved, but eventually the union compromises or gives in entirely.

The ability of the ministry to ignore labor conflicts depends on two variables: the security of the government itself, and the general attitude, especially in trade union circles, about the importance or justice of the particular conflict. Operating in light of these two considerations the minister may decide how much assistance the workers will receive from the government. The harshest treatment the ministry can employ is to ignore the organization; it would not use direct repression (arresting all union leaders, for example).

Although the ministry's role is highly political, most ministry officials like to maintain the fiction that they employ objective criteria as bases for their decisions. If the dispute involves wage demands, officials present their decisions as based on the rise in the cost of living and the workers' "real needs." Since ministerial resolutions usually grant at least double the rise in the cost of living,[5] and workers' needs extend into infinity, such reasoning seems flimsy indeed.

For example, in the 1960 key wage demand of the entire mining industry—that of the 13 unions of the Cerro de Pasco Corporation which sets wage increases for many other firms— the departmental resolution awarded the workers a 13 per cent increase (management had offered 10.5 per cent, the workers demanded 33 per cent). Four days later, the ministerial resolution gave 14 per cent. Rather than pretend that workers' "real needs" increased by one per cent in that period, it would be more realistic to acknowledge the pressure exerted by the general strike of the Federation of Mineworkers of the Central Zone which was to materialize the next day. The Minister guessed at the minimum which the Federation would accept—in this case guessing right, because the strike was called off.

If the conflict involves other aspects of labor–management relations, such as discharge, layoff, and working conditions, then an attempt is made to present the ministerial decision as the simple administration of a legal disposition. Insofar as the legal framework corresponds to both accepted norms and attitudes and the power of configuration on a given issue, then the ministerial

5. The cost of living rose about 8 per cent a year during the 1957–61 period. The wage increases awarded by the ministry were usually between 14 per cent and 20 per cent. Technically, the ministry cannot award an increase greater than the cost of living increment unless management offers more. Very seldom, however, does management hold out at or below this low cost-of-living figure.

decisions may be considered administration. But when legality
and power are in conflict, new implementations or decrees must
be created. Of course, the presidential or ministerial decrees can
always be, and are, interpreted as the implementation of an
existing law or an article of the Constitution. For example, the
disposition which forbids the discharge of labor leaders (except
for criminal behavior) was issued in 1958 to settle a conflict
but was interpreted as implementing the article of the Constitution that guarantees freedom of association.

In July 1961 the Confederation of White-Collar Workers was
on the verge of a strike and the CTP was preparing to support
them in defense of one worker who had been discharged because,
so the labor leaders argued, he was a member of the union. The
workers viewed this action as an attempt to destroy the union by
discharging members. The ministry ordered the replacement of
the worker. Lawyers for the company produced articles of the
Commercial Code concerning the right of management to employ
and discharge, but to no avail.

It seems that in the voluminous body of legal documents there
is ample wordage to supply the ministry with authorization for
anything it might find necessary to do. It is difficult to conceive
of a situation where the survival of the government is seriously
threatened by a labor conflict and yet the ministry refuses to act
for lack of legal authorization.

From time to time ownership threatens to take, and occasionally does take, a ministerial resolution to the courts. But on
issues of political importance the courts seldom question the
legality of a ministerial disposition. Even if they should, it is
doubtful that the Ministries of either Labor or Interior would
step in to create a new conflict where one had been settled. And
since court decisions usually arrive many months or years late,
after the issue is forgotten and different norms have been established, the role of the courts in collective matters of political
importance is usually quite irrelevant.

In individual claims, on the other hand, the legal framework
is quite important, for political forces are removed from the

context. In addition, when the minister judges, for political and economic reasons, that a certain issue should not be resolved favorably to the workers and need not be, then he will publicly base his nonintervention on legal dispositions, a more discreet way of saying, "Go back where you came from." But, on questions of political importance, labor law is a highly flexible framework, created largely by the ministry itself to end specific conflicts and subject to continuous modification and addition as necessity dictates.

The key man in the ministry is, of course, the minister himself. He is responsible for balancing all the conflicting forces and considerations in solutions that minimize the dissatisfaction of the interests concerned. Unlike the head of the Department of Labor in the United States, the Peruvian Labor Minister is not and cannot be partisan, for he is situated directly at the center of the political battleground between employers and employees. He must cooperate with and try to please both workers and management, striking a balance between the economic and political needs of the government. Neither employers nor a wise president would approve the appointment of a minister partisan to labor; to appoint an individual with antiworker sentiments would endanger the survival of the government.

So that the reader may grasp the complexity of the minister's job, some of the major variables which he must consider in making his awards are listed below:

1. The demand intensity of the workers: the expected length of the strike and the probable tactics.
2. Worker organization size and cohesion.
3. Worker organization location, regional (in Lima or in the provinces) and strategic (essential or nonessential service).
4. The probability of solidarity strikes and demonstrations, the size, cohesion and location of the organizations which might engage in such solidarity actions.
5. The positions of newspapers, Congressmen, student groups, and political parties.

6. The position of the armed forces.
7. The demand intensity of the employer.
8. The degree of commitment of employer organizations to the issue, on one side or the other.
9. The impact of the decision on production at the firm and in the country generally.
10. The impact of the decision on inflation.

To arrive at a successful decision the Labor Minister must have full information and he must be able to evaluate this information in a very short time. His job is to be a "survival maximizer." He must be sensitive to the many signals constantly flowing from the environment, and he must be able to interpret them correctly. Then he must make decisions which maximize the government's chance of surviving. It should be clear that moralists, idealists, and partisan politicians are not suited to the job of Labor Minister.

In the period 1956–61 Peru had six labor ministers. Although in most cases the changes were for personal or intraexecutive reasons, in one case, that of Antonio Pinilla, the change was the result of basic political forces. A brief discussion of the background leading to censure of Pinilla after only four months in office is instructive in understanding the role of the Labor Minister.

Pinilla's term, April–August 1958, coincided with the long bank clerk's strike of April–June. Because of his timing of the emission of a resolution concerning the strike, extremists took advantage of the delay and forced the APRA leaders of the union to resign. Whether true or not, APRA labor leaders considered this delay of a crucial resolution as intentional, done to prejudice APRA in the union. From that time on, relations were strained between APRA labor leaders and the minister.

Secondly, Pinilla gave certain employers, especially agricultural producers, the impression that he intended to make sweeping reforms quickly. As Minister of Labor and Peasant Affairs, he might well take certain steps, but in their view he spoke of leaps.

Finally, during the time Pinilla was in office, the extremist strike of the year was carried out. The issue was the increase in the price of gasoline, and there was nothing the minister could have done to prevent the disturbance since the matter was handled by the Ministry of Finance. However, it is the labor department's responsibility to keep trade union activity at a tolerable level, regardless of the cause of the disturbance.

Hence, when he was called before the House of Deputies, Antonio Pinilla had very little support. The APRA and APRA-sympathizing deputies were against him for his supposed role in helping the extremists capture the National Union of Bank Clerks; sympathizers with management were uneasy about the future plans of the Minister; extremists and members of the opposition parties were always anxious to censure any minister; and those who knew nothing about the man were aware that organized labor had gotten out of hand during those few months. Under these circumstances, censure was inevitable.

Although the minister himself is subject to removal at any moment, the subordinate officials—department and subdepartment heads—seem to have considerable security in their positions. However, if either management or labor feels itself treated unfairly by a particular official, the individual may be transferred. For example, the regional labor inspector in Nazca was considered intolerable by the leaders of the labor organizations of that region. According to the charges, this inspector had actually used physical violence on a labor leader with whom he was dealing.[6] With the assistance of the CTP officers and under the threat of a general strike in Nazca, the minister removed the official in question.

On the other hand, workers are anxious to protect officials whom they feel support them. The Chimbote Regional Federation came out publicly in support of the local inspector and urged the minister that he not be transferred. The labor leaders in that region had heard the rumor that the management of a certain fishmeal factory and a large hacienda had applied pres-

6. *La Tribuna* (Lima, June 1, 1961).

sure for the inspector's removal, as the workers put it, "in reprisal for the upright conduct which he always displayed in
making those firms comply with our social legislation." [7]

Although the ministry's role in resolving conflicts is perhaps
its most significant, the functions it performs are many. The
ministry and its regional offices process a large number of individual claims, such as cases involving one or several workers
who have not been given the wages, working conditions, or
social benefits provided for by law. The claims are processed in
one of several ways and if the complaint is justified the ministry
orders the employer to comply. The inspection services of the
ministry also bring to light abuses of laws pertaining to working
conditions—laws which the workers themselves may never have
heard of.

Since 1958 the construction industry has had a department
of its own in the subdepartment of worker affairs to deal with
individual claims. Certain officers of the several construction
workers' organizations spend practically their entire day in the
office, meeting workers who cannot write, helping them find
necessary forms, and getting documents approved and signed.

Other industries have departments or officials to deal with
certain technical problems of workers in their employment. The
textile department is headed by a past officer of the Federation
of Textile Workers. It provides technical assistance relevant to
the enforcement of the *régimen textil* which establishes norms
for the entire industry. There are also offices which deal with
problems of transport workers and printing workers. It must be
noted, however, that these offices provide legal or technical services; when organizations and political considerations are involved, the conflict is handled by the minister and his immediate
subordinates.

When laws affecting the workers are passed by the legislature,
the Ministry of Labor has the task of drawing up a plan of

7. *Noticiario Sindical* (organ of the Chimbote Regional Federation),
(Chimbote, January 12, 1961), p. 8. The inspector, incidentally, was transferred.

implementation. Congress gives only the general features; the ministry must decide how the entire plan will operate in practice, a job which is by no means free of political pressures. For example, the law giving all workers pensions after the age of 60, passed by Congress in March 1961, was handed to the ministry for elaboration. After discussions with the social security committee of the CTP, management representatives, and officials from the National Social Security Administration (which would administer the law), a long, detailed plan of implementation was drawn up which attempted to include the suggestions of all interested parties. Other functions of the ministry include awarding official recognition (largely a formality) and the supervision of technical and statistical studies, an employment service, and projects of technical assistance to the Indian population and a limited defense of their interests.

In summary, the Ministry of Labor is the agent for adjudicating labor conflicts within the existing configuration of power and possibilities. It is perhaps unfortunate that political expediency rather than economic considerations plays such an important part in resolving labor conflicts. For example, if it is politically necessary, the executive will decree a wage increase even if it will put the firm involved out of business. But given the existing political context, there seems no other way to handle such things. During the years 1956–61, the system of political bargaining was successful in the following senses: inflation was kept at a reasonable level (about 8 per cent yearly); employers were not brutally mistreated and the investment climate was considered "promising"; organized labor made significant gains in wages and working conditions.

As indicated before, the executive is anxious to remove itself from the direct responsibility of decision-making. A promising step toward industry bargaining without direct ministerial intervention has been taken in the textile industry. In 1958 the Ministry of Labor created the Permanent Board of the Textile Industry (*Comisión Permanente de la Industria Textil*). Although advised by officials of the ministry, the board is bipartite:

only management and labor, each with one vote, have the power to reach decisions. The textile committee of the National Society of Industrial Producers selects representatives for the employers, and the Federation of Textile Workers chooses the representatives of the workers. The purpose of the Permanent Board is to reach industry-wide agreements whenever possible. Even before the board was created, the textile industry had been subject to a number of special regulations which together form the régimen textil. The board has become the official decision-making center for expansion and modification of these regulations.

For a number of reasons, bargaining at the industry level offers a more satisfactory method of resolving conflicts than if decision-making is confined to the unions. First, when issues are settled on the industry level once and for all, the many probable flare-ups at the union level are avoided. Secondly, the members of the board are better informed than participants at the union level and are more likely to reach agreements which best take into account certain technological considerations. Lastly, the individuals representing both ownership and the workers on the board are culturally and intellectually prepared to discuss their problems rationally and amicably. According to one of the employer representatives on the Board: "Many of the union leaders are crude and narrow-minded—it is impossible to deal intelligently with these men. And many factory managers are even worse. But here [on the board] we have labor leaders with more understanding, with 'culture.' And we [ownership] recognize the problems and needs of the workers. We try to be fair."

The problem the Permanent Board faces is to reach agreements that the member organizations of each side will accept. Some employers are reluctant to abide by the decisions of the board and for this reason the management representatives must be cautious in making concessions. In 1961 the board was occupied with establishing standard wage rates for each job. If it succeeds, industry-wide bargaining on all major issues will not be far off.

Such industry-wide bargaining would not represent collective bargaining, however. The executive will continue to stand behind both parties defining their relative power positions. If the workers cannot obtain concessions from the bargaining table, they will still have the alternative of overt activity designed to provoke executive intervention. In addition, these bipartite agreements would be enforced not by the parties themselves but by the ministry. Already the régimen textil is maintained as a set of legal dispositions, not private party contracts. What bipartite, industry-wide negotiations will achieve is the reduction of strife and a lessening of direct executive responsibility for the details of the normative framework regulating worker–manager relations.

4

The legislative branch of the Peruvian government is bi-cameral, composed of a Senate and a House of Deputies. It is elected in its entirety in the presidential elections held every six years—when the Constitution is followed. Because the conditions under which elections are held differ from election to election, it is difficult to generalize about the nature of Congress. And because the context in which political conflicts arise is constantly changing, the role of Congress cannot be defined with any degree of precision. However, it is useful to make a few observations that applied to the 1956–62 body and would probably be true, to some degree, for future congresses.

The Senate is smaller than the House of Deputies (52 members, as compared to 156 in the House), its members tend to be older (35, minimum age, House, 25), and are elected on a regional basis whereas House seats are accorded on the basis of population. Because in the rural areas the upper classes have the opportunity to manipulate both the circumstances under which elections are held as well as the actual election results, and because illiterates (the great bulk of the rural population) are denied the franchise, the Senate tends to be more conservative than the House. Coming largely from urban areas, the deputies are more responsive to demands of the lower classes, organized workers in particular.

Another general feature of the legislature which is more than a passing phenomenon is its subordinate position as a decision-making body. The president's preeminence as decision-maker is firmly established both by custom and fact. In Peru the legislature has never received the reverence which it is accorded in the United States. Congress tends to be thought of as a debating center or an advisory body, not a policy-making center coequal with the executive. Unfortunately, we cannot undertake here the analysis (which would be lengthy indeed) necessary to explain this subordinate position. We shall merely proceed from this fact.

Although Congress plays a subordinate role it is not without influence, especially in a free regime. On the surface it appears that the president could completely disregard the legislature by refusing to promulgate its laws, by issuing decrees with impunity, or even by dissolving the body and locking the doors. The fact that presidents have resorted to these measures indicates that such actions are quite within the scope of possible presidential alternatives. But the president of a free regime wishes to avoid such forceful tactics if at all possible, for they usually weaken his position vis-à-vis the military.

The legislature serves—albeit partially—as a mechanism for eliciting consent. Being a body of several hundred presumably wise and independent politicians, Congress acts as one mouthpiece voicing the "popular will." If this body supports the president then he can more readily present the image of popularity. If he is opposed by Congress, then charges that the president is unpopular and alone are more easily sustained. Consequently, the president wants a contented legislature. It is an asset to him in his struggle for survival. He is therefore willing to make concessions to Congress; he is willing to relinquish some of his decision-making authority to the legislature in return for a certain measure of approval from that body. However, Congressional support is neither the only nor the most important requisite for survival, and the subordinate role of the legislature reflects this fact.

The range within which the president will honor the will of Congress is bounded on one side by the actions he must take for survival and, on the other, by firm personal or political party commitments to programs or policies.[1] Hence, if the security of the government is not immediately threatened and if the president is not intensely concerned about a particular issue, there is a high probability that Congress will have its way—if indeed it has a clear position.

On labor matters the executive must and will respond to those demands which the workers support with violence, for otherwise his survival is immediately endangered. Congressmen may complain that they were not consulted about certain decrees or resolutions, but there is nothing they can do, directly. If the workers present their demands in a nonviolent fashion, the legislature probably will play an important role, the president willingly standing aloof from a conflict and allowing the bickering and bargaining to take place elsewhere.

There is, then, no legal boundary which determines the matters to be decided upon by Congress. For example, the law establishing the legal working day of eight hours was decreed by the President, José Pardo, on January 15, 1919, to end a general strike. But in December 1959 it was to Congress that a six-hour day proposal was submitted. This proposal originated with the first convention of mineworkers and was recognized by even the workers to be extravagant. It was quietly introduced by one of the deputies from Cerro de Pasco (a mining district) and then forgotten by all parties concerned.[2] Twice in 1961 Congress played a deciding role in labor matters. One case involved the passage of a new pension law (which will be discussed below), and the other awarded all obreros 30-day paid vacations yearly. In both cases the demands were presented nonviolently and on both issues it appeared that President Prado was uncommitted to any specific outcome.

1. In the case of President Prado, we might add, such commitments were minimal; his attitude of astute indifference on practically all specific issues accounted, in no small measure, for his relatively long term.

2. La Tribuna (Lima, December 17, 1959, and January 28, 1960).

The power of censuring a minister (held by both houses) illustrates the secondary role of Congress. Censure of a minister, in itself, hardly represents a serious check on the president since another man may be appointed to pursue the same policy. And if the minister were so unpopular as to incur censure, he probably would be damaging the popularity of the government and a wise president would be glad to let him go. Consequently, congressional censure represents, at best, a minor harassment of the chief executive.

The Peruvian legislature, then, plays a secondary role compared to the executive, but it is not wholly without influence. Its power is not based on a constitutionally established right. Instead it flows from the president's need for support, from his desire to placate potential opposition and to convince the military that all is well. It is difficult to generalize about the political composition of Congress since the conditions under which elections are held as well as the political party scene at the time of elections may vary widely. The political conflicts in the nation may be injected into the legislature causing the congressional scene to accurately and dramatically reflect the bipolarity of Peruvian political society. Or the legislature may be tranquil, composed largely of independents and presidential supporters with only a small scattering of opposition members. The Congress of 1945–47 (see Chapter 2) was of the former, polarized type. President Bustamante found himself in constant battles with that body; the extreme conflict between the APRA and anti-APRA factions made it difficult for him to gain the support of Congress, and his failure to do so probably contributed to his downfall.

The legislature under Prado, 1956–62, was particularly tranquil. There were only a few opposition members (Popular Action Party, Christian Democratic Party, and the Progressive Socialist Party) while the rest of the members were independents or supporters of the regime. Hence, with relatively little effort, President Prado was able to retain the support of the legislature and thereby enhance his chances of surviving in office.

Access of labor leaders to the 1956–62 Congress was largely

along political lines. APRA forces worked through a tiny group of worker representatives, men who were workers and trade union leaders before their election. In the Senate there was one such individual, Victor Salas, a past officer of the Federation of Textile Workers; in the House there were five—past leaders of organizations of footwear workers, taxi drivers, bank clerks, textile workers, and construction workers. All of these men, members of the APRA party or close sympathizers, were elected as independents since the party was outlawed at the time of the 1956 elections. But they were in fact selected and supported by the APRA party.[3] The selection of these men and the industries they represented was not haphazard, but reflected the influence the various APRA labor leaders had within the party in 1956. For example, in the case of the Senate, no worker representative appeared on the initial list of APRA-backed independents. However, the APRA leaders of the Federation of Textile Workers threatened to withhold support from the entire list if the textile workers were not represented in the Senate. The party then removed one of the candidates from the list and substituted the Federation representative, who won the seat.[4]

Extremist labor leaders obtain access to Congress through opposition and extremist party members. During the bank clerks' strike of 1959, a deputy from the Popular Action Party accompanied the extremist officers of the National Union of Bank Clerks in discussions with the Minister of Labor.[5] Extremist-led organizations of construction workers, taxi drivers and farm laborers worked closely with deputies of the Progressive Socialist Party.

This polarized access pattern contrasts with the American congressional scene where constituency interests and personal philosophy determine access on labor questions, party identification being much less important. But in Peru party affiliation

3. Interview with Elías Sipán, Deputy and past leader of the Federation of Footwear Workers, Lima, August 11, 1961
4. Interview with Senator Victor Salas in Lima on August 14, 1961.
5. El Comercio (Lima, June 2, 1959, afternoon edition), p. 1.

seems to be most significant. An APRA labor leader would be loath to call upon a Progressive Socialist deputy for assistance; and this deputy would be most hostile to him—in spite of the fact that the deputy gladly helps extremist and other opposition labor leaders. This pattern of access illustrates the point made in the first chapter: political party conflicts in Peru overshadow social and economic divisions. Even on questions affecting workers, labor leaders and "labor" congressmen are bitter enemies if they are on different sides of the political fence.

To a limited degree one could find nonpartisan access in Congress. The Federation of Public School Teachers and the Federation of Farm Laborers and Peasants, moderate groups, worked successfully with legislators who, for reasons other than political party affiliation, took a special interest in the organization and its problems. In such cases either the organization or the legislators were independent or nonpartisan themselves. For example, the APRA-led Federation of Farm Laborers and Peasants was assisted by several deputies who were neither APRA nor opposition party members.[6]

The most energetic labor lobby before Congress was the national center, the Confederation of Peruvian Workers (CTP), which was controlled by APRA labor leaders; Although the officers of the CTP had occasion to work with congressmen for other reasons, their efforts in the legislature in 1961 were largely directed toward approval of the two laws mentioned above. Perhaps the best description of the operation of the CTP as a lobby and of the legislative process itself is a brief account of the passage of the workers' pension law.[7]

Although a comprehensive pension system had been contemplated by labor leaders at least since 1956, the concerted effort to establish such a system did not begin until the latter part of 1960. A nonviolent approach was adopted, first because it would

6. Interview with Raúl Carrasco and Miguel Cabrera, officers of FENCAP, in Lima, April 16, 1961.

7. The information in the following section was taken largely from files kept by Víctor Zárate, head of the CTP Pro-Pension Committee.

have been difficult to sustain violence on an issue removed from
the immediate interests of most workers, and second because the
APRA leaders of the CTP preferred not to endanger a government
they supported. The nonviolent approach combined with President Prado's apparent indifference to the issue made the pension
question a matter for Congress. The Pro-Pension Committee of
the CTP, headed by the secretary of social security, was formed
on September 19, 1960. Although at first it included only six
officers of the CTP, it was later expanded with the addition of
labor leaders from organizations of farm laborers, power company
workers, and others.

The Committee first organized a national demonstration—sup-
posedly effected simultaneously in different cities—which took
place on September 27, 1960. In Lima a large number of workers attended the open-air meeting in the Plaza Bolívar, in front
of the Congressional Palace. The purpose of the orderly demonstration was to gain publicity, show worker interest on the issue
of pensions, and convey the physical aspect of the workers'
strength to congressmen.

The struggle in Congress centered on the Senate. The House
of Deputies had previously approved several proposed laws for
a pension system but all had died in the more conservative upper
chamber. The new effort, therefore, was begun in the Senate.
Introduced by the APRA worker representative, Victor Salas, the
CTP bill was sent to three committees: Labor; Commerce, Industry and Banking; and Legislation "B." The Labor Committee was
headed by Senator Salas himself and it was there that the real
bill was composed. The task before the committee, as Senator
Salas saw it, was to produce a bill which would meet the minimum demands of both employers and the CTP and which would
be practicable in its implementation.

To discover the positions of the interests concerned and the
difficulties that might impair the utility of the pension system,
the committee (three members) held hearings. Members of the
CTP Pro-Pension Committee testified many times, as well as
representatives from the Chamber of Commerce, the National

Society of Industrial Producers, the National Agrarian Society, the National Mineral Producers' Association, and the National Society of Fisheries. Also called upon to testify were officials from the National Social Security Board, which was to administer the system. From over twenty separate proposals the Labor Committee pieced together one. In substance it provided for a pension fund created by equal contributions from the workers and their employers and managed by the Social Security Board. All workers at the age of 60 and with 30 or more years of employment for the same or different firms would receive a pension equal to the salary which they last received from their employer.

Although neither the CTP nor all employers were completely satisfied with the bill, they considered it a satisfactory compromise. The CTP wanted the retirement age lower and the administration in the hands of a separate board, so that the few workers already receiving certain retirement benefits from the Social Security Board would not lose these. The smaller firms wanted to escape paying toward the fund and had backed a measure which put the responsibility for providing pensions directly on only those companies of large capital. The larger companies had maintained that if there was to be a new pension system at all, all employers, regardless of size, should contribute according to the number of their employees.

The existent pension system was, incidentally, deficient in many respects. Each firm of over 500,000 sols capital was supposed to provide pensions for its workers. Placing the responsibility on the individual employer gave rise to numerous legal battles, the firms insisting or feigning that a certain employee was not entitled to pension benefits for various reasons. In some cases delinquency simply passed unchallenged. Those workers who were highly mobile or who worked for small firms or firms that had gone bankrupt were deprived of pension benefits. Two expected effects of the new system are an increase in labor mobility and a reduction in employer–employee conflicts over the issue of pensions, as well as, of course, more complete pension coverage.

After the bill had been drafted in the Labor Committee, it went to the Committee on Industry, Commerce, and Banking. In contrast to the former committee which favored labor's (that is, the CTP's) point of view, the Committee on Industry was composed of individuals sympathetic to the employers' position. It was feared that this committee might delay the bill or weaken it. However, Senator Salas, by including all points of view in the composition of the measure, had constructed a bill which was acceptable to the Committee on Industry. Only a few minor alterations were made, and even the CTP leaders felt these were helpful. The bill was released with unanimous committee approval in the middle of March 1961 (the Legislation "B" Committee played no active role). Put on the agenda, it was briefly debated, voted upon, and approved almost unanimously. What was apparently an effortless victory, however, had been the result of considerable persuasion.

The worker senator, Victor Salas, had, in addition to selecting a measure which carefully balanced the demands of the CTP with the possibilities for approval in the conservative Senate, employed personal ties to gain support for the bill. Known as one of the most cooperative men in Congress, Senator Salas had since 1956 quietly built up many friendships. When he came to ask for assistance, many of his colleagues supported his bill simply because he was "such a nice guy." But there was another factor that affected the Senate's decision. The CTP had mounted a continuous publicity campaign pointing out the gap in existing social legislation and its undesirable effects on human welfare and social peace. On the night of the passage of the bill CTP officers and other leaders were in the Senate gallery and, as is the custom, cheered and applauded the speakers supporting their position, thus creating a favorable atmosphere for approval.

Once approved in the Senate, the bill went to the House of Deputies. On the advice of Senator Salas, the CTP Pro-Pension Committee judged it unwise to permit the bill to be sent to House committees. They wished to avoid the delay which committee consideration would entail. Also, if the House should approve a bill different from that passed by the Senate, the modified House bill would have to be passed without alteration by the Senate, or die. There is no joint committee mechanism to effect a compromise between the two chambers. Since the bill approved by the Senate was probably the maximum which that body would accept, another bill coming from the House would either be inferior, in labor's view, or, if too liberal, would be rejected by the Senate.

The Pro-Pension Committee next sent mimeographed letters to all the deputies asking them to vote for immediate approval of the bill without committee consideration. With the aid of the President of the House, who supported the CTP's position, and the worker deputies, the members were persuaded to pass the bill immediately and without amendment. The law was formally promulgated on April 21, 1961, by President Prado and given to the Labor Ministry, which drew up the implementation (see Chapter 3). The system would go into effect in June 1962, when a fund had been built up. Although ignored by extremist and opposition forces, this new pension system represented a substantial achievement by worker organizations employing the method of legal enactment.

It is significant to note, however, that in presenting its position, the CTP was unable to exhibit a single table of relevant figures to Congress. On an issue of such financial complexity, this failure certainly weakened the CTP's effectiveness as a lobby.[8] The conclusion we may draw from this fact is that the Peruvian labor movement, indeed even its national center, is not oriented toward the method of legal enactment. As we shall see in Chapter 8, the CTP was primarily concerned with political bargaining, including ministerial intervention, solidarity strikes, and threats of general strikes. It found the role of lobbyist a new and somewhat unfamiliar one.

We might point out in passing that congressmen can play a contributing role in political bargaining. The publicity a con-

8. In an interview, Senator Salas regretted this shortcoming. He found it somewhat disturbing to be unable to provide fellow senators with exact figures.

gressman can give a labor organization is helpful, especially in a system where labor conflicts are settled largely on the basis of public knowledge and interest. Mentioning an organization and its problems in a public session strengthens the workers' position. For example, in the House session of September 13, 1961, when the censure of Prime Minister Beltran was under debate (a motion which was easily defeated), one of the deputies said, "I will vote in favor of Beltran, asking that he deal with, as he ought to, the wage demand of the [organization of] workers in the state-run public restaurants." [9]

Congressmen can also be useful in prodding and prompting Labor Ministry officials, especially on minor matters. When a senator comes to the ministry with a labor leader—as frequently happens—the official concerned does his best to satisfy the congressman. This does not mean that the labor leader immediately gets what he wants, nor is that what the senator would expect. Rather, the official agrees to speed up the process under consideration. Sometimes the presence of a congressman enables a poorly dressed, self-conscious labor leader to gain access and make his view known. Hat in hand, the tattered labor leader might never have had the courage to knock on the door.

Another service which legislators perform for labor organizations is arranging government donations of property or headquarters buildings. Presenting gifts of this nature to all types of organizations is an old custom in Peru, rather like pork-barreling on a diminutive scale. Since the property comes into government hands through bankruptcy or other painless ways, giving it away is quite simple. Usually a special law is drawn up by a senator and passed without question. An outstanding example of such a gift is the large plot of land given to the Federation of Textile Workers, arranged by Victor Salas.[10] Another case was the donation of a headquarters site to the Mechanics' Union of Callao, initiated by the two senators from that district.[11]

9. El Comercio (Lima, September 14, 1961), p. 9.
10. Norte Sindical (Lima, May 1959), p. 9.
11. Ibid. (November 1960), p. 15.

The resolution of conflict on general labor matters by the Congress rather than the executive seems desirable for two reasons. First, a certain decentralization of decision-making would free the executive from the precarious position of being responsible for everything that happens. Secondly, the congressional decision-making process is more open. The many interested groups may confront their opposition and maneuver toward a solution which satisfies their minimum expectations. The resulting decision is more likely to be understood and supported by the contending parties than would be an executive pronouncement formed in a context of semisecrecy which excluded many interested groups from participation.

Whether Congress becomes more important as a decision-making body on labor questions depends on the following conditions: (1) that worker organizations have sufficient access to and support in Congress to make success possible and so encourage their use of this body; (2) that worker organizations can rely upon the bureaucracy to implement congressional decisions; (3) that the executive is sufficiently insecure to require the support of Congress and to desire to pass some decision-making responsibilities on to it. If the president's tenure is secure, for one reason or another, he may snap his fingers at Congress; if his survival is made uncertain by widespread opposition and a reluctant military, then he will make special efforts to appease the legislature and obey its will. That is to say, this feature of constitutional democracy, legislative decision-making, is more likely to be utilized when "instability" is most prevalent. For those who equate "democracy" with "stability" and the absence of violence, this paradox may well be most unsettling.

2 LABOR AND POLITICAL PARTIES

5

POLITICAL PARTIES: EXTREMISTS

As pointed out in Chapter 1, the labor movement in Peru and political parties are closely connected. This connection is quite unlike that in Great Britain where the worker organizations shape the policy of the Labor Party and where the party is relatively uninterested in specific labor disputes. The reverse is true in Peru. The parties tend to shape worker organization policy and, because labor conflicts have important political consequences, party leaders are quite concerned with particular instances of strife.

The relationships between worker organizations and political parties are constantly in flux. The battle for control of the labor movement is much like guerrilla warfare; the formal control of territory seldom signifies victory. This chapter and the next will explore the dimensions of this warfare in the period 1956–61. While statements made refer to this period, the general theoretical perspectives adopted herein should be useful in analyzing other political configurations.

The basic explanation for political activity in the labor movement is found in the political structure of the country. It is this structure which makes the control of worker organizations, particularly as reflected in the ability to influence strike activity, a resource of enormous political power in Peru. In the United

States it is inconceivable that a strike would force the President to resign. But in Peru strikes are frequently crucial in persuading the military to force an incumbent from office. The political party which controls important worker organizations holds high cards when bargaining for a coalition. It also possesses one of the most efficacious instruments for effecting a change in government. In the Peruvian context, where violence has partisan political implications, the holder of the means of violence is politically powerful.

Consequently all parties have a strong motive for attempting to control labor organizations and thereby to influence strike activity. As will be pointed out in the following pages, the parties differ widely in their degree of success in obtaining such control. Nevertheless, they all seek influence in worker organizations. In this respect the Peruvian pattern is quite distinct from the American. In the United States a strike seldom has partisan political implications. Therefore, the major parties have neither a "strike policy" nor the desire to influence strike activity.

The mechanism whereby party control of worker organizations is exercised is quite simple. Many labor leaders are members of or sympathizers with one or another party, as are many American labor leaders. The Peruvian labor leader, however, faces a political situation where the strike policy of his organization will affect the fortunes of the party with which he identifies. He sees that a strike will weaken or strengthen his party (depending on whether it is in the government or opposition), and he tends to influence strike policy accordingly. The American labor leader, be he Republican or Democrat, does not face this situation. Except in an unusual case, the strike policy of his organization has no effect on the tenure of the President of the United States. Consequently party welfare does not enter into his calculations. It does not enter simply because it is irrelevant in the political context.

Peruvian labor leaders allied with political parties, whatever their orientation, face a common problem in attempting to control worker organization activity: rank and file resistance. Opposition party and extremist labor leaders find the rank and file too conservative; workers are reluctant to lose wages by engaging in a solidarity strike for distant causes. Since the goal of an opposition party is to create as much disturbance as possible, there emerges a tension between labor leaders of such parties and most worker organization members. The rank and file resistance to opposition and extremist party leaders may be reflected in many ways: worker withdrawal from the union, rank and file rejection of leadership at elections, or membership apathy.

Labor leaders of government-supporting parties face the same problem from the other side, although not as acutely. They would wish to prevent overt worker organization activity. Their goal is to keep the labor movement as calm as possible, to prevent workers from shaking the incumbent president. But rank and file workers cannot easily be dissuaded from taking violent action when they have a specific, immediate grievance. The labor leader who refuses to employ the strike will face the same problems as the leader who refuses to stop striking. However, in the usual case, the labor leader who sympathizes with a government-supporting party does not need to espouse an absolute no-strike policy. He may carry on the fight for limited worker objectives, making brief jabs at the government which are unsettling, but not fatal, to the existing regime. Nevertheless, there will be times when he must curtail activity and risk rank and file displeasure.

This tension between partisan labor leaders and the rank and file provides a basic analytical perspective for our discussion of political party influence in the labor movement. Generally speaking, we can say that in the period under study the extremists tended to follow party directives while disregarding rank and file demands with the result that their position in the labor movement deteriorated. The APRA party leaders, on the other hand, struck a productive balance between the needs of the party and those of the rank and file. They circumscribed the more common global uses of violence and maximized the use of threats as opposed to actual strikes. But they engaged in many limited strikes and usually succeeded in winning important gains

for the rank and file. In the following pages these basic propositions will be elaborated upon and documented.

The Extremist Parties

This discussion of political influences is simplified by dividing
the political groups acting within worker organizations into two
categories: extremists (E) and moderates (M). The former will
be dealt with in this chapter, the latter group in the next chapter.
The distinction between the two groups is made thus: extremists
are those parties and individuals who seek total, revolutionary
change in the social, economic, and political structure; moderates
are those who, while they may advocate extensive changes, are
satisfied with the basic political and economic institutions. Whenever the terms "extremist" or "moderate" have been used in this
study, they are to be understood as defined above. Further distinctions between the two groups on the basis of tactics or immediate objectives cannot be made. One of the greatest difficulties in understanding Peruvian politics arises from similarities in
the behavior and immediate objectives of both extremists and
moderates.

There were in 1961 seven distinct extremist party organizations, all of the left:

1. Trotskyite party (old Fourth International faction)
2. Trotskyite party (new Pablo faction)
3. Leninist committee
4. Rebel APRA party
5. Communist party
6. Progressive Socialist party
7. Socialist party

Within these groups there were numerous crosscurrents of political thought and ideology, variously supporting Stalin, Khru-
shchev, Mao Tse-tung and Tito. These currents were usually sub-
dued, but occasionally they came out into the open. In 1961
the Fidel Castro government was formally supported by all of

these parties. In addition to the party members there were many individuals too independent to join an extremist organization, but who thought and acted as extremists.

The attitude of each extremist party toward the government cannot be predicted a priori. For example, during the 1939–45 rule of President Prado, the Communist party apparently supported the government, while the Trotskyites were clearly in the opposition. During the period under study, however, all extremists were in the opposition. Against the Prado administration extremists utilized every weapon: the press, declarations and condemnations, demonstrations and riots, and—of particular interest to us—strikes of the worker organizations they controlled.

To further complicate our understanding of the situation, extremists were not alone in this aggressive activity. When a moderate party is out of power, it tends to become part of the total opposition. Being without influence in the civilian government and facing the prospect of several years more out of office (the Constitutional interval between elections in Peru is six years), an opposition party loses little if the military takes over. Instead, it may gain from a coup. New elections may be held which will give the party more representation, or the military junta may favor the former opposition parties by appointing their leaders to important positions and leaving the former governing parties powerless or even persecuted. From the point of view of getting back into power, it makes sense for an opposition party to work toward a military coup.

Hence, the extremists were not alone in their attacks upon the Prado government. The moderate opposition parties, having the same short-run goals, also adopted an attitude of hostility and intransigence toward the government. In 1961 the major opposition parties included the Popular Action Party (*Partido Acción Popular*), the Odría Party (*Unión Nacional Odriista*), and the Christian Democratic Party (*Partido Demócrata Cristiano*). These three moderate parties were quite weak in the labor movement; they usually depended on genuine extremist elements to call strikes and organize riots and then publicized these events

as proof of the "nefarious policy of the government." As far as
the labor movement is concerned, extremists can be considered
to be members of the above seven parties and their sympathizers,
keeping in mind that moderate parties of the opposition, antigovernment newspapers, and individuals with personal grudges
cooperate with and support extremists when the opportunity
arises.

But it has to be emphasized that the term "extremist" must be
used in a very general sense; to use the word "Communists,"
for example, to describe these elements is inaccurate. There was
no labor organization that was completely controlled by any
single extremist party. In some cases, one party's influence, although not total, was considerable: the Lima Union of Printing
Workers—Trotskyites; the Lima Union of Construction Workers
—Communists; the extremist Federation of Petroleum Workers
—Socialists. In other cases the extremist influences in the same
organization were multiple. The Arequipa Regional Federation
(FDTA), included both Communists and Trotskyites as well as
other extremist elements. The National Union of Bank Clerks
was without doubt the most multifarious extremist organization
in Peru. It appears that nearly all seven of the above mentioned
parties had a finger in that pie, so to speak; also the Popular
Action Party, the Christian Democratic Party, and even the
tiny Llosa faction of the National Revolutionary Union (a
small opposition party) were tangibly involved. It must be noted
that in almost all organizations dominated by moderate elements,
extremists were constantly at work, attacking moderate labor
leaders and the government, urging strikes regardless of the
circumstances, and maneuvering for control of the organizations.

Although a membership count of the extremist parties was, of
course, not available from any source, an estimate of 20,000 to
40,000 for 1962 is accurate enough to put the size of this force
in perspective. Surprisingly enough, only a very tiny proportion
of these individuals was found in the labor movement; university students, middle class intellectuals, and others accounted for
the largest part. Judging from observation of extremist activity,

it does not seem that there were even 1,000 extremist party members in the labor movement.

However, the power of this small group of individuals lay in its ability to gain the support of unconcerned or unaware rank and file. The total number of workers controlled by extremists was about 25,000 to 30,000 in 1961, a figure considerably lower than in 1957. This figure represented about ten per cent of the entire number of organized workers.

Dynamics of Extremist Control

The subject of extremists in the labor movement will be treated in three parts: their rise to power, their maintenance of position, and their loss of power. Extremists usually gain control of labor organizations in a very simple and open way: by elections—elections which in themselves are almost always quite fair. This may come as a surprise to some readers who imagine that extremists use rigged elections or other underhanded tactics to come to power. Such is not the case (see Chapter 10). Of course, the extremists, like the moderate forces, do take full advantage of the objective conditions under which elections are held.

In the unions where the rank and file votes, extremist strength lies in the energy of a few enthusiastic individuals. It is the extremists who come to all the meetings and participate energetically, who circulate daily among the rank and file. During the period under study they made vigorous attacks on management, the government, moderate leadership, and the APRA party. When elections came they were the ones who were well known for toughness, a quality which frequently means more to rank and file than party labels.

In the industrial and regional federations, and in certain unions where elections are not direct but are carried out by delegates, the situation is somewhat different. The voters in such assemblies are officers themselves. Each usually has a clear idea about policy and about which men represent each political tendency. Since attendance is usually quite good for federation elections, there is very little margin for doubt. In most federations the delegates know a month in advance what kind of officers' board will be elected. There are occasional cases, such as the elections held by the Federation of Hotel Workers in 1961, where the balance may be very close and one or two switches would change the entire complexion of the new officers' board. In the case of the hotel workers the moderate forces expected a victory, but the absence of two members at elections gave extremists and their sympathizers a one vote margin.[1] Hence, in 1962, the Federation was run by a moderate assembly of delegates and an officers' board which tended toward the extremists' side.

Obviously, then, the struggle for control of organizations where elections are carried out by intermediaries centers around the delegates. Extremists naturally realize that it is very important to capture the position of delegate. Moderate forces, however, are also aware that delegates are important and, except in occasional cases, offer considerable competition. Another simple way in which extremists may control a worker organization is to found it themselves. For example, the extremist leaders of the Lima Union of Construction Workers, unwilling to be outvoted by the numerous moderate provincial organizations in the existing Federation of Construction Workers (M), withdrew from that organization and founded their own federation in 1958.

To maintain themselves in power, the extremists use several devices. In the unions of the concentrated type, where members are closely knit in the same work center, there is usually no way for extremists to counter membership dissatisfaction. Further attacks and demagoguery are much less effective after the rank and file have had experience with extremist leadership. When extremists lose an election in such an organization, they must, except in very rare circumstances, step down. Not to do so would leave them alone and ridiculed. The members of the union would follow the new board.

1. Interview with Santiago Tamariz, secretary of organization of the CTP, Lima, July 13, 1961.

In unions of the dispersed type, where members are scattered over the city, more manipulation is possible, for the rank and file of these dispersed organizations have a tendency to lose interest when their organization is poorly managed. They stop paying dues, stop coming to meetings and elections, and eventually stop obeying strike orders. This is in direct contrast to the behavior of members of a concentrated union where close contact of the members and close dependence on the organization mean that the membership will evidence concern if the organization is badly managed.

In a dispersed union extremist leadership continues regardless of policy or rank and file opinion. What eventually happens is that the organization loses so many members that it really ceases to exist in fact. This is what happened to the Lima Union of Printing Workers, which had been mismanaged for four years (1957–61). In 1961, dues had fallen to practically nothing, the extremist leadership could not call a strike even for issues concerning their own workers, let alone for political purposes, and there were about 40 voters at the 1961 officers' board election. It was in this same direction that the Lima Union of Construction Workers was heading. It would be generous to estimate that it had, in 1961, 700 dues-paying members and 4,000 effective striking members out of a possible 10,000 construction workers in the city.

In the industrial federations the problem of remaining in office does not present itself. In the four industries where extremist industrial federations exist (taxi drivers, construction workers, petroleum workers and peasants), there are competing moderate organizations. Moderate unions affiliate with moderate federations, leaving only extremists in the other organization. Thus there is continuous competition between the two organizations for member unions. Of the two federations of taxi drivers the moderate group had all but won the battle; with both the two construction workers' and two petroleum workers' federations the situation remained static during 1958–61 (see Tables 11 and 13).

100 LABOR AND POLITICAL PARTIES

To stay in power in the regional federations, extremists use the device of claiming as members many tiny or, in effect, nonexistent organizations. Their only significance is that at election time one or two men (extremists) appear claiming to represent a member organization. Since dues are never a requisite for membership, there is no way of excluding such "organizations" if the leadership wants them as affiliates. For example, the extremist Arequipa Regional Federation (FDTA) claimed 24 members, among them "unions" of tailors, shoemakers, carpenters, and ornamental metal workers. An examination of the membership of this organization revealed that the number of genuine member unions was three, or perhaps, at the most, five or six.

The extremist Puno Regional Federation (*Federación de Trabajadores de Puno*—FTP), in addition to the usual fictions, claimed to have a member union of journalists. This "organization" consisted of one member, the secretary-general of the regional federation—an international agent who came to Puno after activities in Bolivia. He did, however, study journalism in Argentina.[2] It should be noted, though, that moderate regional federations also employ phantom organizations to insure control.

The most significant feature of extremist activity in the Peruvian labor movement during the period under study was its lack of success. Once in control of a body of workers through a labor organization, extremists demonstrated a marked inability to maintain that control. They were either voted out of office or, more frequently, their organizations lost members or member unions. Table 11 gives a rough picture of the extremist strength in the labor movement in the period 1957–61. As can be seen, the total number of workers they controlled fell during this period with the 1961 strength at perhaps the lowest point since 1930.

When it is realized that the number of organized workers increased by about 20 per cent in the period 1957–61, so that even to maintain their proportion of strength extremists should have controlled about 65,000 workers, the total figure of 21,000

2. Interview with Sr. Morales, secretary-general of the extremist Puno Regional Federation on September 2, 1961.

TABLE 11

Important Worker Organizations in Extremist Control, 1957–1961
(effective membership)

Organization[a]	1957	1958	1959	1960	1961
Lima Union of Construction Workers	25,000	15,000	10,000	8,000	4,000
Federation of Construction Workers (E) (excluding Lima Union)[b]		4,000	4,000	6,000	6,000
Lima Union of Trolley Operators			1,000		
Lima Union of Bus Workers				5,000	
Lima Union of Printing Workers	3,000	3,000	2,000	1,000	negl.
Arequipa Regional Federation (E) (FDTA)	10,000	3,000	2,000	1,000	negl.
Puno Regional Federation (E) (FTP)		500	500	500	negl.
Cuzco Regional Federation (E) (FTC)	2,000	3,000	3,000	3,000	2,000
Huancayo Regional Federation (E) (USTH)	1,000	1,000	1,000	1,000	500
Federation of Taxi Drivers (E)	12,000	4,000	3,000	2,000	1,500
National Union of Bank Clerks		7,000	7,000	7,000	7,000
TOTALS	53,000	40,500	33,500	34,500	21,000

a. All of the key organizations have been included in this table. However, a number of smaller unions, several inactive regional federations, and certain weak industrial federations (e.g., Farm Laborers) have not been included. The number of workers controlled by these organizations would be about 5,000—a figure which seemed to be about the same in 1961 as it was in 1957.

b. The Federation of Construction Workers(E) was founded in 1958 with unions already in extremist hands. Hence, it may not be quite accurate to consider them not in extremist control in 1957, as we have done.

(or, including the 5,000 not mentioned in Table 11, 26,000) is a clear demonstration of their failure.

There are several factors accounting for this loss in power. In essence, the explanation lies in the orientation of extremists and the policies which they followed, and the high degree of flexibility and freedom within the labor movement. Extremists were almost completely uninterested in the immediate tangible demands of the workers in the organizations they led. Their attention was concentrated on problems of broader political scope, national or sometimes international. Extremists used the labor organizations which they controlled to agitate for these issues, sometimes by press releases, sometimes by public demonstrations, and frequently by strikes.

However, the rank and file members, despite their ignorance of the details of these broader issues, are aware of results. And for better or for worse, the results in which they are interested are of the tangible, immediate kind. When leaders call a strike to defend an issue unrelated to present worker conditions, the membership tends to become annoyed. Or if a federation calls a strike in support of some external issue, the leaders of the member unions know that such a strike will be unpopular with the rank and file in their own organization.

This discontent might well have no effects in a rigid, authoritarian labor movement, but in Peru the labor movement is neither inflexible nor tightly controlled. The small size of most of the concentrated unions (which results in membership awareness, interest, and good attendance at elections) gives ample opportunity for changes in leadership and policy. In dispersed organizations, where leadership is distant from the rank and file, members are perfectly free to retire from the organization. In both regional and industrial federations member unions may withdraw and remain independent, or join a competing federation, or even found a new secondary organization of their own. From top to bottom there is considerable opportunity for mobility and change. The labor movement in Peru hangs together, in parts or as a whole, only if members and member groups are satisfied with the policy and activities of the organization to which they belong.

The combination of this opportunity for mobility with the dissatisfaction which extremist behavior created is the fundamental reason for the extremist decline in the labor movement in the period under study. A few pertinent cases illustrate this view well. In support of the strike of the extremist-led Federation of Construction Workers (June–July, 1961) the already weak Arequipa Regional Federation(E), received the cue to carry out an indefinite strike. This direction had very little to do with the construction workers, although their wage demand was said to be the ostensible reason. The alacrity with which every extremist-controlled organization in the country supported the strike showed that it was part of a general move (made periodically by all extremists) to weaken and discredit the government.

The leadership of the federation followed what may have been a good political policy, from the extremist point of view, without thinking in terms of the strength and cohesion of their organization. The result of the "total and indefinite strike" was complete failure. Life continued as normal in the city. All the key transportation and factory workers' organizations had long before withdrawn from the federation because of its tendency to call strikes for nonmember issues, and in this case they completely disregarded the strike order. The few remaining members of the federation, such as the Arequipa Union of Printing Workers, refused to obey the order because the leaders realized that their rank and file would resent the loss of pay for no apparent reason.[3] It was not surprising to find that at the end of 1961 the federation was openly divided; after such a disgraceful public failure, "reorganization" was the first move of several factions.[4]

Following the same order, the National Union of Bank Clerks contributed a one-day work stoppage. This was the most extremists could urge the assembly of delegates to accept. Even this one day, insignificant as it was, represented a sacrifice. The rank and file complained about the double amount of work there was to do the next day. In an attempt to quiet criticism, the leaders demanded that the banks pay double for the day on which the clerks worked extra hours, a demand which the bank owners rejected. The clerks, in an uncoordinated fashion, began to effect

3. Interview with Claudio Gutierrez B., secretary-general of the Arequipa Union of Printing Workers, on August 31, 1961.
4. See *El Pueblo* (Arequipa, September 1, 1961), p. 1.

slowdowns in some of the banks. This move was answered by a total lockout by the owners. Then with the union leaders confused and uncertain, the banks began to undermine their authority by reopening and employing only those clerks who had signed statements of cooperation. In a very few days all banks were operating normally and the union officers were in the embarrassing position of not being able to prevent either their members or the banks from taking this course of action. The results were loss of prestige for the organization and its leaders and dissatisfaction among the rank and file.

Another aspect of the failure of the extremists in the labor movement was their incapacity as labor leaders. Since they were not interested in the union as a tool of defense of the workers, their thinking and energy did not go into activities designed to strengthen their federations. Important aspects such as finances, organization structure, bargaining techniques, and productive tactics were all but ignored. A wise, circumspect policy of the extremists might well have been to strengthen and vitalize the organizations they controlled in order that they might be effective tools for their political designs, but apparently they lacked the patience or the insight, or both, to go about things in this manner. For example, in both the extremist Federation of Taxi Drivers and the Lima Union of Bus Workers, the scandalous mismanagement of funds by extremist leadership in 1960 was an important factor in its loss of rank and file support. In the Lima Union of Printing Workers the leaders failed to take the steps necessary to keep such a dispersed organization firmly united.

In the regional federations, extremist incapacity was more evident. Although the scope of such federations is limited, there are certain opportunities for assistance, opportunities which leaders of extremist regional federations did not grasp and exploit. In the Cuzco Regional Federation (FTC)—the most powerful organization of its kind in Peru—it was evident, upon investigation of the activities of the FTC, that practically nothing constructive was being done. That the Federation maintained considerable control in that city is largely because it had partaken in very little destructive activity (see below). The Trotskyite criticism did seem to be accurate in this case: "For more than 30 years the bureaucrats of the Communist party have controlled the FTC but nevertheless, what have they done in the field?" [5] In dealing with management and government in wage claims, extremists sometimes demonstrated appalling incompetence. To a certain extent this was a reflection of their strategy, which was to make the greatest public disturbance possible. But in a number of cases, which because of their insignificance went almost unnoticed by the public, extremists, with almost inconceivable shortsightedness, worked themselves and their organization into a ridiculous mess. For example, in 1961 an item in a small Cuzco newspaper mentioned that the "strike" of Indian sharecroppers at the Hacienda Chaupimayo was entering its fifteenth month.[6] Under the guidance of the extremist Cuzco Regional Federation (FTC), the Indians of this hacienda had effected a slowdown in working their own pieces of land. Told by leaders of the FTC that they would be given the land, the sharecroppers had been slowly starving themselves. The two longest strikes in 1961, both of about two months' duration, were precipitated by the clumsy dealings of extremist officers in the Arequipa Committee of Bank Clerks, and in the Union of Workers for the Bata–Rimac Shoe Factory. In such instances, the rank and file began to question the competence of their leaders.

Furthermore, extremists had trouble both in coming to power and staying in control of labor organizations because the labor leaders of the APRA party made persistent, organized efforts to keep them down or throw them out. However, the importance of this factor must not be overrated: first, because the APRA label often did moderate forces more harm than good; and second, because a situation favorable for moderate takeover had to be created first by extremist failure. In general it did not seem that Peruvian extremists had either the ability or orientation to be

5. *POR* (organ of the Trotskyite party of Peru) (Lima, August 7, 1961), p. 3.
6. *El Comercio* (Cuzco, July 3, 1961), p. 1.

successful as labor leaders. The best proof of this is their failure to maintain their strength. Leon Trotsky was aware of the problem extremists face in controlling labor organizations when he wrote:

> The unions, being organizations of the superior levels of the proletariat, as all historical experience demonstrates, develop powerful tendencies toward conciliation with the democratic regime of the bourgeoisie . . . the labor unions are not ends in themselves but only one of the means to employ in the march toward proletarian revolution.[7]

To put it another way, Trotsky is admitting that the great bulk of organized workers are simply not dreamers. This being the case, what Trotsky did not tell his followers was how they were to maintain control of the workers while at the same time carrying out their political projects. Without any solution to this very important problem, Peruvian extremists tried to get along as best they could.

Three Case Studies

The National Union of Bank Clerks

A more complete picture of extremist activity in the labor movement can be provided by presenting certain aspects of the recent history of three important Peruvian labor organizations: the National Union of Bank Clerks, the Cuzco Regional Federation (FTC), and the Lima Union of Construction Workers.

The National Union of Bank Clerks came into extremist hands during a strike in the middle of 1958. An exception to the normal pattern, the change in leadership came about as the result of the resignation of the incumbent moderate officers. However, in the elections of 1959 extremists maintained their leadership

7. Article entitled "Sindicato y Revolución," by Leon Trotsky, republished in El Trabajador (organ of the Trotskyite party of Peru, Pablo faction) (Lima, May 1961), p. 2.

position, the assembly of delegates having shifted in their favor. As noted before, the leadership of the Union contained different extremist influences, all of which had very little in common. In fact, aside from their desire to weaken the government, the only point of unity was their common opposition to the APRA party. For the extremists this antipathy was a useful tool for maintaining themselves in power. In elections, the choice they presented to the rank and file was not between "moderate" or "extremist," but between "APRA" or "us." Whether the general dislike of the APRA party by even independent elements of the rank and file was based on fact or fiction is of little importance. It existed and the extremists made full use of it.

When the time came for election of the 1960 officers' board, the internal divisions of the National Union of Bank Clerks could no longer be contained. Two men (German Ugarte and Humberto Damonte), representing equally extreme factions of the leadership, contended in an election which was voted upon by the entire mass of the union membership, because no candidate could receive a majority in the assembly of delegates. In this election the Apristas, aware of their unpopularity, backed an independent candidate (Sergio Arboleda) in an attempt to avoid the APRA label. The extremist Damonte won the election, the APRA-supported candidate taking second place.[8]

Beginning with the 1959 strike which, despite its length (62 days), was settled on terms unfavorable to the clerks, extremist popularity began to decline. For example, in the committee magazine of the clerks in the Banco de Crédito—perhaps the largest banking company in Peru—a note appeared concerning the new 1960 officers: "Our votes must not be betrayed; the new officers ought to pledge themselves to seeing that the FEB [Union] recovers all its prestige." [9] Clearly there was some misgiving about the way the organization had been handled in 1959. In the election for the 1961 officers' board the extremists could no longer

8. *Alerta* (organ of the committee of the Banco de Crédito) (Lima, January–February–March, 1960), p. 17.
9. Ibid., p. 19.

afford the luxury of partisan division. The two factions drew up a combined officers' board which won in the assembly of delegates, where the extremists still had a majority.

More recently, as the Cuban Revolution became an issue supported only by extremists, most of the leaders continued to support the Castro government despite the fact that such a position was not popular with the rank and file. Union officers spoke at pro-Castro demonstrations and signed bold statements in support of the Cuban revolution. One of the members of the officers' board for 1960, Proel Merino, returned from a trip to Cuba and made such inflammatory statements that the assembly of delegates found it necessary to remove him. Furthermore, a number of officers and delegates made Castro-financed trips to Cuba;[10] rank and file were becoming aware of the pro-Soviet-Cuba allegiance of the union leadership. The press organ of the union read, as one committee leader put it, "like a Moscow newspaper."[11]

The 1961 sympathy strike with construction workers and then the leadership's loss of control of the membership (see above) were also points of rank and file dissatisfaction. The situation at the end of 1961 showed an extremist-led organization with moderate forces in control of two fifths of the assembly of delegates. The extremists discovered that control of a very cohesive organization (built for them by previous moderate leadership) was actually a clumsy tool of limited usefulness. Every step that the union leadership took in defense of the Cuban revolution and other extra-bank clerk issues, no matter how feeble a step it may have been, only weakened its position. And in the meantime, while attempting to use the organization for their own purposes, the extremists were forced to do a minimum amount of legitimate trade union business, concerning such matters as wage increases

10. From past experience, Peruvians know that such a trip to Cuba is not a sign of curiosity, but of partisanship. The Communist party itself distributes these free trips.

11. Interview with César Diaz, grievance secretary of the regional committee (sección regional) for Western Peru of the National Union of Bank Clerks, in Iquitos on May 13, 1961.

and assistance to workers in the realization of their social benefits, in order to satisfy the increasingly restive rank and file
members.

The Cuzco Regional Federation

It was a general tactic of extremists in the labor movement to
engage in ad hoc general strikes. The strike usually began with
one key organization in a strike over an issue of concern to its
members, and then the others joined. These ad hoc political
strikes could be distinguished from ordinary solidarity strikes
quite easily. First, an ad hoc strike was not decided upon or
coordinated by any permanent central organization. It was effected "spontaneously" by extremist-led organizations in diverse
industries and different regions. Secondly, whereas the usual
federation strike takes three to four weeks to materialize, the
extremist ad hoc political strike usually took place one week or
ten days after the initiating organization began its strike. The
only requisite for such a strike was that the issue have a certain
degree of popular appeal. It is instructive to note that extremists
never appealed to the lofty concept of "solidarity of the masses"
when a small extremist-led organization was on strike over an
issue which did not have important political overtones. And, as
noted before, extremists seemed never to consider the effects such
a strike would have on the strength of their own organizations.

The purpose of ad hoc strikes was to weaken and perhaps destroy the government. However, such activity might also be useful in forcing the government to deal with extremists. With their
threat of calling another such strike, the extremists have a bargaining lever with which they may exact concessions of long-run
utility. However, with one exception, the Prado government did
not make concessions to the extremists. To have done so would
have given them the power to destroy from within, thus making
further strikes of a political nature unnecessary. But, as we have
seen, it was precisely these political strikes for nonworker issues,
more than any other factor, that weakened extremist control of
worker organizations. Instead of capitulating to the extremists,

the government left them in a position of non-access. In that condition they were obliged to strike again and again, further weakening their control of rank and file. Whether the government officials reasoned in this fashion is not known, but the effect of the government's policy was quite evident in 1961.

The extremist effort of July 1961 was, in terms of shaking the country, very weak. In fact, it would have gone unnoticed except that at the same time two moderate organizations—bus workers and telephone workers, both highly strategic services—were waging brief strikes of their own. It may have been somewhat painful in the heavy strikes of 1958 and 1959 for the government to withstand newspaper headlines and opposition party ridicule. However, the extremists were left far weaker than they would have been if the government had yielded to them by appointing an extremist to a ministerial post, for example.

The one place where the government had capitulated to the extremists was in Cuzco, a city with a population of about 100,000, located in the Andes to the southeast of Lima. For a variety of reasons, extremists have been quite strong in that city for many years. The extremist-led Cuzco Regional Federation had absolute control of the entire working force of that city.

The Federation willingly supported the April 1958 extremist effort and succeeded not only in paralyzing the city, but in controlling it as well. The FTC had called upon students from the local university (who never miss a good riot) and numbers of totally ignorant Indians. The mobs overturned trucks, smashed car and store windows, and even captured the general of the army division stationed in the city. The armed forces held back, realizing that an attempt to establish order might, in view of the state of agitation, result in a massacre of enormous proportions.

The government was aware that the FTC had a position of power. Unwilling to oppose this force, it made a bargain. A prefect (mayor) sympathetic to the extremists (or perhaps actually a Communist, as some claim) was appointed. This man would prepare the ground for his victory as a senator in the 1962 elections, thus giving the extremists a voice in the Senate (which

they lacked in 1961). In addition, the prefect would give the
FTC freedom to carry on its activities. In return, the leaders of
the FTC agreed to be orderly and refrain from violence. Since
that time, Cuzco, aptly named the "Moscow of America," has
been surprisingly quiet.[12] For example, the FTC refused to participate in the extremist effort of 1961. While the Arequipa
Regional Federation(E) finished destroying itself in an indefinite strike and the bank clerks threw themselves into the embarrassing episode mentioned above, the FTC remained quiet. In
the last days of the strike of the construction workers, the harassment of moderate leaders forced the FTC to call a strike—not the
indefinite type which such an effort should merit, but a stoppage
of 48 hours. The strike lasted only one day, for it was learned that
the issue had already been settled in Lima on the same day.

The prefect held his part of the bargain by ordering police to
permit pickets to close down the entire city. Stores, movie houses,
even the workers' cafeteria, were all closed down by the faithful
little bands. But even this one-day stoppage was sufficient to create discontent in certain sectors. Many people claimed that the
pickets might as well have been delivered the city. As El Comercio (of Cuzco) put it: "those present complained that the
political authority [the prefect] had not given the necessary
guarantees to the rest of the population not connected with the
strike." [13] The workers in Cuzco's only two factories were annoyed at the loss of a day's pay.[14]

Toward the end of 1961, the FTC received several blows. The

12. The Trotskyites, incidentally, were furious at the pact made by the
Communist leaders of the FTC. They held the situation on April 9, 1958,
was the closest Peru had ever been to violent revolution (the FTC gained control of Cuzco on that day) and insisted that calling off the strike was
treason to the cause of the revolution. See POR (organ of the Trotskyite
Party of Peru) (Lima, April 21, 1958), p. 3.

13. El Comercio (Cuzco, July 12, 1961), p. 6.

14. Interview with Jaime Castro, secretary-general of the Union of Brewery
Workers (Cuzco, September 4, 1961). It should be noted that when Peruvian
workers lose one day of work, they lose not only the pay for that day but
also the weekly bonus (dominical) given by law to all workers who miss no
day of the work week. This bonus is equivalent to a full day's pay.

prefect was replaced by a new appointee instructed to maintain order if the FTC should call a strike. The test came on October 17, 1961, when the Federation called a one-day stoppage in repudiation of Peru's Prime Minister, Pedro Beltran, who was visiting Cuzco. The strike was first intended to last until the Prime Minister left the city, and when he replied that he would not leave until the strike was over, the FTC limited the stoppage to one day.

The strike itself was only partial. Beltran urged the merchants to open their stores, which they did. Bus transportation and market operation continued, and all APRA-influenced workers (a sector which had gained strength since 1956) stayed at their jobs. All this was possible because the police gave—as they had not previously given—protection from the bands of university students which the FTC employed as pickets, bands which nevertheless did manage to hurl a few rocks at those who had defied the FTC's order.

On October 23, 1961, shortly after the October 17 strike, the APRA forces founded a competing regional federation, the *Unión Sindical de Trabajadores de Cuzco*.[15] Although weaker than the extremist FTC, the USTC provided a nucleus around which opposition to the extremists might coalesce. Now that the pact between the FTC and the government was broken, the FTC was free to strike itself into oblivion. In a very few years it may well be in the same condition as the extremist federations of Puno, Ica, and Arequipa: merely a name and a handful of agitators.

The Lima Union of Construction Workers

The Lima Union of Construction Workers was, in 1961, one of the most extreme of the extremist-controlled labor organizations. Although during the Odría dictatorship its officers publicly supported the government, their policy changed abruptly in 1956 when Manuel Prado took office.[16] From that date, the leaders

15. *El Sol* (Cuzco, October 24, 1961), p. 1, and *La Tribuna* (Lima, October 26, 1961), p. 5.
16. See *El Obrero de Construcción Civil* (organ of the Lima Union of Construction Workers) (Lima, issues from 1954 to 1958).

attacked the government, the CTP, the APRA party, and the United States with a vehemence unsurpassed by any group in the country.[17]

Of all labor organizations in Peru, the Lima Union of Construction Workers offers the greatest potential for violence. Its large size (at the height of its power in 1956, the union probably could have mustered 25,000 workers into the streets) is only one factor. Excluding the small number of skilled workmen, the workers in the construction industry are of the lowest level of urban society. Many of them are Indians recently arrived from the mountains, unable to read or write, confused and insecure. With energetic oratory, these individuals could be mobilized to do anything the leadership might urge.

On June 24, 1961, the leaders of the union attempted to mobilize a strike, ostensibly for higher wages (wages are set by the government in the construction industry). The strike itself was only partial: instead of 20,000 workers marching through the streets, there were perhaps 500 willing to participate in violence and about 3,000 who stopped work in Lima.[18] There were two reasons for this poor showing. First, the construction industry in Lima had suffered a decline since 1956. The number of workers employed had fallen by at least half from the 1956 figure. Secondly, the leadership of the union had ignored the structural aspects of the organization. In the dispersed construction industry where all jobs are temporary, officers must make continuous, imaginative efforts to organize the new labor centers and integrate the workers into the life of the union. This had not been done.

Although the strike itself was quite feeble, the union managed

17. During my trip to the Cangallo Street headquarters of the union, which coincided with the early part of the April 1961 invasion of Cuba, I was told that my head would be smashed in if I ever returned. This was the only occasion where an actual threat of physical violence was made by extremists. Generally speaking, extremists were surprisingly cordial.

18. Technically, the strike was called by the extremist Federation of Construction Workers. Although a few unions in the provinces were involved, the strike was made primarily by and for the Lima Union.

to get considerable publicity. The opposition newspaper, *El Comercio*, which always ignored strikes of moderate-led organizations, gave the construction workers' strike full coverage. Although antiunion itself (*El Comercio* is the only daily in Lima which does not permit its workers to organize), this paper always gave open support to any worker organization which attacked the government. Another aspect of the publicity the union received concerned the violent methods that leaders instructed pickets to use. On one occasion, when a band of 40 to 50 strikers surrounded and attacked two policemen who were protecting nonstriking workers on a job, one of the Indian picketers was killed. As usual, the opposition forces came forth with the old clichés: "tyrannical oligarchy," "oppressive government." It is interesting to note that the Indian killed in the violence did not even speak Spanish, but only his native dialect, *Aymará*.

Perhaps the most significant aspect of the construction workers' strike was that it was successful from the point of view of the workers. Beginning with a totally unrealistic demand for wages and working conditions, and a strike designed to have political overtones, the leaders found it necessary to go through the motions of handling a worker issue, by appealing to the Ministry of Labor. The ministry responded eleven days after the strike had begun with a resolution raising the wages of the workers. The leaders refused to accept the disposition on the grounds that "all the points of demand had not been settled." [19] The real reason was that the political effects of the strike were just beginning to build: meetings and parades (which with luck might have turned into riots) were being planned in protest of the death of the worker mentioned above; the opposition in the House of Deputies was attempting to censure the Minister of Interior (police); the Arequipa, Cuzco, and Callao regional federations looked as if they might create some genuine disturbances. When nothing materialized and people began to forget about the construction workers and their strike, the Ministry of Labor issued another resolution which gave construction workers a

19. Reported in *El Comercio* (Lima, July 5, 1961), p. 1.

slightly higher wage increase than did the former measure. In view of the quieting political atmosphere, the extremist federation and union accepted the new resolution, even though no more points of their demand had been considered.

Although the moderate-led federation of construction workers was pressuring for higher wages at the same time, the 12 to 15 per cent increase (depending on the category) granted by the ministry was primarily the effect of the action of the extremist organizations. A significant point arises from this fact: although extremists use labor organizations for political purposes, they are forced to clothe their policies in worker demands. And although the tactics may be clumsy and destructive, in the process the worker sometimes receives greater benefits than would be obtained by nonpartisan or government-supporting labor leaders.

But in the long run extremists in the Peruvian labor movement were detrimental to the effectiveness of the worker organizations. While their activity occasionally resulted in temporary gains for the worker, extremists usually tended to destroy themselves or the organization they controlled. This latter case was the most unfortunate, for it meant that workers were without the defense of any organization. The 2,000 Lima printing workers, for example, were without such protection in 1961. Their organization, in extremist hands, had disintegrated, leaving the workers at the mercy of their employers, with only a hope that in three or four years the new printing workers union, formed under APRA leadership, would come to their assistance.

6

POLITICAL PARTIES: MODERATES

Extremists are not the only ones anxious to control worker organizations for political purposes. Moderate parties—both those which support the government and those in the opposition—are also keenly interested in capturing and manipulating these centers of power. And from the viewpoint of the party, such interest is justified. Labor leaders of opposition parties wish to control worker organizations for the same reason as extremists: to weaken and destroy the government through the use of strikes. Labor leaders of government-supporting parties want to prevent extensive worker organization violence.

The most important moderate party connected with the labor movement is APRA.[1] During the period 1956–61 this party supported the Prado government. In 1961 it had more members in leadership positions in the labor movement than any other party. In fact it seemed that perhaps a majority of labor leaders in the country were Apristas. The APRA success in gaining and holding positions of leadership can be accounted for by the following facts:

    1. Although they by no means form a majority of organized workers, APRA rank and file workers form a relatively large group.

1. See Chapter 2 for a brief account of the history of this party.

2. The party has been active in the labor movement for many years—since 1931.
3. The party is tightly organized and its members well coordinated.
4. The labor leaders of the party followed a productive strike strategy during 1956–61, minimizing the use of strikes and violence while maximizing the use of negotiations and threats, and avoiding strikes for political issues extraneous to the membership.

The following discussion is an attempt to elucidate and amplify points 3 and 4 above.

It is extremely difficult to describe the APRA party since it is in a period of transition and attitude changes have been uneven throughout the membership. Aprista political viewpoints range from naive idealism to a pragmatic bargaining orientation. Individual views on what the role of the party should be and how it should act differ. Nevertheless, there are certain general characteristics which most party members seem to hold in common.

First, Apristas view their party as more than a means of effecting political and economic changes. It is an end in itself, although less so than formerly. Founded and developed in an atmosphere of intolerance—an atmosphere which was created in part by the Apristas themselves—*Aprismo* became a near-religious doctrine, promising glorious futures if the party came to power. Because of the utopian content of the APRA doctrine, the party has commanded a devotion and zeal which no other moderate party possesses. In worker organizations in particular, Apristas are characterized by an energy which equals that of even members of the Communist or Trotskyite parties.

A second aspect of the APRA party is its organization. The Aprista zeal and intense desire to gain power have resulted in a tightly knit party structure which reaches into all group activity of the nation, including, of course, worker organizations. Third, perhaps even more so than extremist parties, APRA has generated a strong current of hostility, not just distaste or disagreement but a fierce dislike. This strong anti-APRA sentiment extends quite widely through the society, touching not only the army and members of the upper classes but also many white- and blue-collar workers. Aware of this hostility, most Apristas are hesitant about announcing their party affiliation publicly. In worker organizations they attempt to minimize their tie with the party.

Lastly, the Aprista party is today a party of reform, not of revolution. Although Apristas still speak of a grand future, it appears that their practical political objectives include only moderate proposals (to assist the Indian population, promote housing cooperatives, expand educational facilities, promote foreign investment). The Apristas respect the norms of private property (albeit with a social interpretation), of political and religious freedom, and of constitutional democracy in the Western tradition. Apristas today seem quite willing to work for human betterment within the existing broad economic and political framework. One important teacher for the Apristas on this subject has been Fidel Castro, who did in Cuba exactly what APRA had been considering for some time: turn everything upside down in one sweeping blow. The results, the Apristas have decided, were extremely disappointing.

Aprista activity in worker organizations is carried out through the party's labor affairs bureau, the *buró sindical*. The buró itself is a secondary organization composed of delegates from *agrupaciones* and *centrales,* as well as top APRA labor leaders without specific member organizations. The agrupaciones are formed on the union (plant) level and include all militant APRA party rank and file and APRA leaders of the union. A central is technically composed of delegates elected from each agrupación in the same industry, but in practice it is an informal collection of labor leaders in the same industry.

In general, the structure of the buró and its subordinate bodies is quite informal. Representation, for example, is haphazard and is not accorded on the basis of APRA strength in the particular industry, nor is it weighted according to the number of organized workers involved. Rather, the most militant APRA labor leaders tend to find their way to the buró sindical. Of course, close personal and ideological ties make a highly formalized structure un-necessary for effective activity. Although the existence and struc-ture of the buró are made public, its activities are not.[2] It seems, however, that in the period 1956–61 the buró was largely con-cerned with curtailing extremist activities in the labor movement. One indication of this function was the relatively high level of activity of the centrales and agrupaciones in those industries where extremists presented a serious threat. The APRA centers of metallurgical workers, footwear workers, and taxi drivers were quite active in 1961, holding meetings almost every week. In these three industries extremists were contesting APRA leadership keenly. On the other hand, the APRA centers of textile workers and white-collar workers—in industries where extremists were weak—were relatively inactive.

When elections are coming up in a federation or union, the respective central or agrupación meets to decide the best way to use APRA strength: determining which APRA men will be nomi-nated, which independents will be supported, and so forth. On issues of political importance, such as solidarity strikes and the formation of competing regional or industrial federations, the matter is thoroughly discussed and decided by a vote. There is no need to suppose that on issues which come before the APRA labor bodies, the executive committee of the party gives orders to the labor leaders. Rather, the labor leaders themselves decide the course of action, keeping in mind the needs of their party.

To a certain extent the buró acts as a coordinating body for party policy. If the buró decides that publicity is needed in one area, then the labor editor of La Tribuna (a member of the buró) handles the task. If APRA labor leaders decide that a par-ticular wage demand of a union is especially important for the prestige of the APRA leaders involved, then all party leaders in in-fluential positions (Congressmen, top government officials) are asked to make special efforts to urge a favorable solution. If the buró decides it needs a group of 500 or 1,000 energetic demon-

2. While confided in by many APRA labor leaders, I was not permitted to attend a meeting of the buró.

strators, the order is sent to the APRA student group of San Marcos University; if the leaders decide that demonstrations are undesirable, the student groups are notified to prevent, if possible, action by the university students.

On matters of general party policy the buró, which meets weekly with the attendance of forty to eighty top APRA labor leaders, might be expected to have considerable influence. Most of these men are highly active and prominent in the labor movement generally. In 1961 three APRA officers of the CTP were on the 21-member executive committee of the party—the policy-making board.[3] In general, it does not seem at all accurate to view APRA labor leaders as "tools" of the party, forced to act against their will by party leadership. Rather they are party leaders in their own right and to a large extent determine what the party labor policy should be.

The coordination which the buró sindical and its subunits provided, combined with the energy of APRA labor leaders, were significant factors contributing to APRA success in the labor movement during the period under study. But equally important was the policy the APRA labor leaders followed. The position of Apristas in the worker organizations was a delicate one. In accordance with the general position of APRA as a government-supporting party, APRA leaders were anxious to avoid any extensive violence which might have caused the president's downfall. However, as noted in earlier chapters, the power of Peruvian worker organizations depends largely on their ability to employ violence. Labor leaders of a government-supporting party cannot flatly reject violence as a strategy, for to do so would render the organizations they controlled virtually powerless. The strike, the demonstration, and the parade (which are the precursors of actual violence) are the lifeblood of the labor movement. Rank

3. These men were Fortunato Jara R., subsecretary-general of the CTP and secretary-general of the Moderate Federation of Taxi Drivers; Efigenio Zamudio L., grievance chairman (secretario de defensa) of the CTP and secretary-general of the Moderate Federation of Construction Workers; and Francisco Taboada A., secretary of worker education of the CTP and past (1960) secretary-general of the Lima Union of Trolley Operators.

and file workers would not tolerate leadership which refused to employ these tactics. Consequently, the labor leaders of a government-supporting party must retain violence as a worker organization strategy.

However, the actual use of violence by an organization controlled by government supporters will be considerably less than it would be if the same organization were in the hands of opposition or extremist leaders. Eager to avoid violence, government supporters rely heavily on threats. They squeeze every possible drop of power from the threat and carry out the strike only as a last resort. This behavior contrasts with that of opposition leaders, who refuse to bargain realistically until after a strike has begun.

Government-supporting leaders have much better access to the decision-makers, namely the president and his labor minister, than do the opposition leaders. The simple fact of direct, continuous contact with officials in the Ministry of Labor enables government-supporting leaders to avoid misunderstandings, to make clear threats, and to voice explicit demands. Also the claim which government supporters have upon the executive serves to stimulate a higher level of ministerial generosity. Consequently the actual gains made by government-supporting labor leaders tend to parallel the achievements of extremist and opposition party leaders, although the amount of violence employed is considerably less.

APRA labor leaders followed this general pattern. They maximized use of their access to and ability to communicate with government officials. They attempted to extract the utmost coercive value from their threats. And they avoided all but the most cautiously planned solidarity strikes. But when a showdown was necessary, Aprista labor leaders were willing to act, hoping the government would yield before the issue built to dangerous proportions. Because rank and file workers prefer to make their gains without sacrificing wages in a strike, the APRA limited strike policy was successful. Substantial gains were made, cohesion was maintained, the government survived the occasional jabs which the leaders found it necessary to make, and Aprista leadership in the labor movement was strengthened. The APRA-controlled national center (the CTP), for example, threatened a general strike several times in the period 1956–61, but actually effected only one such strike (see Chapter 8). But this one-day stoppage was highly effective, more effective than a longer strike would have been. The CTP gained a position of respect without sacrificing cohesion.

When the government was threatened by extremist solidarity strikes, Apristas were careful not to add to the confusion. The strike committee of the Federation of Hospital Workers called off its strike on April 9, 1958, as the extremist general strike of that date grew serious. The action was taken "in order that our activity be not identified with another [the extremist attempt to destroy the government] of which we have no part." [4] Although they refrained from overt attacks upon the government in such moments of crisis, the Apristas certainly did not relinquish the use of the strike and its related tactics. The Federation of Textile Workers, the National Union of Bank Clerks before 1958, the Federation of Metallurgical Workers, and many other organizations where APRA had a controlling position, all engaged in strikes —but always for limited worker objectives. In fact, in the period 1956–61, APRA labor leaders were strict trade unionists, and largely for this reason they were successful.

The process of leadership selection (discussed in Chapter 10) tended to place energetic, responsible individuals in positions of authority. Because the party tactic corresponded to responsible, specialized behavior in labor organizations, Apristas were frequently the individuals selected. To a certain extent extremists prevented or overthrew APRA control by attacking Apristas as overly conservative. In the extremist (and opposition) view Apristas had betrayed the workers by "selling out" to the Prado government. In general, however, it seems that rank and file workers were more sensitive to the gains made by APRA leadership than to the extremist charges.

Although APRA labor leaders made considerable progress with the limited strike policy, there exists the danger of a shift in their

4. *Comunicado* published in *El Comercio* (Lima, April 10, 1958), p. 4.

policy if the party should find itself in the opposition. There are several reasons, however, why a change to a maximum strike policy is less likely today. First, APRA labor leaders recognize the non-APRA nature of their support. Although Apristas claim the allegiance of the working class, they are aware that, if alone and isolated, they would be weak. They realize that a maximum, "irresponsible" strike policy would be highly unpopular and probably would destroy their position of authority almost overnight.

Secondly, many of the organizations are developing strength and self-sufficiency. For the same reasons that university students no longer play a role in directing labor organizations (see Chapter 10), the APRA party is becoming less important as a source of guidance and leadership. With a cultural background superior to that of earlier leaders, and with considerable trade union experience, the newer APRA leaders appear less inclined to put party before union. The emergence of this trade union loyalty is seen particularly in the older, stronger organizations, such as the textile workers, bus drivers, and tobacco workers. The APRA leaders of the newer units, whether regional federations or farm workers' organizations, are less likely to express a distinct trade union loyalty.

Lastly, the worker organizations themselves have gained considerable power. In earlier years, when dictatorial regimes prevented workers from employing the method of political bargaining, leaders were encouraged to see the destinies of the party and of the working class as inseparable. But today, given the size of the labor movement and assuming the more or less continuous existence of free government, many worker organizations may employ political bargaining with success. Salvation-by-party as a doctrine of betterment now tends to stand in opposition to political bargaining. It is not unreasonable to suppose that many APRA labor leaders will elect the latter in the future.

Whether APRA will ever become a workers' party, with the labor movement as a formal part of the party, seems doubtful. The relationships between parties and worker organizations are today entirely informal. No worker organization is a formal part of any party; in fact, the statutes of most unions explicitly state that politics should have no part in the life of the organization. Although Apristas point to the British Labor Party as a model to be copied, it appears that they are unaware of certain fundamental differences in political environments. The intense and multiple political divisions in Peruvian society would make it very difficult to tie a labor organization overtly to a party. Only if the vast preponderance of rank and file workers became Apristas could such a formal link be made with the APRA party.

Moderate Opposition Parties

The other moderate parties were also anxious to control worker organizations, but lacked the zeal and discipline of APRA. Recent arrivals on the scene (since 1949), they have not had time to penetrate the labor movement extensively. The labor affairs bureau of three major opposition parties—the Popular Action, Christian Democrat, and Odría parties—seemed small and inactive. The meetings of the labor affairs bureau of the Popular Action Party, for example, were attended by fifteen to twenty individuals, most of whom were merely rank and file workers.

The most significant feature of the activity of these moderate opposition parties in the labor movement was their close cooperation with extremists. Although perhaps difficult to understand at first, such cooperation, given the principle of total opposition which the moderate opposition parties employ, is a consistent tactic for them to use. Both extremists and moderate opposition parties had the same short-run goals: to discredit and weaken the government, and to destroy APRA influence in the labor movement.

For example, several members of the labor affairs bureau of the Christian Democratic Party were leaders of or close collaborators with the extremist Federation of Farm Laborers and Peasants, the nucleus for rural agitation. The object of the Trotskyite and APRA Rebelde leaders of this Federation was to foment a Castro-type revolution. But the Christian Democratic Party depends ostensibly on the support of devout Catholics. Such a paradox demonstrates the extreme limits of "total opposition."

Although absent from the country for several years, Odría began to take an active interest in organized labor after returning to Peru in April 1961. Relying upon collaborators from his former dictatorship, he managed to capture a few labor organizations, the most important being the Lima Union of Trolley Operators, in 1962.[5] Whether Odría becomes a genuine threat to the labor movement will depend on his future career as a politician.

The Popular Action Party of Belaúnde was equally dependent on extremists for influence in the labor movement. In May 1958 the *Comando Nacional Obrero* (labor affairs bureau) of the party published the first and only issue of *Frente Obrero*. In this publication the leaders of the CTP, the National Union of Bank Clerks, and the Lima Union of Bus Workers—all APRA-led organizations at the time—were openly attacked. The Lima Union of Construction Workers and the virtually fictitious Confederation of White-Collar Workers, both extremist organizations, were warmly supported. Probably one of the reasons why *Frente Obrero* never appeared again was that party leaders found it rather embarrassing to play the extremist line publicly, note by note.

5. *Comunicado* of the *Unión Nacional Odriista* published in *Expreso* (Lima, December 20, 1961), p. 2.

3 INTERNAL FEATURES
OF THE LABOR MOVEMENT

7

ORGANIC STRUCTURE

The pattern of political bargaining, in addition to determining the relationship of worker organizations to political parties, has many implications for the internal features of the labor movement. Some of these consequences will be explored in the next four chapters. In this chapter on the structure of the labor movement attention will be focused on the problems of cohesion. This is a key variable because it determines, in large part, the degree to which any group of workers or the labor movement in general is able to threaten the executive, and thereby gain concessions. As will be pointed out in Chapter 13, cohesion also influences the pattern of industrial strife through its effects on threat reliability and the flexibility of strike policy.

The total number of organized workers in Peru in January 1962 was about 329,000 (see Table 12). The concept of "effective membership" has been used because it describes organization strength most accurately. "Effective membership" is that number of workers who will obey a strike order when given under suitable conditions by the organization to which the workers immediately belong. Leadership estimates or membership lists (when they exist) usually overstate effective membership. The former tend to be exaggerated guesses, the latter include deceased members and workers who have changed employment. The

TABLE 12

Effective Membership of Organized Workers in Peru, by Industry[a]

Manufacturing			Transportation		
Textiles	22,000		Truck and taxi		
Garment making	1,000		drivers	13,000	
Footwear	6,000		[b] Bus drivers and		
Metallurgical	4,000		related	6,000	
Printing	3,000		Trolley operators	1,000	
Glass and tile	3,000		[b] Railroads	12,000	
Paper	1,000		[b] Aviation	1,000	
Rubber and chemical	2,000		[c] Dock and maritime		
Cement	3,000		services	4,000	
		45,000			37,000

Food and Beverage			Communication		
Bakery and pastry	3,000		Telephone	4,000	
Milling and indus-			[b] Telegraph and		
trial baking	1,000		radio	2,000	
Confections	1,000		[c] Postal service	5,000	
Brewing	3,000				11,000
Soft drinks	3,000		Services		
[c] Tobacco	1,000				
		12,000	Construction	20,000	

Extractive Industries			Hotels and		
			restaurants	5,000	
Mining:			[c] Public school		
Northern region	4,000		teachers	45,000	
Center region	30,000		[c] Street cleaners	4,000	
Southern region	8,000		Electric light/and		
Fish meal	2,000		power	2,000	
Petroleum	5,000		Market vendors	20,000	
[c] Guano	3,000		[c] Hospitals	3,000	
		52,000			99,000

Agriculture			Miscellaneous		5,000
Sugar	35,000		TOTAL		329,000
Other (excluding					
sharecroppers, small			a. Public employees have been in-		
owners, and indige-			cluded only when they belong to active		
nous communities)	20,000		organizations capable of sustaining a		
		55,000	strike.		

Commerce			
			b. Includes some public employees.
			c. Composed entirely of public em-
Banking	7,000		ployees.
Retail	3,000		
Wholesale	1,000		
Other	2,000		
		13,000	

figure for dues-paying membership would be smaller than effective membership; regular dues-paying membership might be roughly estimated at 50 to 60 per cent of the total figure given above. Unless otherwise stated, all figures of organization size given in this study are estimates of effective membership.

The usual comparison of union members to the nonagricultural work force is difficult in the case of Peru since no precise figures of work force size are available. The Economic Commission for Latin America estimated that in 1955 the number of "economically active" persons was 3,696,000; of this number 2,176,000 were in agriculture and 1,520,000 in nonagricultural pursuits.[1] If we assume that the estimate of "economically active" populations is a reasonably close approximation of "labor force" as it is measured in the United States, then we may calculate that nonagricultural union members (274,000) constituted about 15 per cent of the nonagricultural work force in 1962 (estimated at 1,850,000). In the United States union members constituted about 30 per cent of the nonagricultural work force.

In one sense the above figure misstates the density of union membership in Peru. In this underdeveloped country the proportion of independent workers who are difficult to organize, such as shopkeepers, street vendors, artisans, domestic servants, is much higher than in the United States, where economic concentration has greatly reduced the number of self-employed or singly-employed workers. If one examines the degree of unionization in firms of over 50 workers he discovers that in Peru practically all private firms of this size or larger are organized. In the United States, of course, unionization is far from complete among firms of this category.

In an overall view, the structure of the Peruvian labor movement is as diagrammed in Figure 6. For simplicity the structure has been presented as monolithic, without competition or division. Such a presentation, as already shown, is somewhat arti-

1. Economic Commission for Latin America, *Analysis and Projections of Economic Development VI: The Industrial Development of Peru* (United Nations, Mexico, D.F., 1959), pp. 4–5, 41.

FIGURE 6.

Outline of the Structure of the Peruvian Labor Movement

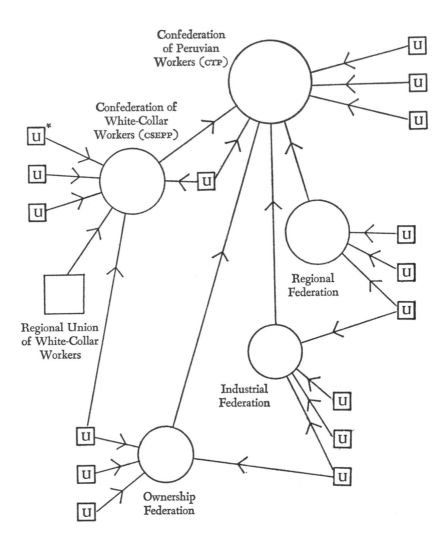

* Union

ficial. The base units have been designated "unions." In the terminology employed in this study a union is a specific type of organization. It is that organization which (1) bargains for a majority of its members, and (2) receives (or retains) the greatest proportion of all membership dues. With few exceptions, the use of the word "union" will refer to organizations bearing the title *Sindicato de* . . . in Spanish.[2]

With the exception of the four national unions of school teachers and the National Union of Bank Clerks the unions are local organizations. Usually they group only the workers in one work center. Even workers employed by the same firm but working in plants some distance apart will have two unions, one in each work center. Later in this chapter we shall contrast this type of union with the less common unions in such dispersed occupations as construction.

Division along craft lines is practically unknown in Peru. With few exceptions, men who work together are in the same union.[3] The Peruvian labor movement is organized almost entirely along industrial lines, broken down into factory-level, or, in dispersed occupations, citywide unions. The absence of craft divisions can be explained by reference to the nature of the strike weapon which, as was pointed out, is not economic but political. The

2. It would be well to prepare the reader for a few exceptions. For example, titles such as *Asociación, Unión, Sociedad* and others are occasionally applied to organizations which, in function, are unions as defined above. In addition, the title *Federación* is occasionally applied to organizations which, for the purpose of clarity, will be treated as unions. The two important organizations of this type, the *Federación de Empleados Bancarios,* and the *Federación de Motoristas, Conductores, y Anexos,* the National Union of Bank Clerks, and the Lima Union of Trolley Operators respectively, despite complexities of structure, bargain for the majority of their members and receive the largest proportion of dues from more than half the membership.

3. The most important exception to this generalization is the distinction (actually a class difference) between obreros (manual laborers) and empleados (white-collar workers) which is discussed at the end of this chapter. Other exceptions include the Lima Union of Bricklayers (which groups its members apart from the Lima Union of Construction Workers), plasterers (*albañiles*) in some of the provincial towns who have an organization apart from that of other construction workers, and brakemen, engineers, and maintenance men on the Southern Railway System who have separate organizations.

logic of a craft organization is based on the economic strike which withholds the labor of the particular craft from the employers. The bargaining unit becomes that group of workers which achieves a monopoly of the supply of their particular skill, e.g. a craft union. In Peru, where the political strike is labor's weapon, craft divisions are not functional to the workers. The strength of a political strike depends on numbers and coordination; craft divisions would introduce barriers to such coordination. The unit of structure which succeeds, and hence survives, is that which includes all the workers in one work center in a single fighting organization.

The unions, as shown in Figure 6, usually affiliate with industrial and/or regional and/or ownership federations. The first type is composed of unions of workers in the same industry; the second, unions in the same city or region; the third, unions of workers employed by the same company. The federations of unions, in turn (with the exception of some extremist-led organizations), are affiliates of the Confederation of Peruvian Workers (*Confederación de Trabajadores del Perú*, the CTP), the national center. As shown in Figure 6, the CTP also has individual unions as members. The Confederation of White-Collar Workers of Peru (*Central Sindical de Empleados Particulares del Perú*, CSEPP) affiliates unions of white-collar workers employed by private firms. Briefly then, this is the outline of the structure of the Peruvian labor movement. A closer examination begins with the base unit, the union.

According to Ministry of Labor statistics, there were on January 1, 1960, a total of 712 labor organizations with official recognition.[4] If we subtract the estimated number of federations and nonexistent organizations (30) we obtain the figure 682 as the number of unions with recognition at that date. Correction for the increment in 1960 (52) and 1961 (about 70) would put the total number of recognized unions at about 805 on January 1, 1962.

4. Ministerio de Trabajo y Asuntos Indígenas, *Estadísticas de Trabajo* (Lima, 1960), p. 13.

Of the 712 organizations mentioned above, 455 or 64 per cent were in the Lima–Callao area.[5] Since the largest organizations (sugar workers' and miners' unions) tend to be located in the provinces, we may estimate the proportion of organized workers found in the greater Lima area to be about 60 per cent. As stated earlier, the typical union is composed of all the workers in one factory (a textile mill, a brewery, a shoe factory) or one work center (a hospital, a hotel, a sugar plantation). This type of union will be termed "centralized" to differentiate it from a second type termed "dispersed."

The dispersed unions are those organizations grouping workers employed by many different firms and working in different centers. For example, construction workers engaged in work on many temporary projects in different parts of the city are grouped into one union of construction workers. Other examples of dispersed unions are the Lima organizations of printing workers, pastry workers, and bus workers—these latter working for many different bus companies with separate routes through Lima. However, dispersed unions are still industrial in structure. The members are physically dispersed but not divided by craft lines. The Lima Union of Bus Workers (*Sindicato Único de Trabajadores en Autobuses*—SUTA), for example, includes drivers, fare collectors, and mechanics. The Lima Union of Construction Workers (*Sindicato de Trabajadores en Construcción Civil de Lima*) includes carpenters, cement workers, crane operators, unskilled workers, tile setters, and (with the exception of bricklayers) anyone else who happens to work on the projects.

The distinction between concentrated and dispersed unions has been made because the simple fact of whether the members work together or in many different places has important implications. While dispersed unions still bargain for their members and receive the greatest proportion of dues, their problems are quite different from those of concentrated unions. The Union of Domestic Servants (*Sindicato de Trabajadores Domésticos del Perú*) stands as an extreme example of the dispersed union. With its

5. Ibid.

"members" scattered all over Lima, one or two in every middle class home, this organization can scarcely hold meetings and would never contemplate a strike. The organization is composed of a handful of dedicated APRA party members, mostly women, who act as personal, self-appointed champions of the over 100,000 servant girls in Lima.

In comparison with American unions, the size of Peruvian worker organizations is relatively small. It does not appear that any union of the concentrated type has more than 10,000 members; the number of such unions with more than 1,000 members is less than twenty. A few of the dispersed unions are sizable: the Lima Union of Construction Workers had 12,705 dues-paying members in 1957,[6] the Lima Union of Taxi Drivers had about 8,000 members in 1961, the National Union of Bank Clerks, 7,046,[7] and the National Union of Primary School Teachers, about 30,000. On the other hand, dispersed unions in the provinces are usually quite small (less than 100 members).

The City of Chimbote offers a fair cross-section of the labor movement. Of the 22 member unions of the regional federation in that city (all but two of the concentrated type) the median size was found to be 124 members, the average, 360.[8] If we estimate total labor union membership in Peru at 329,000 (see Table 12), then with 805 unions the average number of effective members in each union would be about 410; the median size would be much smaller.

6. *El Obrero de Construcción Civil* (organ of the Lima Union of Construction Workers) (Lima, December 1957), p. 3. This is one of the few times in Peruvian labor history that a labor leader has actually bothered to look at the records to discover the actual number of dues-paying members and publish the figure he found. In this particular industry in 1957 it seems that the figure for effective membership was about 20,000.

7. *Alerta* (organ of the committee [Centro Federado], of the Banco de Crédito del Perú) (Lima, January–February–March, 1960), p. 17.

8. Compiled on the basis of information given in *Noticiario Sindical* (organ of the Regional Federation of Santa) (Chimbote, January 12, 1961), p. 3.

Concentrated Unions

The structure of most unions of the concentrated type is quite simple. Major decisions—strikes, elections, affiliation to higher labor organizations—are performed in an assembly of the rank and file. Leadership is provided by an officers' board of from twelve to twenty-six members. Although it might appear that the assembly has considerable part in the decision-making process, it is, in fact, the officers' board which controls and directs the union. This is true for several reasons.

First, the officers are usually the best informed about union problems—a natural consequence of their position. It is they who have contact with officials of government, management, and other labor organizations. Secondly, since the officers are entrusted with bargaining and representation of the union before other organizations, the officers themselves form, to a large extent, the reality in which the organization must operate. It results then that the assembly of the rank and file must decide on the basis of information from the leaders about situations which, to a large extent, the leaders themselves have created. If, for example, the officers report that negotiations for a wage increase have failed and urge a strike, the rank and file have little alternative but to accept both the leaders' reasons for the failure and their suggestions for action.

Another reason for the officers' control of the union lies in their personal abilities for leadership. They are chosen in an election in which a substantial proportion of the rank and file participates.[9] Consequently, the officers will usually command respect. In addition, because of the informal selection processes operating before and during an election, officers frequently are drawn from different parts of the working force of the firm. The leaders, therefore, are men with popularity and authority throughout the work center.

9. See Chapter 10. This generalization does not apply to unions of the dispersed type which are discussed later.

It is indicative of the importance of the officers' board as compared to the assembly of the rank and file that the officers hold formal meetings about once a week while the assembly meets less than once every month. For example, the officers' board of the union of empleados of the Corporación Peruana del Santa (*Sindicato de* CPS with about 400 members) met fifty times in the same period (approximately one year) during which the assembly of the rank and file met eight times.[10] From observation, it seems that a six or seven to one ratio is the usual relationship between meetings of the officers' board and assemblies of the rank and file.

Apart from its function of electing officers, the assembly serves as a means of uniting and directing the membership. Before a strike, for example, an assembly is always held, and the members are informed of the situation and urged—usually with heated oratory—to adopt the recommendation of the officers. Thus, the officers are protected from charges of acting against the will of the rank and file, and membership participation in the strike is encouraged. Naturally, poor attendance would impair the utility of the assembly in its function of enhancing the cohesion of the group. It appears from observation that between 20 and 50 per cent of the members usually are present at a meeting of the rank and file. Since this number will include the most interested members, the secondary leaders or opinion formers, this figure represents good control of the organization.

Some unions have a majority clause which states that an assembly cannot transact business with less than one half of the members present. But invariably there also exists an escape clause which states that if for the first citation a majority was not present, the second meeting announced will transact business, regardless of the number. In any case, if a substantial portion of the membership is present at a meeting a roll call is seldom considered necessary.

The officers' board, then, determines the policy of the union.

10. *Central Sindical* (organ of the CSEPP) (Lima, September 15, 1961), p. 2.

The assembly serves primarily as a means of uniting and directing the rank and file. Only in cases where the officers are divided or indifferent does the assembly play a decisive role in decision-making. Of course it must not be overlooked that the threat of a division between the officers and the opinion of the rank and file as voiced in the assembly is a force which keeps the leadership within certain bounds. Similarly, in the yearly elections, the membership does make very important decisions. Nevertheless, once in office, the leaders have a considerable margin of freedom in the policy which they choose to follow. A few of the most significant aspects of the decision-making process within the officers' board are noted below.

Although the meetings of the officers are small, an even more intimate process of creation and formulation of ideas takes place before the meeting itself. Groups of two, three, or four leaders discuss an idea and bring it before the full board in the later meeting. This saves time and insures support for the proposal when it is presented.

Second, the decisions taken within the board are effected by a democratic process. This is so by necessity, for a divided board means a divided organization, because the officers usually represent different sectors of opinion within the union. If, for example, the secretary-general and two or three other officers attempted to call a strike when the majority of the board was against such action, the strike would probably not materialize. Only by giving every member the opportunity to express his opinions, and deciding issues by majority vote, can the officers' board maintain its unity.

Thirdly, power seems to be distributed evenly throughout the entire board. No office or position receives special or additional weight in the decision-making process. The secretary-general usually presides over the meetings, but apart from this each officer has influence according to his experience, insight, and character.

In an attempt to establish better control of the membership in the larger unions (of the concentrated type), many organizations have diversified leader responsibility by employing a system of delegates from different parts of the plant. The primary function of the delegates, elected by the workers in each section, is to service the immediate demands of workers on the job. They provide a link for communicating personal grievances to management. Instead of going to a member of the officers' board with a complaint about working conditions, the worker goes to his delegate, who works in the same section and is aware of the problems peculiar to that part of the plant. Especially in the larger firms leaders have found it helpful to rely on delegates to iron out personal problems.

In the sugar and mining establishments, the delegate system is well developed. For example, the Union of Metallurgical Workers of La Oroya (4,000 workers) has about 30 separate sections, each of which has three officers.[11] The union of workers on the Paramonga sugar plantation (3,000 workers) had, shortly after its formation in 1956, 22 delegates from different parts of the plantation (as of February 1957). As the union developed and the need for better control and diversified responsibility became apparent, the number grew to 80 by July 1960.[12] Even the smaller unions have a limited system of delegates. The union of workers in the Leche Gloria condensed milk plant of Arequipa (300 workers) has four delegates, one from each section of the plant.[13]

In addition to the delegates' function in handling grievances, there is a tendency to use an assembly of delegates instead of a meeting of the rank and file to communicate opinions and unite the organization. On many of the sugar plantations, for example, the assembly of delegates replaces the meetings of the rank and file, except for elections. In view of the difficulty in achieving satisfactory attendance at meetings of the large unions, the use of

11. Interview with Claudio G. Salazar, managing secretary of the Union of Metallurgical Workers of La Oroya on April 28, 1961.
12. Interview with Carlos Orams, director of industrial relations, Cía Agrícola Paramonga in Paramonga on June 28, 1961.
13. Interview with Alfredo Gutierrez, grievance chairman of the Union of Workers of Leche Gloria (Arequipa, August 31, 1961).

an assembly of delegates seems to be a wise alternative. The delegates are leaders and opinion formers in their sections; they provide an alert, relatively active cross-section of the entire membership.

Dispersed Unions

In the unions of the dispersed type, cohesion is much more difficult to maintain. Here an assembly of the rank and file seldom draws but a tiny fraction of the membership, usually two to five per cent. Even elections are poorly attended (see Chapter 10). In an attempt to establish contact with this group, dispersed unions usually adopt a subdivided structure. In such an arrangement each center of employment elects a committee of three to twelve members which functions like the officers' board in a concentrated union. In addition, the committee officers serve—or should serve—as the link with the union.

For example, the Lima Union of Taxi Drivers (*Sindicato de Choferes de Servicio Público de Lima*) has over 80 of these committees, each grouping from 30 to 100 drivers on the same *colectivo* line.[14] The five- or six-man officers' board of the committee handles the problems particular to its members, such as admission of new members and traffic problems. The committee leaders also serve as intermediaries in cases when difficulties can only be dealt with on the union level.

Other dispersed unions have similar arrangements. In the Lima Union of Construction Workers, committees are organized at the project. These committees may have from 20 to 2,000 members, depending on the size of the project. In the printing industry, committees are organized in the small shops (30 to 100 members), each having an officers' board of three to twelve members. The large newspapers (*La Prensa, La Crónica*) have separate unions organized apart from the Lima Union of Printing Workers. In the national unions of school teachers and bank clerks,

14. A *colectivo* line is a bus route on which privately owned cars are also found charging the same or perhaps slightly higher fares than buses.

the committees are formed in Lima in the various work centers. In the provinces, a regional committee is formed, with representation in the national union. This regional body groups numerous subcommittees, one in each town of the area (see Figure 7).

Ideally in a dispersed union the assembly of delegates should take the place of the assembly of the rank and file of a concentrated union. Its function should be the unification and control of the diverse member committees. The delegates should be representative of the different committees, and should also perform functions of unification and control in their respective committees. In practice, this two-step process of control has been difficult to operate successfully. The delegates, key men in the process, have a responsibility to fulfill but obtain few of the rewards of leadership, such as power, prestige, or financial remuneration. Theirs is a messenger boy function, vital to the life of the organization but offering little incentive.

Consequently, the delegates and other committee officers are likely to be irresponsible or to lack interest. Or, equally detrimental, politically motivated individuals tend to occupy the position of delegate. These men are willing to perform the unattractive chores of attending meetings and settling small matters knowing that in the long run, if others in their party do the same, the party will achieve a large degree of control over the organization.

The assembly of delegates is further impaired in its function by the presence of "interested" elements who hold no office in the organization, but are permitted full participation in the meetings. This dilution of delegate authority occurs especially in the Lima organizations of construction workers and printing workers. A meeting of the union turns out to be an assembly of some delegates and anyone else who decides to participate. The result is to undermine the authority and usefulness of the few delegates who choose to attend meetings.

The result of this state of affairs is that the officers' board of the dispersed union has far more autonomy than it would have

FIGURE 7.

Outline of the Formal Structure of the National Union of Bank Clerks[a]

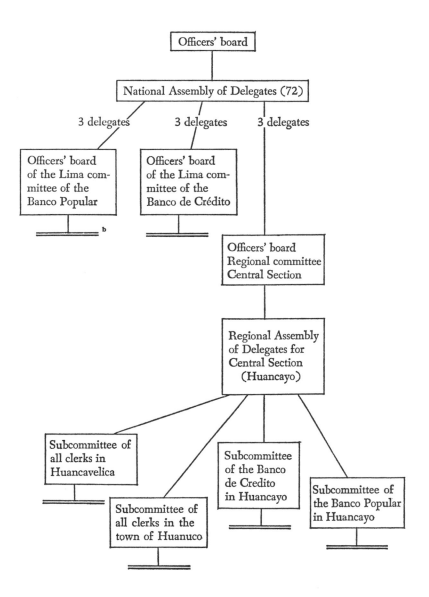

a. Cohesive union of the dispersed type.
b. Assembly of the rank and file.

in a union of the concentrated type. Its only formal connection with the rank and file is through assemblies of the few elements which have bothered to come across the city for a meeting—perhaps half of them delegates. For this reason, degeneration and division are disproportionately common within dispersed unions. Having only minimal contact with and responsibility to the rank and file, the leadership of the organization may drift farther and farther from the interests and opinion of the body of the membership, without there being any process to correct this tendency.

For whereas in a concentrated union elections would certainly be the turning point in this drifting process, it happens in dispersed organizations that dissatisfied members do not come to elections. In the usual circumstances, a member of a dispersed union has very little sense of belonging. His tie with the organization is strong only insofar as he is made a part of it by active committee life and is made to perceive the organization's utility to himself and his friends. When degeneration both of the committee structure and the leadership occurs, very few members consider the possibility of changing officers; generally they simply lose interest.

Another aspect of some dispersed unions that tends to lower their cohesion is the weakness of the individual committees. Instead of being independent centers of power with leaders in positions of authority and respect, they are frequently weak, noncohesive, and inactive. Although this weakness is partly the result of a lack of interest and incapability of the committee leadership (for the reasons mentioned above), it is also a reflection of shortcomings of the officers of the union. There are many things union officers can and should do to maintain committee strength and cohesion, including visits, assistance in elections or in handling problems, calling special meetings, or organizing social events on a committee basis. The Lima Union of Taxi Drivers, for example, devotes two pages of its monthly newspaper to committee activities such as elections, outings, and problems. The result of an active, integrated committee life is to give the worker a sense of belonging to an organization with vitality, strength and purpose.

A glance at the divided or degenerated unions reveals that, with very few exceptions, all are of the dispersed type: the Lima Union of Construction Workers is degenerate—strikes are incomplete, dues have fallen to practically nothing; the Cuzco Union of Construction Workers is divided. The Lima Union of Printing Workers has been steadily losing membership and dues for the past two years. In the middle of 1961, after a reduced number of Trotskyites and other extremist elements renewed the leadership of the same tendency, moderate elements announced the formation of a competing organization intended to organize the 4,000 potential members who had lost interest in the existing union.

The Lima Union of Taxi Drivers, after a turbulent history of past divisions, had by 1961 succeeded in rendering the competing organization little more than a name. In other occupations of a dispersed nature, division and weakness are frequently the case. There are, for example, two unions (one is called Asociación) of newspaper vendors of Lima. Bakery workers have a number of unions in Lima, all of them quite weak.

To demonstrate the preceding points it is useful to consider three dispersed unions which are both cohesive and powerful: the National Union of Bank Clerks, the Lima Union of Bus Workers, and the National Union of Primary School Teachers. The members of each are in the upper strata of the working class. Their level of cultural sophistication is relatively high and consequently the rank and file are more aware of the importance of unity. They are more alert than workers in the construction industry, for example, and more active in their group life. But membership attitude is only one facet of the success of these organizations. Disagreement and conflict, as sharp as found in any labor organization in the country, are present in each of these as well. In large part, it is the structure of these unions which prevents the occurrence of open division.

Each of these unions is characterized by: committees with vitality and considerable autonomy; an assembly of delegates that is not simply a collection of interested elements but a representative cross-section of committee opinion; and, elections performed by the assembly of delegates, not the rank and file. For example, in the National Union of Bank Clerks the individual committees (*Centros Federados* or *Secciones Regionales*) are quite active. In Lima they publish monthly magazines of high quality, hold sport and social events, and engage in the active defense of their members. In addition, they receive a 20 per cent rebate on the dues that their committee members have paid to the national union. In the provinces, the committees have an equally active role, many of them engaging in strikes of their own. Because of membership interest, the officers and delegates of each committee are elected by a fairly large proportion of the membership. For example, in the 1960 elections of the *Centro Federado* (committee) of the Banco Internacional del Perú, of 612 dues-paying members, 271 or 44 per cent voted for committee officers.[15] This is a surprisingly high figure when one realizes that this committee itself is dispersed, having members in many branch offices in Lima.

The union's national assembly is composed of 72 delegates from the various Lima and regional committees. A roll call is taken, quorum rules followed, and visitors are not permitted to vote. In addition, the assembly of delegates elects the officers' board of the union.[16] As a reflection of its importance, the assembly of delegates usually meets twice a month, about as frequently as the officers' board. The assembly of delegates, then, provides a firm link to the committees in both directions. If committees are dissatisfied with either the officers or the policy of the national union, this dissatisfaction is reflected by the actions of the dele-

15. *El Defensor* (organ of the *Centro Federado* of the *Banco Internacional del Perú*) (Lima, January–February, 1961), calculated on the basis of information given on pp. 6 and 29. In this case, effective membership is nearly equal to dues-paying membership.

16. However, when no candidate for secretary-general can obtain a majority in the assembly, the entire rank and file votes.

gates in the discussions of policy and election of officers. And it is just this control of the organization by the various committees that maintains the unity of the organization. For given a voice in both elections and policy decisions, the committees attempt to influence policy by working within the structure of the organization.

The clearly defined system of representation of the National Union of Bank Clerks is diagrammed in Figure 7. When the assembly of delegates decides to strike, this decision is backed by the committees and ultimately by the rank and file. The strike is complete and cohesion maintained. Employing similar systems of representation, the primary teachers and Lima bus workers have organizations equally as cohesive and as effective.

Figure 8 diagrams the structure of a degenerate, dispersed union such as the Lima construction workers. Neither committees nor delegates serve as rigid links to the rank and file. When the nearly autonomous officers' board chooses to call a work stoppage it never knows how many of the committees will be able and will want to strike.

The Federations

There are three types of federations a union may join: industrial, regional, and ownership, affiliating, respectively, unions in the same industry, in the same geographical area, and unions of workers employed by the same firm. The industrial federations are the best developed of the three types; the first of them were founded in 1919 (textile workers, printing workers, and taxi drivers).[17] The size of these federations varies between 35,000 members (13 unions) of the Federation of Sugar Workers, or 30,000 members (35 unions) of the Federation of Mine Workers (Center) to 1,250 members (three unions) of the Federation of Aviation Workers.[18] It appears from observation that there are

17. Neither the taxi drivers' nor printing workers' organizations became federations, in the sense that they grouped unions, until much later. In 1919 they were, in effect, dispersed unions with direct members.

18. *Norte Sindical* (Lima, January 1961), p. 6.

FIGURE 8.

Outline of the Structure of the Lima Union of Construction Workers[a]

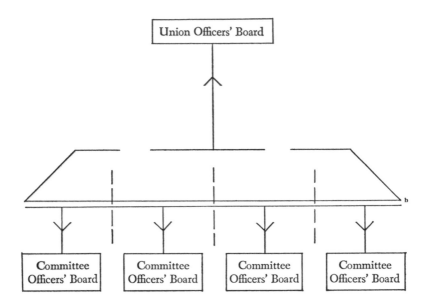

a. Noncohesive union of the dispersed type.
b. Represents assembly of the rank and file.

about 26 active industrial federations, including divided organizations (see Table 13).

Not included in Table 13 are federations in the process of being organized (brewery workers, fishmeal industry workers, bus workers, and miners of the Southern zone), or very weak, inactive organizations (Federations of Garment Workers (*Confecciones*), Daily Workers (*Ordeñadores*), and other practically nonexistent bodies.

The organic structure of the industrial federations is similar

TABLE 13

Active Industrial Federations in Peru, October 1961: Effective
Base Membership,[a] and Number of Member Unions

	EFFECTIVE BASE MEMBERSHIP[b]	MEMBER UNIONS
1. Federation of Textile Workers (*Federación de Trabajadores en Tejidos del Perú*)	21,000	82
2. Federation of Metallurgical Workers (*Federación de Trabajadores Metalúrgicos del Perú*)	3,000	23
3. Federation of Public School Teachers (*Federación Nacional de Educadores del Perú*)	43,000	4
4. Federation of Hotel and Restaurant Workers (*Federación Nacional de Trabajadores en Hoteles y Ramos Similares*)	5,000	25
5. Federation of Mineworkers (Center) (*Federación de Trabajadores Mineros del Centro*)	30,000	35
6. Federation of Footwear Workers (*Federación de Trabajadores en Calzado*)	5,000	9
7. Federation of Aviation Workers (*Federación de Trabajadores en Aviación Civil*)	1,250	3
8. Federation of Lima Department Store Workers (*Federación de Trabajadores de Tiendas de Comercio de Lima, Callao, y Balnearios*)	2,000	14
9. Federation of Taxi Drivers (M) (*Federación de Choferes y Anexos*)	10,000	34
10. Federation of Taxi Drivers (E) (*Federación de Choferes*)	1,500	5
11. Federation of Stevedores and Maritime Workers (*Federación de Estibadores y Obreros Portuarios*)	2,000	9
12. Federation of Cement Workers (*Federación de Trabajadores en Cemento*)	2,500	7
13. Federation of Sugar Workers (*Federación de Trabajadores Azucareros*)	35,000	13
14. Federation of Petroleum Workers (M) (*Federación de Trabajadores en Petróleo y Anexos*)	3,000	7
15. Federation of Petroleum Workers (E) (*Federación de Trabajadores en Petróleo*)	2,000	5
16. Federation of Construction Workers (E) (*Federación de Trabajadores en Construcción Civil*)	10,000	6
17. Federation of Construction Workers (M) (*Federación Nacional de Trabajadores en la Industria de Construcción Civil e Industrias Similares*)	10,000	16

TABLE 13 *(Continued)*

	EFFECTIVE BASE MEMBERSHIP[b]	MEMBER UNIONS
18. Federation of Railroad Workers *(Federación de Trabajadores Ferrocarrileros)*	12,000	11
19. Federation of Hospital Workers *(Federación de Servidores de Hospitales y Ramos Similares)*	2,000	6
20. Federation of Textile White-Collar Workers *(Federación de Empleados Textiles)*	700	5
21. Federation of Printing Workers *(Federación Gráfica)*	2,000	8
22. Federation of Bakery Workers *(Federación de Obreros Panaderos "Estrella del Perú")*	2,000	3
23. Federation of Mineworkers (North) *(Federación de Trabajadores Mineros del Norte)*	2,000	7
24. Federation of Market Vendors *(Federación de Trabajadores en Mercados)*	8,000	20
25. Federation of Farm Laborers and Peasants (M) *(Federación Nacional de Campesinos)*		
26. Federation of Farm Laborers and Peasants (E) *(Confederación de Campesinos)*		

a. Effective base membership represents the total number of workers all member unions could bring out on strike, each striking under suitable conditions. It does not refer to the number of workers who would go on a federation-called strike. However, Table 13 has been so arranged that the federations most capable of calling all their members on strike appear toward the top of the list. Specifically: for federations 1 to 5 we can expect quite complete member organization participation; for 6 to 11 we may expect satisfactory participation under good conditions; for 12 to 19 we would find satisfactory participation of most member organizations only in exceptional circumstances; and numbers 20 to 26 have not had federation strikes as such and probably could not effect a strike under any conditions.

b. In general, figures on total effective membership (with respect to member or base organizations) have an accuracy of plus or minus 20 per cent. Figures on the number of member unions are particularly difficult to collect since leaders frequently claim member organizations which do not exist in fact. An attempt has been made to present figures as meaningful as possible. No attempt has been made to estimate figures for the agricultural workers' federations because of their extensive scope and weak, undefined structure (see Chapter 10).

to that of the dispersed unions. There is an officers' board of 14 to 30 members and an assembly of delegates composed of representatives from each member union. The leadership of the federation controls and directs the organization to a lesser extent than it does in the unions. Indicative of this, one finds that meetings of the assembly of delegates are usually held at least as frequently as those of the officers' board—usually about twice a month.

The importance of the assembly of delegates is primarily a reflection of the nature of the organization. Being composed of many unions, each an independent center of power, the federation serves largely as a coordinating body. Whereas a union must deal with all the intricate problems of workers in the plant— wages, working conditions, social assistance plans—the federation is primarily a mechanism for effecting industry-wide strikes. And the decision to strike necessarily requires agreement among the representatives of all the unions. Another indication of the reduced importance and limited functions of the industrial federations is the relatively small proportion of membership dues that it receives. As shown later in Table 18, very few federations receive more than ten per cent of the dues which the member unions collect.

It may be that in the future industrial federations will come to play a more intricate role, perhaps even bargaining for the entire industry. But although some federations have made steps in that direction,[19] the union remains the bargaining unit and the center of power. In general, member unions are accorded equal representation in the assembly of delegates. In this manner the smaller unions tend to be overrepresented with respect to their membership. In a few federations, an attempt has been made to weight representation according to membership, but the weighting is done so imperfectly (see Figure 9) that its effects are hardly noticeable. And in practice both roll calls and strike votes are taken by organizations, not delegates.

19. See Chapter 3.

FIGURE 9.

Statutory Representation Accorded to Member Unions of the Federation
of Taxi Drivers[a]

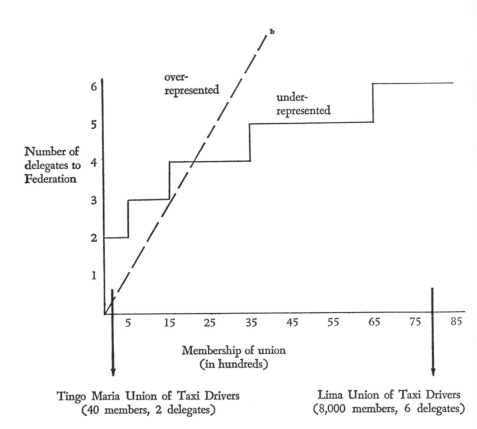

Tingo Maria Union of Taxi Drivers   Lima Union of Taxi Drivers
(40 members, 2 delegates)   (8,000 members, 6 delegates)

a. Moderate rather than extreme leadership.
b. The diagonal line indicates perfectly proportional representation.

There are two situations in which the nonrepresentative nature of the assembly of delegates can lead to friction. The first is where strong, cohesive Lima unions and a number of small, weak, provincial organizations are included in the same federation. Since the provincial organizations frequently cannot strike, and if they could their efforts would go largely unnoticed, a situation of inequity results: those without power participate in making decisions which those with power must carry out. In order to avoid this unsatisfactory situation, federations in this category have, in effect, excluded the provincial unions from the decision-making process and from the responsibility of striking as well. For example, in the Federation of Textile Workers the 60 Lima unions decide on and carry out most of the strikes of the federation, the provincial organizations (about 22) participating neither in the decision nor the strike. Of course, in not contributing, the provincial unions are in the position of not receiving as well. When the provincial unions find themselves in difficulties, the federation is usually slow to come to their assistance. In the Federation of Hotel Workers a similar procedure is followed. During that federation's strike of July 1961 (in defense of a Lima union), only the member unions in the Lima area (about 17) went on strike while the provincial members (about eight) were not included.

Misrepresentation in the assembly of delegates may have another consequence in cases where one very large Lima union dwarfs the other member organizations, as in the Federation of Taxi Drivers where the Lima union has well over half the membership. If the leaders of this union are in disagreement with the policy advocated by the many small provincial organizations, the Lima union, in view of the disproportional representation accorded to it (and still inadequate in terms of its importance) may well break away from the federation. This actually took place in 1958 when moderate elements controlled the Lima organization and extremists controlled the federation by means of the provincial delegates. Another example of this phenomenon is the breaking away of the extremist-led Lima Union of Construction Workers in 1957 from the federation of that industry, and its formation of a competing, extremist-dominated federation. Another case concerns the Lima Union of Printing Workers, which separated from the Federation of Printing Workers in the period of 1960–61. Of course, in such cases acute political disagreement is the primary motivating force for division. But this understanding of the distribution of power explains why organic splits and the formation of competing organizations are the result. The single, large-membership union could never alter the policies of the federation.

The delegates to the federations are usually officers of the member unions or men with past experience in either the union or the federation. However, one point must be noted: the delegates are usually elected separately from the officers of the union. That is, the position of delegate is distinct from that of the other officers. It does not go automatically to the secretary-general, for example, although the secretary-general is quite frequently elected as one of the delegates.

In addition to the officers' board and the assembly of delegates, the industrial federations have a third body, the national congress. Usually meeting once every two years, the congress provides a forum for thorough discussion of federation policies and goals. The congress has two major functions: election of federation officers and formulation of plans for action. This last function is performed first in a number of committees which discuss proposals in a certain area, such as wages, working conditions, and education. Later these proposals are presented and usually approved by the plenary sessions.

As would be expected, the resulting "plan for action" includes so many proposals of such extravagant scope that they could not be put into effect, even with luck, in a half century. However, the real function of formulating such goals is to enhance the cohesion of the organization. For in formulating and debating the proposals for action, the participants become aware of the many possibilities for group action, as well as the many needs for such action. In addition, a considerable amount of personal contact takes place at these congresses, which usually last three to five days and are attended by large delegations from each member union. Thus the bonds of unity become strengthened by inter-organization personal relationships.

The regional federations[20] tend to be less cohesive and less effective than federations organized along industrial lines. Because of a number of objective circumstances, a regional federation cannot have either the scope of activity or the cohesion of an industrial federation. In the first place, a regional federation groups unions of workers in many different trades and industries. Consequently, the bond of common interest, the feeling of solidarity, is relatively weak. All taxi drivers, textile workers, or miners have, respectively, both common experiences and common problems and, frequently, common solutions; the regional federation includes many diverse elements, each of which has very little in common with the other members.

In addition to the diversity in trade of the member unions, there is also a wide variation in the size, cohesion, and power of these organizations. Since representation is on an equal basis, the larger, more cohesive organizations will be dominated by numerous tiny, weak groups of plasterers, wool-washers, or tinsmiths, which cannot pay dues and have practically no membership with which to strike. The leaders of the larger unions, then, usually refuse to pay dues and resent and resist a general strike which means no loss for the tiny organizations but a considerable sacrifice in the cohesion of their own organization.

A third reason for the weakness of the regional federations is their disadvantageous situation within the power structure of the country. Both government and employers are influenced primarily in centers other than regional ones. The government is most sensitive to events in Lima, while employers respond most readily to pressure applied along industrial lines. An industrial federation (all but two of which are located in Lima) has greater opportunity to influence the government by strikes, demonstra-

20. The term regional federation has been used to describe organizations named *Unión Provincial, Unión Departamental, Federación Departamental,* etc.

tions, or newspaper coverage, and the firms by means of industry-wide strikes.

For example, in April 1958, the city of Cuzco was completely overpowered by extremists who organized a general strike through the regional federation. Although the strike had strong political overtones, it was staged ostensibly to prevent an increase in gasoline prices. Despite the degree of control which the federation obtained (it even demanded and obtained the withdrawal of army reinforcements sent to establish order), the price of gasoline still went up. If the same incident had occurred in Lima, governments, not gasoline prices, would have been changed.

All the indices of organization strength testify to the weakness of the regional federations. In finances, for example, there are few regional federations that maintain even their low level of activity on the income from member organizations. Dances, raffles, political parties, or other nonmember sources provide the funds in almost every case. Regional federations frequently lack a headquarters building (Puno, Arequipa—FDTA, Cerro de Pasco, Nazca, Pucallpa) and in cases where they do have one (Iquitos, Cuzco, Lima), the rent or purchase cost is borne directly by some of the member unions or the government.

Although the regional federations are usually quite weak, there are certain instances when these organizations may act successfully. If the issue is one of immediate concern to the entire local labor movement, and if local officials are in a position to resolve the problem, then a local general strike may be possible and may produce favorable results. For example, in Arequipa the three different regional federations (FDTA, USTA, FECIA) periodically unite and, along with independent unions, strike for blanket, citywide wage increases which the local office of the Ministry of Labor can and does grant.

But strikes for nonpartisan worker objectives are the exception, not the rule, for the regional federations. Usually these organizations are led by devoted party members who repeatedly attempt strikes for partisan objectives. When added to the centrifugal tendencies already present, an aggressive, partisan strike policy virtually destroys a regional federation. Through their delegates the rank and file workers express their displeasure at losing wages in strikes for distant, nonmember objectives. The federation leaders, through the use of phantom organizations, escape the control of the genuine unions, so the latter find it necessary to withdraw.

In Arequipa, Peru's second largest city, politics has all but destroyed regional labor organizations. The degeneration began in 1956 when the extremist-led regional federation (*Federación Departamental de Trabajadores de Arequipa*—FDTA) espoused an aggressive strike policy toward the Prado government. The Apristas formed a competing federation (*Unión Sindical de Trabajadores de Arequipa*—USTA) which at first was quite weak. Successive antigovernment strikes urged by the leaders of the FDTA drove some members to the USTA, which was following a limited strike policy. But the situation in 1961 was one of independent unions: the four strongest organizations—unions of workers in the condensed milk plant and the industrial baking plant, railroad workers, and taxi drivers—were affiliated with neither federation. The textile workers were tepid supporters of the USTA, and the printing workers rather reluctant members of the FDTA.

The only regional federation which is both powerful and in the control of extremists is in Cuzco. The success this organization has had in retaining its membership is largely due to the conservative strike policy which it followed (a result of an agreement made with political authorities; see Chapter 5). Since the federation was not demanding any sacrifice from the member organizations, there was little pressure for withdrawal. However, at the end of 1961 the agreement with the government was broken and the FTC, starting with a protest strike against Prime Minister Beltran, began to call strikes for nonmember issues. At about the same time the Apristas set up a competing regional federation to encourage unions to defect from the extremist-led FTC.[21] In many other places—Ica, Huancayo, Puno, and Callao

21. The Cuzco situation was discussed in detail in Chapter 5.

—this political struggle for control of regional federations, combined with sharply differing strike policies, has produced divided organizations.

It is interesting to note that the most vigorous supporters of regional federations are the extremists. Especially in the case of Lima, they have been particularly annoyed that the regional federation (in APRA control) groups only those unions without industrial federations. It is their dream to form and control a Lima regional federation with every union in the area as a direct member: "A regional federation of Lima and Callao must be formed in order to unite the forces of the proletariat of Lima, achieving thus an enormous potential." [22] Another example of extremist inclinations toward regional federations is found in *Cursillo-Manual de Sindicalismo*. Writing primarily to encourage cooperation of independent moderates with extremists in the labor movement, the author holds these organizations capable of playing an important role. As examples of regional federations he points to the extremist "organizations" of Puno, Callao, Arequipa, and Huancayo (which are so weak that it is difficult to ascertain their existence), and of Cuzco, which maintained cohesion largely through inaction. [23]

What the extremists tend to overlook in their ardor, however, are the structural requisites for a cohesive organization. It may appear feasible on paper that a regional federation including Lima and Callao, having about 600 unions as direct members, would be an immensely powerful organization. But, in fact, the problems of decision-making and cohesion in such an organization would practically preclude concerted action. The Confederation of Peruvian Workers overcomes some of these problems by having unions represented through federations and by relying on APRA party discipline. But even that organization faces serious problems of cohesion in the event of a strike (see

22. *Voz Obrero* (organ of the Trotskyite Party) (Lima, December 1960), p. 6.
23. Jorge del Prado, *Cursillo-Manual de Sindicalismo*, pp. 90–98.

next chapter). One suspects that the extremist fascination with regional federations comes more from their dogmatic belief in the unity of the proletariat than from any calculated appraisal of the limitations of these organizations. It is difficult to estimate even the approximate number of regional federations because of the low quality of most of them. In fact many names do not represent organizations in a meaningful sense. There are relatively stable organizations in Chimbote (Santa), Iquitos (Loreto), and Lima, under moderate leadership, as well as the Cuzco organization controlled by extremists. Beyond these, there are about 20 names representing organizations of varying degrees of activity.

The third type of federation is termed "ownership." These federations group unions of workers employed by the same firm. A relatively recent development, the ownership federations are designed to enhance the power of the workers by facilitating strikes made against all branches of the firm. The oldest of these is the Federation of White-Collar Workers (*empleados*) of the Cerro de Pasco Corporation. Founded in 1947 with the encouragement of the company, it includes about eleven unions of empleados in the different branches of the corporation. It provides a convenient unit for contract bargaining and serves as a mechanism for resolving collective conflicts. It is dispersed and inactive; if it were not for the company's role in bringing the members together for bargaining, it would probably disappear. Significantly, it has never called a strike.

Another example is the federation of workers employed by W. R. Grace and Company, founded in 1961. It has 15 unions of workers for the Grace sugar plantations, transport company, air line system, textile mills, wholesale and retail establishments, and others. Also founded in 1961 is the federation of five unions of workers employed by the commercial organization, La Fabril.

Whether ownership federations will ever develop into active, viable organizations remains to be seen. Certainly they will be troubled by the same diversity of trade, size, and strength of member organizations that weakens the regional organizations. In addition, there is some doubt as to whether the member organizations really have as much in common as might be supposed. The problems faced by employees of Panagra Airlines, for example, are totally different from those with which a sugar workers' union must deal. Nor does it appear that the tactical advantage is actually as great as it might seem. In Peru the economic pressure of a shutdown has been only a secondary element in forcing the firm to a solution. Rather it is usually the government, influenced by workers and occasionally employer organizations of the same industry, which coerces the individual employer.

In addition to the more or less permanent secondary organizations already described there is a wide variety of temporary bonds joining two or more unions together. Sometimes an ad hoc committee might be set up and the alliance given a title: *Bloque* . . . , *Grupo* . . . , *Frente.* . . . Or union leaders may simply agree to a pact of mutual assistance. These groupings may unite two unions located close to each other but in dissimilar industries, as seen in the case of the mutual assistance pact between the Union of Leche Gloria (condensed milk) and the Union of Victoria (industrial baking) in Arequipa. Or unions of the same firm may join together, as did three unions for Duncan Fox Enterprises in a solidarity strike in support of the workers in the Duncan Fox textile plant "La Unión." The *Bloque Marítimo de Callao* grouped various maritime unions, including organizations of longshoremen, customs agents, and sailors. All such groupings are ad hoc in the sense that no formal structure exists, no dues are stipulated, and no permanent officers elected.

These ad hoc alliances are, of course, a manifestation of the acute need for political support which Peruvian labor leaders feel in times of crisis. The first thought in the mind of a labor leader preparing a strike is "Who will join us?" He realizes that on the economic level he cannot adequately coerce the firm. If he does not expect to be assisted by a federation, then he must look about for temporary allies who will join with him in making the greatest possible political disturbance.

Such temporary alliances, however, have certain drawbacks. They are instruments for action but lack the safeguards necessary for sustained, effective activity. First, there are no leaders who hold the interest of the alliance above the needs of any particular member. In a well-developed industrial federation, the federation leaders are likely to consider the welfare and cohesion of the federation above any claim that a member union might make. Thus the leaders investigate the particular conflict and evaluate the chances for success. They sound out opinion within the organization to discover if a solidarity strike will severely impair cohesion. They make contact with the employer and the government in order to judge the range of concession possible and to make maximum use of their threats and thus avoid a strike.

Secondly, the industrial federation has well-developed processes whereby a solidarity strike is decided. Successive meetings are held where deliberation takes place. Although the officers cannot control the decision to strike, they can shape the decision of the assembly of delegates in favor of or against a strike, depending on their evaluations of the situation. A union desiring a solidarity strike must go through many steps and sacrifices before it is likely to gain federation support. Consequently a solidarity strike will probably not be requested and certainly not granted for trivial reasons.

Finally, the formal status of the organization, the existence of an established decision-making process, the commitments which members have made in their contribution of dues, specific federation officers, a headquarters building, past congresses, and so on—all combine to give an established federation a position of respect in the eyes of the members. Leaders of the member unions are more inclined to obey a solidarity strike order even when unpalatable because membership in the federation is prized in itself.

But in an ad hoc alliance, all of these elements are substantially lacking. There are no leaders who are primarily interested in preserving the alliance. Instead each organization acts freely to extract the maximum from the arrangement. One organization may urge a strike for what appears to be a trivial reason. The other refuses to strike and is condemned by the first as a traitor. How long should the other unions wait before starting a solidarity strike? How long should they strike if the issue is not resolved? These questions are argued repeatedly but cannot be settled since no agreed decision-making process exists. The problem of reciprocity is left unresolved. The alliance may begin with one union supporting a sister organization in a successful strike. But when the situation is reversed and the sister union is requested to return the favor, it is very probable that bickering over the nature of the obligation to reciprocate will break the alliance apart.

The difficulties faced by temporary alliances in dealing with solidarity strikes only point up more clearly one general problem of cohesion in the Peruvian labor movement. Except in the most unusual circumstances, a solidarity strike involves sacrifices for those who effect it. Ideally, for maximum cohesion, no solidarity strikes should be attempted. But in the system of political bargaining, solidarity strikes are key weapons. The federations exist, in fact, primarily as mechanisms for effecting such strikes. Consequently, a federation must employ solidarity tactics.

However, if cohesion is to be maintained, the following principles must be observed in employing solidarity strikes: (1) the objective of the strike must be seen by the rank and file workers as important in their frame of reference; (2) solidarity strikes must be infrequent and of short duration; (3) the leaders of the organizations effecting the solidarity strike must feel committed to this course of action (by agreed decision-making processes, loyalty to the federation, etc.), so that momentary expediency does not determine behavior. Expediency, as suggested above, would argue against taking solidarity action (assuming that partisan political considerations are absent). Consequently a deeper commitment or long-range loyalty is necessary if union leaders are to engage in solidarity strikes in support of other organizations.

Empleados

Although the labor movement in Peru has very few divisions that exist along purely craft lines, so that workers in the same establishment might be organized in more than one union, there is one important division of this nature: the distinction between white-collar and manual employees. The white-collar workers, or *empleados,* are office workers, foremen, and salesmen, while the laborers, or *obreros* are those individuals doing largely manual work. The distinction is not completely logical; for example, trolley car operators are empleados while bus drivers are not. However, in general, the division reflects a social line or status level. Furthermore, the distinction has come to be included in the government dispositions which apply to workers; hence conditions of employment and social benefits are different, with the empleados usually receiving more complete coverage. The legal and social division between empleados and obreros tends to be reflected in the formation of two unions in the same firm, one of empleados, one of obreros.

Unification of the two groups, or coordination, is in the interests of both. The empleados can contribute sophisticated leadership, information about the company's financial position, and their ability to deal with management. The obreros constitute a unified force, the power behind the demands. Frequently, a union of empleados is lacking in cohesion, the membership being quite close to management itself. Very seldom is a strike of the empleados complete enough to create a political disturbance. With the assistance of the manual workers, however, full pressure can be brought to bear.

The primary impediment to unification of the two organizations seems to be a mutual distrust of the attitudes and tendencies of the other group. The obreros frequently consider the empleados too conservative and lacking zeal; reciprocally, the obreros are viewed as irresponsible or politically motivated. In addition, because of the relatively small size of the typical white-collar workers' union and its formal ties to superior organizations of empleados, the white-collar workers are reluctant to dissolve their organization and enter another in which they would have little voice. The obreros, on the other hand, tend to reject arrangements which would overrepresent empleados.

However, mixed unions have been formed, and seem to function quite successfully. For example, the union of workers for the All-American Cables Company includes both empleados and obreros. The obreros, the minority in this case, are assured of a voice in the organization since, by statutory disposition, they are given two positions on the officers' board. In other cases of small commercial establishments, department stores, and similar firms where the social and cultural distinctions between the two groups were minimal, it has been possible to form a "sindicato único," as they are usually called, including both empleados and obreros.

However, in such cases the union was formed as a mixed organization. In instances where there are two independently existing organizations, total unification is much more difficult. It has happened in only a very few cases. For example, the empleados of the Cartavio sugar hacienda, aware of their weakness, agreed to join the obrero union, their organization becoming simply another member committee of the union. In the same fashion, the leaders of the union of manual workers in the banks agreed to dissolve their organization and become direct members of the National Union of Bank Clerks.

But such instances are rare. In general, some less comprehensive arrangement must be made. Either a third officers' board is set up, with representatives from each of the two unions, or an informal understanding of mutual assistance and advice links the two. The degree to which these methods of coordination actually unify the two organizations varies in the particular situation. In view of the rapid growth in the number of empleado unions, unification, or close coordination with the respective obrero union, is a major task which must be undertaken to enhance the effectiveness of both.

In conclusion, the structure of the Peruvian labor movement is highly flexible and decentralized. The centers of power are the many tiny unions. And while the framework for coordinated action exists, decision-making still centers in the unions themselves. Authority has not been centralized to a greater degree because most secondary organizations have not demonstrated that they can use increased power to the advantage of the rank and file. The frequent use of the solidarity strike for political reasons has led to rank and file distrust, low levels of cohesion, and even to open division. The union leaders will not place greater responsibility in the hands of federation officers until it is clear that this responsibility will be exercised to the long-run advantage of the unions and their members.

8

THE NATIONAL CENTERS

To an extent difficult for an American to conceive, the Peruvian national executive is involved in the social and economic life of the country. It plays the role of American federal, state, county, and municipal bodies all in one, and then some. It appoints governors, mayors, and councilmen, and maintains one police force for the entire country. In the economic realm, the national government regulates, either formally or informally, the prices of items ranging from matches to gasoline, from soft drinks to cement. Indirectly, through its control of tariffs, it fixes the prices of hundreds of imported products from automobiles to pins. Finally, it owns and operates the national salt, guano, tobacco, and cigarette monopolies. On labor issues there seems to be no area with which the central government has not concerned itself. Vacations, retirement, discharge compensation, living and working conditions, housing, hospital care, wages and hours: all have been and are subject to governmental law or decree.

In the first chapter this centralization of decision-making was cited as one basic explanation for the insecurity of the executive in a free context. Centralization has also affected the structure and orientation of extraconstitutional bodies, including worker organizations. Since decision-making centers in the executive, not in state or municipal bodies or in the economic arena, there has been a pronounced tendency toward the formation of a national confederation to influence this executive. Almost as soon as the labor movement emerged a national center was formed. And although dictatorships have suppressed this body, it has sprung up immediately when freedom was restored. The persistence of this institution, in spite of the obstacles posed and the rudimentary state of the labor movement, demonstrates that, for the workers, it plays a highly functional role in the political context.

As noted in Chapter 2, the first central labor organization in Peru was the *Federación Obrera Local*—the Local Workers' Federation—founded in 1918.[1] In 1929 this organization was renamed and reorganized and given national scope (in name) with the title *Confederación General de Trabajadores del Perú* (General Confederation of Peruvian Workers).[2] The CGTP was outlawed in 1932 by Sanchez Cerro,[3] and during the period 1932–44, no national center existed.

The Confederation of Peruvian Workers (*Confederación de Trabajadores del Perú*) was founded in 1944 during Manuel Prado's first term. In 1948 it was destroyed by Odría, but came to life again in 1955, first in extremist hands. As exiled leaders returned to the country and trade union life began once again, the CTP was taken over by APRA forces in the congress of May 1956.[4] In 1961, the CTP affiliated about 240,000 workers through the member regional and industrial federations and a number of separate unions. This figure represented about 75 per cent of the total number of organized workers.

The power of the CTP lies in its potential ability to call a

1. Luis Felipe Barrientos C., *Los Tres Sindicalismos*, p. 149. Another historian, Ricardo Martinez de la Torre, in *Apuntes para una Interpretación Marxista de Historia Social del Perú*, puts the founding date of the *Federación Obrero Local* as 1922, the previously existing organization having the name *Federación Regional Peruana*. See Vol. 3, p. 5.

2. Martinez de la Torre, 3, 6–7. It appears that an attempt was made in 1927 to found the CGTP but a wave of government repression cut short activity. Ibid., 2, 273. Also see Luis Felipe Barrientos C., p. 173.

3. Martinez de la Torre, 3, 466.

4. José Benites, *Realidad del Sindicalismo Contemporaneo* (Lima, 1956), pp. 7–8.

nationwide general strike which would paralyze the country and provoke widespread violence. Such a general strike, combined with the agitation of opposition and extremist parties, would probably sound the death knell for the incumbent regime. However, a general strike is not easily engineered. It is a mistake to imagine that the leaders of the CTP could effect a successful general strike whenever they pleased. Time is required to build up favorable sentiment across the nation and to secure widespread agreement in the labor movement. Also, a general strike usually weakens the cohesion of both the CTP and its member organizations. There will always be workers who are uninterested in or opposed to the purpose of the strike, workers who will disobey the strike order—particularly if the strike lasts more than a few days. These renegades may split their organization into warring factions or force it to retire from the CTP. And since a general strike materializes largely because the participants believe it will materialize, a partial failure of a previous general strike robs labor leaders of their confidence in the CTP. For these reasons the general strike is a finite, limited weapon. The more it is used, the less effective it is likely to be. The leaders of the national center must attempt to use the *threat* of a strike as much as possible, avoiding the actual strike itself.

From 1956–62, when the APRA party supported the government, there was a certain ambivalence on the part of the APRA leaders of the CTP toward the use of the general strike. The logic of a general strike makes it a threat to the existence of a constitutional regime. But the APRA labor leaders in the CTP realized that the Prado government was far more desirable than an anti-labor and/or anti-APRA government which could be brought on by a general strike. As a result, from 1956 to 1962 the APRA-led CTP played an unnerving game of "chicken" with the Prado government. The CTP attempted to frighten the executive as much as possible with threats of a general strike while making every attempt to postpone such a strike, thus giving the executive ample opportunity to move out of the way before a collision occurred.

The only general strike which actually took place in the period 1956–61 was the one-day stoppage on May 13, 1960. From the point of view of the CTP leadership the strike was ideal. First it achieved complete paralysis. Since it was called for only one day, rank and file dissatisfaction was minimal and support was nearly unanimous throughout the labor movement. Solidarity ran high in worker circles in favor of the strike, which was a general protest against "police brutality" that had resulted in a number of worker deaths in clashes across the country. The issue had built to a climax. Even independent nonmembers of the CTP (as well as extremists) joined in.

But the strike itself was carefully controlled. The CTP made it clear that it was protesting not against the government but against the "assassins at the service of imperialistic companies." [5] Careful provision was made to insure continuation of essential services, electricity and water. The demonstrations, which are always an integral part of a general strike, were scenes of flowery oratory, nothing more. Through this strike the CTP demonstrated, apparently, that it could command the labor movement. And it was able to demonstrate this without seriously threatening the Prado government.

The assumed ability of the CTP to call a general strike gave its leaders considerable prestige with the executive. When the secretary-general, for example, came to the Ministry of Labor to complain about something, government officials listened. The visits of confederation officers were not just occasional; scarcely a day went by when one of the top leaders did not walk straight into the minister's office with a problem. Utilizing its position of access and power, the CTP became, in many cases, the link between worker organizations and the ministry. Its leaders took up the problems of the smallest unions and resolved them personally with ministry officials. The CTP was, in practice, a body to which disappointed leaders could appeal for aid. And when

5. *Cetepé* (organ of the Confederation of Peruvian Workers) (Lima, May 28, 1960), p. 1.

their cases were taken up by confederation officers, these lesser leaders usually obtained a satisfactory solution.

The power of the CTP commanded respect from even the extremist-led organizations. Of course, extremists attacked the CTP because it was an APRA-controlled organization which tended to support the Prado government. But when they found themselves in difficulty, extremist leaders frequently turned to the CTP for help. For example, in the long 1959 strike of the extremist-led National Union of Bank Clerks, the officers of that organization called upon the CTP for support. The CTP was in a position to refuse assistance in this instance because the extremist leaders of the union had earlier founded and joined a competing, extremist-oriented national center, the FUT (*Frente Único de Trabajadores*).[6] Like several other attempts the extremists made to form a national center, the FUT had quickly collapsed. Because of their role in openly repudiating the CTP the National Union of Bank Clerks was denied support and, after 62 days of strike, finally accepted defeat at the hands of the bank owners.

The formal structure of the CTP is similar to that of a federation. It has an officers' board of 25 members and an assembly of delegates of about 200 members. The officers are elected and policy discussed at the national congress which is supposed to be held every three years. In addition, there are several committees headed by the officer in charge of the area; among these are a social security committee and a culture (worker education) committee.

In the view of the leaders, the members of the CTP should ideally be only the industrial and regional federations. However, it is evident that there are, in fact, many unions among the members of the CTP. In the 1958 national congress were ten regional federations, 18 industrial federations, and 25 unions were represented.[7] It appears that since that time the number of member

6. *Norte Sindical* (Lima, June 1959), p. 5.
7. *Obrero Textil* (organ of the Federation of Textile Workers) (Lima, January, 1959), p. 1.

unions has grown out of proportion to the growth in member federations.[8]

In some cases the reason for admitting unions to the CTP is immediately obvious. There are several important unions for which no industrial federation exists: Backus and Johnson brewery workers, bus workers, Lima Light and Power Company workers, and a few others. To relegate these organizations to mere membership in the Lima Regional Federation (the body which comprises the many small unions in the Lima area which are without an industrial federation) would offend their leadership and invite open noncooperation. They expect to be given a voice in the national center whose strength depends, in significant part, on their support.

However, there are many smaller unions in the CTP. Most of the 25 to 35 member unions have fewer than 500 members. Some—the unions of obreros and of empleados of the Milne Company, empleados of the trolley company (distinct from trolley car operators), and several others—have fewer than 200 members. These organizations are included because they contribute significantly to the CTP's hard pressed treasury. In addition their inclusion reflects the high value the leaders place on a large membership list (see below). This tendency to reduce the CTP from a tertiary (affiliating only federations of unions) to a secondary organization has had a significant impact on the nature of the body. The first effect of the unregulated membership policy has been the degradation of the assembly of delegates to the point where it has become practically functionless.

The assembly, instead of being a body representative of the power distribution in the labor movement, is nothing more than a gathering of labor leaders. The formal scheme of representation (see Figure 10) if followed in practice, would give a union of 200 members two delegates and an industrial federation of

8. The leaders of the CTP do not make public the list of member organizations. Information about membership has been collected from interviews and observation.

FIGURE 10.

Formal Representation Accorded to Member Organizations in the Assembly
of Delegates of the Confederation of Peruvian Workers

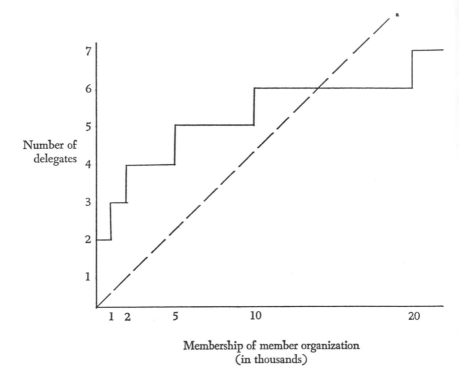

Membership of member organization
(in thousands)

a. The diagonal line represents perfectly proportional representation.
Source: *Carta Sindical del Perú* (Statutes of the CTP) (Lima, Publicaciones
CTP, 1958), Art. 70.

10,000, only six delegates—hardly a 1:50 ratio. In practice, since
organizations usually send only one delegate to the ordinary assembly, regardless of the number allotted to them, the influence
and prestige of the larger, more powerful organizations is further

reduced. The result is, then, that the assembly is an impractica-
ble body for deciding things. Crucial issues—strikes, acceptance
or rejection of laws or decrees, etc.—must, for practical purposes,
be decided by the leadership in accordance with the sentiment
in the labor centers of power. Otherwise, the smaller organizations would be able to determine the policy which the powerful
members would be bound to execute. Even as a sounding board
the assembly gives a poor reflection of the opinions of rank and
file across the country and has been reduced to doing what a
newspaper should do—disseminating information. Because of
poor handling, even this function is diminished.

The statutes of the CTP state that "the assembly of delegates
is the representative body which provides the impetus for the
work of the officers and decides all affairs of transcendent importance." [9] In practice, the assembly is not "representative" and
consequently neither impels nor decides. The meeting time is
spent largely reading minutes, letters, reports, or expositions of
problems. The votes are usually unanimous ratifications of leadership proposals. Very little time is spent on productive discussion or exchange of views. In fact, an assembly of delegates of
the CTP is one of the sleepiest affairs in organized labor in Peru.

The result of the haphazard membership policy followed by
the CTP is, in the final analysis, to endanger the cohesion of the
entire organization. The general assembly should be the body
which decides upon programs and unites the member organizations behind the decisions taken. In its present nonrepresentative
condition, the assembly is not permitted to decide—if it were,
the results would probably endanger cohesion still further.
Clearly, the CTP does not rely on the assembly either for direction or cohesion. The question is, then, how does the CTP continue as a relatively cohesive and surprisingly effective organization? For it is both.

The first answer is that nearly all of the leaders and delegates
of the CTP are members of the APRA party. To a certain extent

9. *Carta Sindical del Perú* (Lima, 1958), Art. 45.

this is a reflection of the fact that the majority of labor leaders in Peru are Apristas. But the CTP's policy of permitting affiliation to only one of two federations of the same industry or region accentuates the proportion of APRA leaders, since the federation chosen is always the APRA–moderate one. Thus the extremist-led federations of construction workers, taxi drivers, farm laborers, and petroleum workers, as well as several extremist regional federations, are not permitted membership. There are a few extremist-controlled organizations in the CTP, such as the National Union of Bank Clerks and the Union of Cristal Ferrand Glass Workers, but these constitute a very tiny minority. Consequently, the parallel views on goals, means, and enemies, and the feeling of responsibility and loyalty to fellow party members, tend to reduce conflict among the many APRA leaders in the CTP. On important issues, delegates and officers may reach a decision either informally or at the *buró sindical*, the labor office of the APRA party, thus rendering the assembly a public body which only manifests decisions already taken elsewhere.

Secondly, in the period 1956–61 the CTP followed, by Peruvian standards, a conservative strike policy. A strike of any secondary or tertiary labor organization tends to create strains within the organization. But the CTP effected only one general strike, and that lasted only one day (see above). It is quite possible that if the CTP had ordered more strikes of longer duration and in support of particular labor organizations, cohesion would have been severely impaired.

In addition, the distribution of member organizations represented on the officers' board (which has an important role in deciding matters) tends to enhance cohesion, and results in decisions that conform closely to the realities of opinion and power in the labor movement. The distribution of offices among the various member organizations is seen in Table 14. Of the 25 positions, 21 are filled by leaders from important organizations. There is some question as to whether the distribution is as broad as it could be and ought to be for maximum cohesion. The large

TABLE 14

Distribution of the Positions on the Officers' Board of the CTP
among Representatives of Member Organizations

Member organization[a]	Effective base membership[b]	Number of positions on board	Effective base membership per position
Federation of Textile Workers	21,000	2	10,500
Federation of Taxi Drivers (M)	10,000	1	10,000
Lima Union of Bus Workers	5,000	1	5,000
Federation of Mine Workers (Center)	30,000	1	30,000
Federation of Metallurgical Workers	3,000	1	3,000
Federation of Footwear Workers	5,000	1	5,000
Lima Union of Trolley Operators	1,000	2	500
Union of Backus and Johnson Brewery Workers	1,000	2	500
National Union of Bank Clerks	7,000	3	2,300
Cerro de Pasco Regional Federation	(8,000)	1	(8,000)
Federation of Construction Workers (M)	10,000	4	2,500
Federation of Farm Laborers and Peasants (M)	(5,000)	1	(5,000)
Iquitos Regional Federation	1,900	1	1,900
Officers from organizations of little or no importance		4	

a. This table has been constructed so that organizations with representation disproportionately high with respect to their power (size, cohesion, strategic position) appear toward the bottom of the list.
b. Figures in parentheses are estimates given for organizations of very low cohesion.

number of positions (four) accorded to the moderate-led Federation of Construction Workers, a relatively weak industrial federation, is one case in point. Also, it seems unlikely that the National Union of Bank Clerks, although a very strong organization and the wealthiest in Peru, would demand three offices as the price of its cooperation.[10] The same reasoning would apply to the two positions allotted to the Union of Backus and Johnson Brewery Workers. In overrepresenting these organizations, other important federations are left out. The most important of the slighted organizations would be the federations of sugar workers, hotel workers, petroleum workers, and cement factory workers. If these organizations are continually denied the prestige and influence associated with a position on the officers' board, their leaders may become dissatisfied and rebellious.

Although it might appear difficult for a congress of hundreds of delegates to elect an officers' board balanced according to the importance of the organizations represented, there are informal processes at work which make this possible. Delegates discuss and bargain, keeping in mind organizations and leaders that will be disappointed if left off the board. The buró sindical of the APRA party is one very important decision-making center for such matters.

The finances of the CTP are in the same disorganized condition as the formal structure. A first explanation for the financial deficiency of the CTP is found in the limited nature of the resources available. As shown in Chapter 9, there is not much money anywhere in the labor movement. In view of the small resources of most of the industrial federations, and the even smaller resources of the regional federations, a large flow of funds to the national center is not to be expected. But this is only a part of the problem. Many of the member organizations are in

10. There is probably far more to these two cases than meets the eye. Both the National Union of Bank Clerks and the Federation of Construction Workers have had serious trouble with extremists. At the time when the CTP congress was held (December 26–30, 1958), the National Union of Bank Clerks had recently fallen into extremist hands and the extremists in the construction industry had just (December 14–20, 1958) formed a competing federation of that industry, designed to strip the moderate-led federation of member unions. It is probable that the leaders of the CTP felt that by giving positions of prestige and power to the APRA leaders of these two organizations, they could strengthen the position of moderate forces. The results, after three years, indicate that this strategy was misguided.

a position to pay several times the tiny (20 sols per delegate, 74 cents) monthly dues, but they are unwilling to pay a higher sum when others continue to pay nothing. However, if the CTP were to require all members to pay dues, it appears that almost every one of the regional federations would lose its membership. The CTP leaders are extremely reluctant to lose an affiliate simply because it cannot pay dues.

Leadership's pronounced desire to keep the organization large can be explained partly by examining the requirements of the bargaining strategy. When legal enactment is practiced, the strength of a national center depends heavily on the financial resources it has at its disposal. Propaganda, election campaigns, court cases, lobbyists, and a legislative research department: these are at the heart of legal enactment and they cost money. If an affiliate does not pay dues, then its utility to the national center is greatly reduced.

In collective bargaining the value of any particular member organization to the national center is also closely dependent on its financial contributions. The major way that the national center can be of assistance to the labor movement in collective bargaining is by giving financial contributions to member organizations on strike. Again, the nonpaying organizations tend to be a burden to the national center.

The Peruvian CTP does not employ either of these methods to any substantial degree. It does not fight court cases. It does not have a lobbying arm. What little attention is paid to elections or legislative action is ad hoc and on a very reduced scale. Nor does the CTP make grants to member organizations on strike, for these are seldom necessary (see Chapter 9). The CTP employs the method of political bargaining. When this strategy is used, however, affiliates are valued per se. The success of the national center in coercing the executive will depend upon the number of affiliates which might be disposed to obey an order for a solidarity strike. Therefore, the leaders of the national center will be reluctant to suspend any member organization and anxious to gain new adherents. Consequently they are encouraged to pursue a lax financial policy in order not to force affiliates out of the organization. This is not to say that the leaders of the CTP would not like to have more money. They would. But they are unwilling to suffer the loss of strike capability which would probably result if they tripled dues and suspended all nonpaying organizations.

As mentioned above, the dues to the CTP are 20 sols per delegate per month. For an industrial federation with six delegates—textile workers, for example—dues come to 120 sols ($4.80). Even if all organizations paid their quota, the total income would be about 3,000 sols ($110). In practice, the CTP manages to collect about half that amount.[11] With a little additional income from the sale of publications, the total income may reach 2,000 sols monthly, or about $75. This amount is perhaps sufficient to cover the wages of one hired employee and the purchase of office materials.

Who pays for the many trips to distant organizations and the many days the leaders lose from work following up numerous problems? The answer is not public, but it seems that the bulk of the CTP's expenses are covered by two sources: ORIT (Inter-American Regional Labor Organization) and the APRA party. Although even the CTP officers are not aware of the total expenditures of the organization, it appears that the figure is around 12,000 sols monthly.

The newspaper of the CTP, incidentally, is almost a complete failure. The *Cetepé* appears about twice a year. The layout is unattractive, the style is dense, and the distribution extremely haphazard. The press organs of the Lima Union of Taxi Drivers, the Federation of Textile Workers, and the National Union of Bank Clerks appear far more regularly and are superior newspapers. What is surprising is that, according to the treasurer of the CTP, the *Cetepé* makes a profit.[12] The lack of attention given to the newspaper can probably be accounted for by the presence of *La Tribuna*. This APRA party organ appears daily and devotes

11. Interview with Eusebio Cabrera, treasurer of the CTP, June 22, 1961.
12. Ibid.

about half of one page to labor matters. The labor editor of *La Tribuna* was, in 1961, the secretary of press and propaganda of the CTP. Apparently many leaders feel that a separate CTP newspaper would be largely redundant. But what they have failed to realize is that the great bulk of rank and file workers (who are not devout Apristas) do not read *La Tribuna* and are therefore cut off from CTP opinion.

As noted in Chapter 4, the CTP has recently employed the method of legal enactment in a few instances. At present, however, the organization continues to rely most heavily on political bargaining and has adapted to this strategy. If basic variables should change so as to make legal enactment relatively more effective, certain changes in the CTP may be expected. First, the CTP would probably form a permanent lobbying department and engage statistical, technical, and legal specialists. Second, there probably would be an increase in dues and income, coupled with a firmer policy toward nonpaying members.

The Confederation of White-Collar Workers

As mentioned in Chapter 7, there is a very perceptible social division between obreros and empleados, or manual and intellectual workers. The distinction has existed for many years and has gradually entered into the formal dispositions of the government. At the present time, two sets of laws exist concerning workers: one for obreros, one for empleados. To a certain extent the two overlap but on many points they are different, with the empleados receiving more benefits.

To defend the empleados' legally distinct position, as well as to affiliate workers whose social background differed from that of most manual laborers, various national centers were established. The first organizations were largely social in function. They included white-collar workers from the various stores and banking houses in Lima as direct members. Because of the dispersed nature of their membership, vigorous activity was not possible. Perhaps one of the first of these groups was the *Sociedad de*

Empleados de Comercio, founded about 1914. In 1920 another organization with a slightly more militant orientation was founded, the *Sociedad Unión de Empleados del Perú.*[13]

A few extracts from its press organ, *Trabajo y Libertad* (Work and Freedom) give an interesting glimpse at the viewpoint of this, then new, sector of society:

> We are not going to begin struggles between capital and labor . . . neither do we intend to raise up with boastful and disgusting bullying the red banner of revolt . . . Our mission is that of protection, of mutual defense, of petitions without intemperance, of disagreement without insults or diatribes.
>
> We shall search for, by all means at our disposal, the close cooperation between management and *obreros,* directors and *empleados* whose interests are parallel lines reaching to infinity without obstructing one another.[14]

It is not difficult to understand why the empleados, with such a reasonable point of view, had little in common with the anarchists of the labor movement at that time. But despite its moderate, even gentle, ideology, the Sociedad was considered a threat by management. Its new secretary-general, a man with 27 years of employment at the National Tax-Collecting Company (a private firm), was discharged shortly after he was elected to his post.[15] This event probably led a number of the members to reexamine the idea about parallelism of interests to infinity.

During the following 25 years, there appears to have been very little empleado activity. The small size of the establishments and the consequent closeness of the white-collar workers to management itself made vigorous, cohesive organizations impossible to form. But the economic changes that were taking place gave rise later to establishments where the many white-collar workers were

13. *Trabajo y Libertad* (organ of the *Sociedad Unión de Empleados del Perú*) (January 15, 1920), p. 1.
14. Ibid., p. 2.
15. Ibid., p. 4.

quite distinct from ownership. The large commercial houses, banks, and industrial companies provided large groups of empleados willing to organize themselves into unions. With these unions, a national center of white-collar workers became a tangible possibility.

An attempt was made in October 1946 to form such a center under the name of *Federación General de Empleados*. A look at the list of organizations represented at the congress explains why the Federation fell apart as soon as it was founded. The groups represented included 91 groups of the most diverse character from the Lima area: societies of public employees, journalists, nurses, actors, musicians, traveling salesmen, drug store clerks, public school teachers, mutual aid societies, and a few genuine industrial unions of empleados.[16] In addition 31 regional organizations were represented—organizations which were usually little more than names. Closer to a circus menagerie than a labor organization, the *Federación* was useful only as an example of what not to do.

Toward the end of the Odría dictatorship, as controls on trade union life were lifted, the white-collar workers began formation of a national center. The result was the *Central Sindical de Empleados Particulares del Perú* (CSEPP—Confederation of Private White-Collar Workers), founded on September 14, 1955. The CSEPP is by far the most cohesive central organization of white-collar workers ever formed in Peru. Unlike previous organizations of empleados, the CSEPP affiliates neither individuals nor public employees. The leaders have applied a firm membership policy, excluding mutual assistance societies and dropping groups which have, in effect, disappeared. The composition of the membership in 1961 is shown in Table 15. Of the 92 member organizations, 78 are industrial unions of white-collar workers. The other 14 are regional unions. With perhaps one exception, the Union of Clerks for Notary Publics (which figures as a regional organization), there are none of the impressive-sounding but

16. *Recommendaciones, Votas, y Acuerdos del Segundo Congreso de Empleados del Perú* (Lima, October 1946), pp. 63–80.

TABLE 15

Composition of the Confederation of White-Collar Workers,
by Member Organizations, September 1961

Type of organization	Number in the CSEPP	Membership of each organization	Total membership
Industrial unions of empleados	75	250 (average)	19,000
Regional unions of empleados (excluding Arequipa)	13	40	540
Other organizations:			
Arequipa Regional Union of Empleados	1	1,000	1,000
Lima Union of Trolley Operators	1	1,000	1,000
National Union of Telephone Workers	1	2,000	2,000
Federation of Petroleum Workers (M) (empleados only)	1	500	500
TOTALS:	92		24,040

ineffective associations of nurses, salesmen, etc. in the membership of the CSEPP.

The regional unions[17] are very weak and in some cases, practically nonexistent. Their few members are isolated individuals
from different stores and offices. A strike, if ever called by one
of these unions, would succeed only in causing the discharge of
the few members from their respective centers of employment.
The one exception is the Arequipa Regional Union of Empleados
(*Federación de Empleados de Comercio y Industria de Arequipa*
—FECIA) which has about 1,000 members and sound finances.

17. Called by many names: *Federación, Unión Sindical, Central Sindical,
Asociación*. These regional organizations group individuals (not unions) and
would bargain for their members if their strength permitted; hence they are
termed "unions."

If its leaders carry out their program it soon will become a federation, affiliating unions instead of direct members.

The leaders of the CSEPP have been accused by extremists of using regional unions as a means of obtaining delegates and votes to support their policies. However, given the overwhelming strength of moderate forces in the CSEPP, such a device is not necessary to keep the organization out of extremist hands. Rather, it seems that these regional unions are maintained in the hope that they will develop as time goes on. Technically, as we have seen, the CSEPP is a secondary organization, affiliating unions, and therefore is a federation according to the terminology employed in this study. However, because of its many member organizations and its special character, the term "confederation" has been applied.

The CSEPP, like the CTP, has an officers' board (24 members), and an assembly of delegates. Officers are elected at the national congress, held every two years. The same conditions of misrepresentation found in the CTP are present in the CSEPP: the non-proportional formal arrangement, and the fact that only one delegate from each member organization usually attends an ordinary meeting. The result is that the representation of member organizations is leveled, regardless of size. But whereas in the CTP this condition tended to threaten cohesion, in the CSEPP it does not. The assembly is a vigorous body where both discussion and decision-making take place. It is, in fact, the key to the cohesion of the confederation. The reason for this is that the CSEPP, with the exception of perhaps two organizations, is a body of near-equals. Because the delegates are aware of the impotence of their individual organizations, they accept equal representation without resentment. One exception is the Lima Union of Trolley Operators, a powerful member. In fact, the trolley operators are the backbone in any strike of the CSEPP. In 1961 the union was in APRA–independent hands and remained within the CSEPP, although not without complaints. The National Union of Bank Clerks was another powerful organization among the many weak members of the CSEPP. When leadership of the union came into extremist hands in 1958, it lost little time in withdrawing.[18]

In contrast to the CTP the officers of the CSEPP apply a moderately firm policy toward organizations which do not pay dues. The constitution of the confederation states that if a member fails to meet its financial obligations after six months it shall be suspended. In practice this rule is not applied to regional organizations. It is carried out, however, in the case of other unions. In 1960 about seven organizations were dropped from the membership list for failure to pay dues.[19] This contrast with CTP financial policy reflects a basic difference in the strategic possibilities of the two organizations.

The leaders of the CSEPP have found that their organization alone is not a potent force in political bargaining (see below). Whatever their conception of the optimal strategy for their organization, they do not expect to bring the government to its knees by a strike. Consequently, the loss of an affiliate is not so important as it is for the CTP since the leaders of the CSEPP do not expect to do much political bargaining on their own. They are therefore willing to pursue a more aggressive financial policy at the cost of a smaller membership list. The monthly dues to the CSEPP are 50 sols (1.85) for each delegate (compared to 20 sols of the CTP). The monthly income of the organization is about 6,000 sols ($220).[20]

Concerning possible scope of action, it must be remembered

18. It frequently happens when a member organization withdraws from a higher organization that a split is claimed and the seceding organization holds itself to be following the "genuine" faction. In 1958 such a "split" was engineered by the National Union of Bank Clerks in order to withdraw from the CSEPP without appearing in the role of "destroying the unity of the working class." Although even in 1961 the extremist leaders of the bank clerks' organization still claimed to be members of an organization with the same name as the CSEPP, but headed by Guillermo Sheen Lazo (Felix Loli was the 1961 secretary-general of the CSEPP), I was unable to find this competing extremist-led organization.

19. Interview with Napoleon Posada L., secretary of organization of the CSEPP, Lima, October 11, 1961.

20. Interview with Florentin Esteban S., treasurer of the CSEPP, Lima, December 10, 1961.

that the CSEPP is much smaller than the CTP (24,000 compared to 240,000). This fact alone would suggest that political bargaining might not be as effective for the CSEPP. But there are a number of other conditions peculiar to white-collar unions which limit the potential of the confederation.

First, a union of empleados tends to be less cohesive than a parallel organization of obreros. The white-collar workers are more conservative than obreros, being closer to management, and many do not participate actively in the union. Second, many white-collar workers are not emotionally or ideologically disposed to take extreme measures to achieve a satisfactory solution. Whereas manual laborers are immersed in a subculture which justifies violent action, the empleados are somewhat separated from this culture—and indeed, many would like to be seen as distinct from manual laborers.

For these reasons the CSEPP is not suited to engage in strikes. They are difficult to effect, and are of little political importance. In the period 1956–61 the CSEPP actually carried out two strikes. The second was a one-day protest stoppage on March 6, 1961, to encourage Congress to deal with the empleado social security bill. The strike would have gone unnoticed without the support of the trolley operators and the bank clerks. The latter union was not a member of the CSEPP, but it complied with the common empleado effort nevertheless. As an indication of the ineffectiveness of the strike, Congress did not take up the bill until four months later. The executive disregarded the strike completely.

When the social security proposal was considered, the lobbying campaign of the CSEPP was feeble. To be sure, the confederation was opposed by the Peruvian Medical Association, a formidable lobby in itself. But, as its officers admitted, the confederation did not make strenuous efforts on its own behalf. It must be remembered, however, that the CSEPP is a very young organization. It was not fully established until its national congress of 1959. At present the organization is experimenting with both political bargaining and legal enactment as trade union methods. Neither has been employed with great energy or success. It seems that any political bargaining will have to be done not by the CSEPP itself but by its powerful allies, the Lima Union of Trolley Operators and particularly the CTP.

The one case in which political bargaining was used successfully concerned the ministerial decree ordering the replacement of one empleado of the Milne Company who had been discharged, so the labor leaders held, because he was a member of the union of empleados. The CSEPP was to have begun an indefinite general strike on September 18, 1961, in defense of the worker and of the general principle of job security. Two days before that date the Minister of Labor ordered the worker reinstated. It appears, nevertheless, that whatever coercion may have been directed at the executive came from the CTP, which had backed the CSEPP position with considerable firmness. Certainly the CSEPP alone could hardly have frightened anyone. Indeed, the officers of the confederation were greatly relieved when they learned that a strike would not be necessary, for they feared that their organization might be wrecked by a strike of any duration.

At the December 1961 congress the CSEPP decided to affiliate to the CTP as a member organization. It would seem apparent, then, that white-collar leaders recognize their dependence on the national obrero center. However, the CSEPP cannot call upon the CTP at will. There are many labor conflicts in the country and the CTP must not expend its resources on all of them. In addition, it is usually a requisite for CTP assistance that the petitioning organization first take energetic action on its own. If the CSEPP cannot strike—and it seems that perhaps it cannot— then it may not receive much assistance from the CTP.

Yet legal enactment may become a highly successful tactic for white-collar workers in the future. If elections should become more continuous and more meaningful, the CSEPP might be the first organization to take advantage of the change. The white-collar workers are a substantial segment of the politically alert and socially skilled population. Although they cannot use the tactics of mass demonstrations and violence to advantage, it is likely that they could generate a significant impact on the legislative process. Signs of this potential are visible already. For example, the Vice-President of the House of Deputies in 1961, Manuel Panizo, was formerly active in the National Union of Bank Clerks and worked closely with the CSEPP. Given a congenial electoral climate and a few more years to develop as an organization, the CSEPP may well become one of the most powerful lobbies in the country.

9

In comparison with the financial resources at the disposal of the North American labor movement, Peruvian worker organizations are poor. The most commonly heard explanation for this difference is that Peruvian workers, having low incomes, cannot afford to make more than a minimal contribution to their unions. Low income, it is true, does establish an upper limit to worker organization finances. But one cannot explain on the basis of worker income why this upper limit is so seldom reached in practice. It may be that a unionist cannot spare more than 40 or 50 sols a month for union dues. But this does not tell us why he in fact pays only five or ten sols. Therefore the problem of finances must be examined more closely.

In the unions the primary source of funds is the monthly or weekly dues paid by the members. In most cases these dues are collected personally by the treasurer, a time consuming and inefficient method. An energetic treasurer, spending every spare moment shoulder-tapping and appealing, might obtain a fair portion of the income which should regularly enter the organization's treasury. But human beings have a tendency to forget and put off: invariably this habit is reflected in the union's intake of funds.

A far better method of collecting dues is the check-off system, relatively new in Peru, but gaining in popularity. The union submits to management a list of members who have agreed to have the company deduct their dues from the weekly pay. The firm then turns over the total sum directly to the treasurer of the union. Although requiring several months to bring into full operation, the check-off system, once established, gives the union a constant monthly income effortlessly collected by the paymaster.

One of the first unions in Peru to employ this system was the Lima Union of Trolley Operators, in 1946. Since that time a number of organizations have adopted the check-off; about 20 per cent now use it. The leaders of the Federation of Textile Workers estimate that about one half of the 82 member unions collect dues with this system.[1] Of the 23 unions in the Federation of Metallurgical Workers, three use the check-off.[2] In many of the larger mining establishments the same procedure is employed. The primary obstacle to more widespread use of the check-off is, as one might suspect, employer reluctance to assist unions in this matter.

The check-off system, it must be noted, is voluntary. Members submit their names to the management if they wish to have their dues discounted from their pay. If a member decides that he does not wish to pay dues, he merely withdraws his name. There is no formal means of coercing members to join the union or to pay dues, either by the collection or check-off system.

The closed shop is practically unknown in Peru for several reasons.[3] First, the closed shop is an organizational goal and not one which brings rewards to the workers directly and immediately. The tiny unions are highly responsive to rank and file

1. Interview in Lima with Vicente Segovia, secretary-general of the Federation of Textile Workers and Jorge Hau Blas, past secretary of publicity, June 4, 1961.

2. Interview with Luis Gutierrez, past secretary-general of the Federation of Metallurgical Workers in Lima, June 26, 1961.

3. The National Union of Primary School Teachers receives one sol monthly from each teacher, deducted by the Ministry of Education. However, each teacher voluntarily pays about 10 sols monthly to his local organization.

opinion and leadership must concentrate on demands of tangible benefit to the members: wages and working conditions. If leadership should demand a costly battle for the closed shop—costly, for the management would not capitulate readily—the rank and file would probably defect. Workers are prepared to sacrifice three weeks' pay for a 15 per cent wage increase, but not for the organizational luxury of a closed shop.

Secondly, many leaders and members are opposed to the closed shop in principle. They hold that the Constitution guarantees freedom of association and a closed shop would violate this guarantee. Trade unionism in Peru, it should be pointed out, is not yet a business. It is viewed as a philosophy which the individual worker should adopt by his own decision.

Lastly, union security is achieved through methods other than the closed shop. The small size of most unions makes it relatively simple to enlist the support of newly employed workers. Face to face contact with leaders and considerable informal group pressure bring new workers into the life of the organization almost as soon as they are hired. On the other hand, the separation benefit law makes management reluctant to attempt destroying a union by discharging its members. Any worker is entitled to receive 15 days' pay for every year of employment on being discharged for any reason except criminal offenses or gross negligence.[4] The leaders of a union are protected against dismissal (except for criminal offenses) by a ministerial decree given in 1957.

It is true that employers do make occasional attempts to destroy a union by dismissing either members or leaders. But in these cases the workers go to the executive for protection, demanding either the implementation of an existing law, or simply that the union not be destroyed. It is significant to note that as the next step in achieving union security, labor leaders are considering not the closed shop but a law which would make it impossible for management to dismiss a worker for any reason except proven incompetence or criminal acts.

4. Law number 8439, August 20, 1936, Art. iii.

The monthly dues vary from three sols (11 cents) in the Union of Tobacco Workers to 20 sols (74 cents) in the National Union of Bank Clerks. The average seems to be about seven sols (25 cents) for Lima organizations and about five sols (19 cents) for organizations in the provinces.[5] Dues (when paid) usually constitute about .4 per cent of the total monthly income of the worker (see Table 16). Because the concepts of both effective membership and dues-paying membership are difficult to apply with precision, any figure of proportion of dues-paying membership to total effective membership would be only approximate. Generally in concentrated unions the figure is quite high, 85 per cent or better. In dispersed organizations it may be rather high if the organization is cohesive—the Lima Union of Bus Workers has about 95 per cent, the National Union of Bank Clerks about 85 per cent—or low in organizations with a weak organic structure, such as the Lima unions of construction workers, printing workers, and pastry workers, all below 30 per cent. Table 16 presents, for the better developed unions, a picture of the proportion of effective membership which pays dues (column C). It also shows the amount of dues (column D) and the proportion which these dues represent of the worker's monthly earnings (column F).

In addition to this primary source of funds, a union may realize a profit on sporting events and raffles. Renting the headquarters to social clubs for dances provides another occasional source. But these incomes, in the case of most unions, are secondary. Thus a well established union with a dues-paying membership of 300, using the check-off, would have at its disposal about 3,000 sols a month, or about $110. When one realizes that a full-time officer would cost about 2,000 sols ($74) or a secretary 800 sols ($30), then the possible extent of operations becomes evident. The expenditures of this union would include: part time of the officers (paid at the rate which they would earn on the job), legal fees, office materials, press releases and bulletins,

5. In all figures in this chapter the exchange rate of 27 sols to the dollar, or the inverse, 0.037 dollars to the sol, has been used.

TABLE 16

Dues, Dues-paying Membership, and Dues as Proportion of Monthly Earnings[a]

	A	B	C	D	E	F
	Effective member- ship	Dues- paying member- ship[b]	Dues- paying member- ship expressed as per cent of effective member- ship	Monthly dues[c]	Average monthly wage[d]	Monthly dues expressed as per cent of worker's monthly wage
Type of union			(B/A)			(D/E)
CONCENTRATED						
Leche Gloria, Arequipa	380	375	99%	5	1,400	.36%
Lima Trolley Operators	900	860	96%	10	2,300	.43%
Textile "La Unión"	640	600	94%	6	1,500	.40%
Metallurgical "Record"	230	210	91%	4.5	1,800	.25%
Metallurgical La Oroya	4,000	3,000	75%	10	1,300	.77%
State Tobacco Monopoly	730	700	96%	3	1,200	.25%
White-Collar Workers of the Lima Electric Co.	600	550	92%	5	2,000	.25%
DISPERSED						
Lima Bus Drivers	5,500	5,200	95%	16	2,000	.80%
Lima Construction Workers (1960)	4,000	700	17%	4	1,000	.40%
Lima Printing Workers (1960)	2,000	640	32%	5	1,200	.42%
Bank Clerks Lima only (1960)	4,500	3,800	85%	20	1,700	1.20%

a. Because it is difficult to collect accurate information on the smaller, less active organizations both in Lima and the provinces, this table is a representative cross section of only the larger, more important unions.

b. The number of dues-paying members (column B) was estimated from publications and interviews with different leaders. It must be considered only approximate.

c. The figures for dues (column D) include all contributions which members regularly make, even though the union may pass a portion of the funds it receives along to federations or to union committees.

d. The monthly dues and earnings (columns D and E) are in sols (3.7 cents/sol). The monthly earnings figures (column E) are only estimates; they may be as much as ±20 per cent in error.

and dues to superior organizations. In addition, many unions have programs of social assistance which frequently are paid for out of dues, but occasionally there are extra contributions to a separate fund made by those who want to participate in such plans.

In the few larger, well-organized unions, the financial resources are greater and the scope of activity wider. The Lima
unions of bank clerks, bus workers, trolley car operators, and
taxi drivers, for example, have both full-time officers and secretaries. Furthermore, these organizations are among the very few
unions in the country which publish newspapers. The number
of unions with full-time officers or secretaries is probably not
over thirty. The number with press organs is somewhat smaller.
However such circumstances are not primarily the result of
inadequate financial resources. In these organizations of 100 to
500 men there is not sufficient need for full-time employees.
Publications of the union, important as they are, do not appear
because leaders lack both the interest and ability to compose
a newspaper, not because of financial limitations. Nor does it
seem that lack of funds can be singled out as the primary reason
for the failure of many unions to carry out adequately other
administrative functions such as grievance handling, correspond-
ence, and negotiations.

An examination of strike funds reveals that practically all
unions are without reserves for times of strife. Even in the case
of the Union of La Oroya Metallurgical Workers, with about
500,000 sols in its strike fund [6]—perhaps the largest in Peru—
this sum would last a very short time paying each striker (4,000)
ten sols a day (one fourth usual wage), perhaps only 12 or 13
days.

But again, probably one should not consider low worker income as an explanation for this state of affairs. In the first place
strikes under political bargaining tend to be quite short and
therefore do not drastically affect worker income. Whereas in
the United States unions have to prepare themselves for economic strikes of many months' duration, Peruvian labor leaders
expect to be on strike only a few weeks and are not greatly concerned with building up large strike funds.

Another reason why excess funds have not been amassed by

6. Interview with Claudio G. Salazar, managing secretary of the Union of
La Oroya Metallurgical Workers, April 28, 1961.

the unions is officer dishonesty and membership fear of future mishandling of funds. Although dishonesty appears to be more common in provincial organizations where members are less vigilant and safeguards less well developed, the phenomenon is not unknown in Lima. In 1960 the leaders of the Lima Union of Bus Workers managed to swindle or misspend the entire savings of that organization, leaving it in debt when new leaders took over.[7] The exact amount is in doubt, but it could not have been less than 100,000 sols ($3,900) and might have been over 500,000 sols ($18,000).[8]

One tactic followed in cases where the leaders cannot be trusted with excess funds is to invest money in fixed resources such as chairs, desks, and typewriters. The Union of Longshoremen of Pucallpa has even purchased three plots of land with surplus funds.[9] The fact that a number of unions have assets of this kind indicates that financial limitations may not be a significant impediment to vigorous activity.

To a minimal extent other organizations assist a union in difficulties by contributions, either collected at meetings or donated from the treasury. For example, to support the 25-day strike of the miners at Huarán in January 1961, other miners' unions donated a total of 39,370 sols ($1,450).[10] The Lima Union of Trolley Operators sent 22,580 sols ($820) to the trolley workers in Arequipa who had been thrown out of work by the damage of the 1960 earthquake.[11] In connection with the same disaster, the Federation of Printing Workers sent 2,000 sols ($74) to the Arequipa Union of Printing Workers,[12] and the Federation of Textile Workers held a collection for the

7. Interview with Benjamin Medina, secretary-general of the Lima Union of Bus Workers, April 26, 1961.

8. The monthly savings of this organization in 1961 were about 10,000 sols. See financial reports in SUTA (organ of the Lima Union of Bus Workers), February 1961, p. 6, and March 1961, p. 5.

9. Interview with Juan Chong Inca, secretary-general of the Union of Longshoremen of Pucallpa, May 7, 1961.

10. La Tribuna (Lima, January 24, 1961), p. 5.

11. Norte Sindical (Lima, May 1960), p. 4.

12. La Tribuna (Lima, January 23, 1960), p. 5.

textile unions of Arequipa which netted 829 sols ($31).[13] Such gifts are motivated partly by disinterested concern and partly by a practical consideration. Help given in time of need tends to obligate the recipient organization to the donor. When searching for allies to bolster its position at a later date, a worker organization may be able to cash a moral I.O.U.

It is interesting to note that in the period 1950–61, the real dues (correcting for inflation) paid by members of labor organizations increased by an average of 90 per cent. This is a very surprising demonstration of the strengthening of union finance in the last eleven years (see Table 17). The finances of the industrial and regional federations seem extremely slender, particularly when the potential scope of these bodies is compared to the activities of a tiny union. The industrial federations, as a result of their higher cohesion, are better situated financially than the regional organizations, but this says little in view of the almost total absence of funds in the regional federations.

The maximum proportion of union dues that labor leaders maintain ought to go to the industrial federation is 25 per cent. In practice the figure is much lower. In the well developed Federation of Textile Workers—again as a reflection of its cohesion and utility to members—the highest proportion (13 per cent) is obtained. The Federation of Sugar Workers probably collects nearly that much.[14] But in other industrial federations the proportion is much lower: .5 per cent to 1 per cent or, in some cases, nothing (see Table 18). Federation dues are almost always assigned in a fixed amount, either per man (textile workers' and mineworkers' [center] federations) or per organization (footwear workers) or per delegate (taxi drivers). In the regional federations, treasuries with a regular monthly income from member organizations are rare. With very few exceptions funds come from outside the labor movement, and the federations thus lead a half life completely dependent on a handful of self-sacrificing

13. Ibid. (January 15, 1960), p. 5.
14. Interview with Leopoldo Pita V., past secretary-general of the Federation of Sugar Workers in Lima, September 16, 1961.

TABLE 17

Changes in Dues, Money and Real, of Representative Unions, 1950–1961[a]

Organization[c]	Money dues 1950	Dues 1950 in 1961 terms[b]	Dues 1961	Net change in real dues 1950–61	
				Amount	Per cent
Sindicato de Pasteleros, "Estrella del Perú"	2.4	5.4	4	−1.4	−26
Sindicato de Empleados Manuales Bancarios	2.0	4.5	20	15.5	345
Sindicato de Trabajadores en Calzado "El Diamante"	1.3	2.9	9	6.1	210
Sindicato de Cobradores de EE AA EE	2.0	4.5	5	.5	11
Federación Gráfica	2.3	5.2	5	−.2	−4
Sindicato de Inspectores de Omnibus	2.0	4.5	10	5.5	121
Sociedad Obrera del Estanco del Tabaco	1.0	2.2	3	.8	36
Simple average	1.9	4.2	8.0	3.8	99

a. Figures for 1950 money dues were taken from Nicolás Mendoza, *Guía Obrera del Perú* (Lima, 1951). 1961 figures were collected by the author. All figures are monthly payments, in sols.

b. Since the cost of living (and running a labor organization) rose between 1950 and 1961, the 1950 money dues must be corrected to 1961 terms. The Ministry of Finance price index figures have been used: 1950 = 44.5, 1961 = 100.

c. Certain organizations have changed names or structure since 1950. The *Sindicato de Empleados Manuales Bancarios* has become a part of the National Union of Bank Clerks. The members of the old organization now pay the National Union's dues of 20 sols monthly. The *Federación Gráfica* grouped individual members in 1950. In 1961 these individuals would be members of the Lima Union of Printing Workers (founded 1956) where they would pay 5 sols monthly dues.

or externally paid leaders, or perhaps struggle along with intermittent income from dances or raffles.

However, it is neither helpful nor accurate to conclude that economic limitations prevent an expansion of activity. In general, the weak financial position of the federations is the result of the officers' inability to convince member unions that the federation can use more funds profitably. It can be said, with a high degree

TABLE 18

Income of Selected Industrial Federations from Payments of
Member Organizations, in Sols

	A	B	C	D	E
	Effective base member-ship[a]	Regular monthly receipts[b]	Monthly receipts per member	Average dues paid by worker to union[c]	Proportion of total dues re-ceived by the unions which go to the federation (C/D)
Federation					
Textile Workers	21,000	18,000	.9	7	13%
Metallurgical Workers	3,000	1,500	.5	7	7%
Mine Workers (Center)	30,000	6,000	.2	5	4%
Footwear Workers	5,000	450	.09	6	1.5%
Taxi Drivers (E)	1,500	200	.13	10	1.3%
Taxi Drivers (M)	10,000	0	0	10	0
Public School Teachers	43,000	2,900	.07	9	.8%
Market Vendors	8,000	0	0	4	0

a. For definition of effective base membership see Table 13.

b. The figures on regular monthly receipts are based on federation publications, leadership reports, and statutory dispositions. They should be considered approximate.

c. The figures for average dues paid by workers to the unions were estimated on the basis of knowledge of some of the member organizations of the federation, not all. These figures include all contributions by the member, before payment is made to the federation.

of certainty, that there is no union in the country which is not in a position to double its contribution to its industrial federation without making any significant sacrifice. It is true that most industrial federations could not greatly expand their activities on the financial resources they now have. But the real reason why these organizations do not receive more funds is that neither members nor most leaders are sufficiently aware of the opportunities for expanded activity which increased revenues would provide.

There are norms that discourage putting more leaders on a full-time basis. According to some leaders, the rank and file tend to be suspicious of officers who leave the shop. In addition, the distant but perceptible link with anarchist world views predisposes a few of the leaders to fear a bureaucracy. In the Federation of Textile Workers, for example, the constitution states that "As a means of avoiding the dangers of a trade union bureaucracy, the FTTP (Federation of Textile Workers) will not establish salaries or full-time pay for any of the officers." [15] If "dangers" means corruption or irresponsibility of leadership, the clause is understandable. If it means a total and permanent negation of bureaucracy—which is probably the case, in light of the way modern trade unionism is carried out in the world—it appears childish. The Federation of Textile Workers, incidentally, puts most of its monthly income into a fund for a new headquarters building.[16]

In addition to these two objections to paid leaders, there is some doubt whether the sudden full-time employment of federation officers would result in a sizable expansion in activity. The process of learning to use a full-time staff depends on a gradual realization by members of the opportunities. An officer may demonstrate his energy and imagination working on a part-time basis. After several years of successful activity, members will become aware of his utility to the organization and of the advantage obtained by employing him full time. If the process were reversed and a leader hired with the hope that he would make himself useful, the officer might, simply because he lacked ideas, spend most of his time playing billiards.

In the same fashion the need for technical information—cost

15. *Planificación Sindical del Gremio Textile* (Lima, 1958), Art. ii.

16. In all fairness it must be pointed out that the Federation of Textile Workers is the best organized, most effective industrial federation in Peru. The restraint put on leadership activity by the clause quoted above is circumvented by extensive part-time employment of leaders. The officers are paid by the federation for days lost from work while attending to federation business.

of living index, wage levels and structure, firm sales and profits, market conditions, and accident rates—has not been grasped. Few leaders of any federation know within an accuracy of 10 per cent the number of affiliates; in fact, most leaders are uncertain about the number of member unions. Even if they should want such statistical information, there is some doubt whether competent and trustworthy specialists are available.

As in the case of the unions, federation publications are infrequent. But again, the intermittent appearance or absence of federation newspapers (the Federation of Textile Workers is the only industrial federation which even approaches the publishing of a regular monthly newspaper) is not at all the result of deficient finances, for almost invariably publications break even or show a profit. Rather, newspapers do not appear more often because leaders lack ability and interest in writing, composing, and distributing them.

Outside Sources of Funds

Finance seems to be one aspect of labor organizations that is built from the ground up; to imagine that by permanently injecting funds at the top the many other aspects will automatically develop is perhaps a mistaken view. Of course, temporary assistance at key points including organizing drives, schools for labor leaders, congresses, and similar activities can be of importance in enhancing the effectiveness of the labor organizations —but only if such aid is temporary. A number of organizations outside the Peruvian labor movement give financial assistance to the worker organizations. The various sources of outside funds, the methods of distributing them, and their effects on the labor organizations are discussed below.

The moderate-led organizations receive aid from the international trade secretariats, from ORIT, and the APRA party. Extremist-led organizations appear to have several sources, most of which cannot be identified with certainty. The international trade secretariats spend their funds almost entirely in maintaining the regional office and advisor, holding schools for leaders, arranging congresses and conferences, and supporting key organizational drives. Little, if any, money is spent for permanent subsidy of either organizations or leaders. The ORIT (Inter-American Labor Organization) is a pan-American labor body with member national centers in almost all of the Latin American countries, the United States, and Canada. Apart from its many other functions ORIT is an instrument for channeling funds from the wealthier United States and Canadian (and perhaps Mexican) labor organizations to the newer, weaker movements in the South.

Although the size of the ORIT contribution to the Peruvian national center (the CTP) is not made public, it appears that the sum is between $500 and $600 monthly (14,000 to 16,000 sols). Even by Peruvian standards this is small. When one realizes that the National Union of Bank Clerks had a monthly income of about 30,000 sols even before it doubled dues in 1961 (and the thirteen full-time leaders are not paid by union dues but are "on leave" with their regular salaries), or even that a healthy union of 800 members would receive 8,000 sols monthly ($300), the conclusion that ORIT is supporting the entire Peruvian labor movement is quite mistaken. ORIT money is distributed around the country to a number of industrial and regional federations, as well as to the CTP. The Arequipa and Lima regional federations and the moderate-led Federations of Construction Workers and Taxi Drivers are among the probable recipients. Judging from hearsay, a number of other leaders attempt to extract a few pennies for their own organizations.

There are several dangers in establishing a direct subsidy, even though quite small, to the labor movement. First, because of the impossibility of evolving a satisfactory public or institutional means of dividing the funds, distribution must be done informally, thus giving rise to haggling, personal feuds, and resentments. Second, because of the informal method of distributing the funds, workers in general are not aware of these funds or their source. They often believe that organizations receiving

ORIT money are subsidized by other bodies. For example, the opinion of non-APRA trade unionists in Arequipa was that the APRA-led regional federation (USTA) was being subsidized by the Peruvian government (the APRA party, it must be remembered, supported the Prado government). Leaders of the non-APRA Union of Taxi Drivers in Iquitos have been heard to state that the moderate Federation of Taxi Drivers, most of the officers of which are Apristas, was supported by the International Petroleum Company. (Neither APRA nor this federation have supported the campaign to nationalize petroleum.) Both were wrong. These two organizations are assisted by ORIT, or by North American labor organizations anxious to see Peruvian organizations reach the same level of effectiveness and success as they themselves have achieved.

Thirdly, because of the hegemony of APRA leaders in the CTP, which receives the ORIT money, these funds tend to become politically colored—exactly what the North American contributors wish to avoid. This is not to say that the money is spent for political rallies or such overtly partisan events, but simply that the APRA leaders have a tendency to favor fellow party members and overlook less partisan leaders and organizations in the distribution of funds. Thus the distance between independent leaders and Apristas is maintained or perhaps widened by resentments, whereas the goal, presumably, is to close the gap.

The fourth, and perhaps most convincing argument against the ORIT subsidy in the form in which it is given is that it does not contribute to the formation of healthy, cohesive labor organizations; on the contrary, it may actually be detrimental to the establishment of tightly-knit organizations. When expenses are covered by outside sources, the leadership does not have to serve the membership. They need not adopt a policy which brings the kind of results members are interested in, nor need they bother about building up strong bonds of cohesion. When an internally supported leadership loses contact with the membership, dues are not paid, member organizations withdraw, and the organization ceases to function. But with externally supported leadership, the organization continues to exist regardless of the policy. In fact, this existence is largely nominal because members themselves may well drift away, leaving a name, a building, and periodical press releases. The present ineffectual state of the moderate-led Arequipa regional federation (USTA) may well be a result, in part, of the officers' independence from internal financial support.

Of course, alert energetic leaders may use outside funds wisely, but when such income is on a permanent basis there is no need to generate internal sources. For example, the moderate Federation of Taxi Drivers, after a relatively profitable three-year period of organizing and establishing the new federation, is now at the point where at least half of its expenses could be covered by dues from the member unions. Nevertheless, it continues without receiving a penny from its own members.[17]

When member organizations do not invest funds in their superior organizations, they are likely to be uninterested in its activities. This indifference may lead to lower cohesion of the entire organization. It is one thing to belong free of charge to a federation, but quite another to contribute part of one's own financial resources. If some of the money comes from them, member unions will want to know how the money is spent and, more important, will want to suggest better ways of spending it. It seems, then, that the ORIT subsidy to the Peruvian labor movement, as administered in its present fashion, may be doing more harm than good. If funds are to be given at all it would seem far wiser that they be distributed by an international representative for specific, temporary projects—as do the inter-American branches of the trade secretariats.

Although evidence is difficult to obtain, it appears that the APRA party assists those leaders and organizations which it finds particularly useful; such contributions are not particularly large, however. The party has its own expenses, and although it is keenly interested in removing communists and other extremists

17. Interview in Lima with Medardo Gomero, secretary of organization of the moderate-led Federation of Taxi Drivers, April 18, 1961.

from positions of power in the labor movement, this goal usually is not greatly furthered by financial assistance. The party does operate its own labor leadership training and indoctrination courses and probably finances the trips of APRA labor leaders when they serve a semipolitical function.

Given the diversity of the extremist left in Peru, it seems certain that there is more than one source for the outside funds received by extremist-led organizations. Exactly what the sources are remains in doubt. The Soviet bloc, Communist China, other Latin American extremist movements, and local sources are the possibilities. The last source may be more important than at first imagined. Extremist parties have wealthy members, and a devotion to the "cause" might well lead them to part with some of their income. In addition, with very few exceptions, extremist-led labor organizations are usually turned over to new leadership in a bankrupt condition. The money drawn from wealthier organizations may well find its way to weaker extremist-led groups.[18]

The external source of funds to any labor organization, extremist or moderate, can usually be discovered by investigating whether the member organizations pay any dues, or whether the dues are sufficient to sustain the organization. Of course, there may be certain other incomes. For example, the extremist-led Federation of Taxi Drivers receives only a few pennies from its member unions, but owns a rather large building, parts of which are rented. However, the income from this source does not appear at all sufficient to cover the salaries of practically all the officers who are apparently working full time, and at least three secretaries. In addition to the staff whom the observer can notice during working hours in the headquarters, there are always light, telephone, transportation, press, and office expenses.

18. In at least one case the money has gone directly from one extremist-led organization to another. In January 1961, the National Union of Bank Clerks—the wealthiest labor organization in Peru—gave 1,000 sols ($37) to the extremist-led Federation of Farm Laborers. This money came directly from the treasury and was reported in the organization's newspaper, FEB (Lima, April 15, 1961), p. 11, *gastos generales*, Item 14.

In general the outside funds, as in the case of moderate-led organizations, go to secondary bodies, such as industrial and regional federations. However, in the case of the Lima Union of Construction Workers, outside funds have been necessary to maintain a dispersed union. A study of some older publications of this organization reveals an estimated deficit of 2,000 to 10,000 sols monthly. It is not accurate to separate the Lima Union from the recently formed extremist Federation of Construction Workers since they work so closely together; thoughtful calculation puts the figure of outside funds received by both organizations at about 15,000 sols monthly ($550). The fluctuations in income from membership dues of the Lima Union of Construction Workers is shown in Figure 11.[19]

19. Utilizing past publications of the Lima Union of Construction Workers, we may construct a graph of the flow of funds, from membership dues, into the organization (see Figure 11). The curve reflects both the decline of the number of workers in the construction industry since 1956 and the crumbling organic structure of the union during the same period (see Chapter 5). Extrapolation of the tendency seems to indicate that in 1961 the income from dues was very close to zero or, as a maximum, perhaps 1,000 sols monthly.

Stated expenses of this organization in 1958 were about 3,000 sols monthly (3,395 for January, 1958, 3,404 for February), as reported in *El Obrero de Construcción Civil* (Lima, June 2, 1958), p. 4. In the same issue it was reported that in January there was a deficit of 115 sols, leaving in February a total deficit (including deficits of preceding months) of 9,120 sols. We conclude that even to cover minimum stated expenses the union runs a deficit of 2,000 to 3,000 sols monthly. If we consider real expenses to be at the 1956 level (12,000 sols monthly), then in 1961 the monthly deficit may be as high as 10,000 sols.

But this is only a part of real expenses. Apart from the officers, the union has at least three full-time "employees," each of whom probably receives about 1,200 sols monthly. In addition, the organization has undertaken a number of expensive extra activities. For example, the National Congress held in December 1958, at which the extremist federation was formed, probably cost at least 25,000 sols for transportation, meals, and perhaps lodging, days lost from work by delegates, publicity, and mimeographing. One month before the congress, the November 16, 1958, issue of *El Obrero de Construcción Civil* (p. 3) stated: "Six delegates of the organization committee of the first national congress of construction workers of Peru have journeyed (into the provinces) to assure the participation of the provincial organizations at our national congress." A conservative estimate of the traveling and living expenses of these six delegates would be about 10,000 sols. On April 12–16, 1961, a similar congress was held with the attendance of 44 delegates (re-

FIGURE 11.

FIGURE 11.

Changes in Income from Membership Dues of the Lima Union of Construction
Workers, 1954–1961

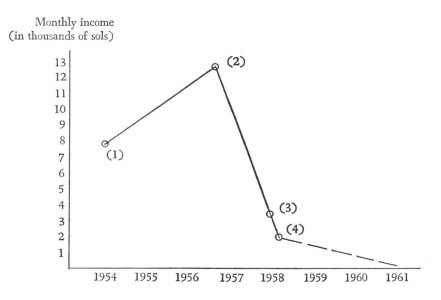

Monthly income
(in thousands of sols)

1. 7,970.31 sols in January 1954.
2. 12,524 sols in October 1956.
3. 3,180 sols in January 1958.
4. 1,908 sols in February 1958.

Source: *El Obrero de Construcción Civil* (organ of the Lima Union of Construction Workers), June 4, 1954, December 1956, June 2, 1958.

ported in *Unidad* [organ of the Communist Party], Lima, May 31, 1961),
p. 3. Because of the notably weak financial situation of the provincial unions
of construction workers, it is extremely doubtful that these organizations pay
any dues or cover even a significant fraction of the expenses for congresses.
Hence, it is not unreasonable to conclude that the Lima Union and its off-
spring, the extremist Federation of Construction Workers, receive a minimum
of 15,000 sols monthly from outside sources.

Table 19 gives a conservative estimate of the amount of money extremist labor leaders receive, sums which are presumably spent on maintaining and using the organization. The figure arrived at is about $2,440 monthly. In view of the relatively large funds

TABLE 19

Estimated Income of Important Extremist-led Organizations
from Outside Sources

Organization	Estimated monthly income, in sols[a]
Arequipa Regional Federation (FDTA)	8,000
Puno Regional Federation (FTP)	3,000
Cuzco Regional Federation (FTC)	10,000
Lima Union and Federation of Construction Workers (E)	15,000
Federation of Taxi Drivers (E)	15,000
Federation of Farm Laborers and Peasants (E)	10,000
Other organizations	5,000
TOTAL	66,000 ($2,440)

a. These figures do not include outside payments for the cost of trips which many leaders have made to Cuba, Russia, Argentina, Uruguay, and Chile.

which extremists receive, the question arises as to why they are not more successful. As seen in Chapter 5, the extremists lost ground during the four years 1957–61. The only real gain they made in that period was the control of the National Union of Bank Clerks, one of the few extremist-led organizations which does not need—and probably does not get—outside funds.

The simplest answer is that money isn't everything. Some of the remarks made about ORIT money and vigorous trade union activity apply to the extremists as well: haggling for the same piece of pie, low cohesion, leaders not dependent on member contributions, and, in the case of federations, membership indifference partly as the result of taking no financial part in the secondary organization. In addition, few of the leaders (with perhaps the exception of the Lima Union of Construction Workers and the extremist Federation of Construction Workers) receiving the assistance are particularly imaginative or energetic. One could almost assume that the leaders receive their allotment, distribute part of it to a few close assistants, and then relax. Occasionally they may organize a strike for partisan political objectives and thus strain the cohesion of their organization. The steady weakening of the regional federations in Arequipa (FDTA), Puno (FTP), and even Cuzco (FTC), as well as of the extremist Federation of Taxi Drivers, is not due only to the efforts made by moderate forces. It is equally the result of the extremists' own misguided strategy, lack of imagination, and indolence.

In an overall view, the condition of worker organization finances is a function of many variables. Among those suggested herein are: (1) the inability of labor leaders to employ more funds productively at their level of skill and insight; (2) the political bargaining pattern which reduces the importance of reserve funds; (3) the fact of and fear of officer dishonesty; (4) the existence of norms which discourage full-time leaders; (5) lack of interest in and commitment to the labor organizations by members and member unions; (6) the absence of effective techniques for collecting dues (the check-off). The level of worker income and its relation to a so-called "subsistence wage" are of minor importance in determining the level of worker organization finances.

10

ELECTIONS, LEADERSHIP, AND ATTITUDES

In concluding this section on the internal features of the Peruvian labor movement, attention will be focused on leadership. In previous discussions it has been suggested that worker organization structure is highly flexible, that the rank and file exercise considerable control over officers, and that a leader's tenure of office was generally an uncertain matter. Now the mechanisms of this flexibility may be viewed more closely. A logical starting point in this analysis is a discussion of the electoral procedures employed in selecting officers.

Elections are held quite frequently in the worker organizations; yearly in most cases, every two years in some federations. In general, two systems are employed for elections: the *list* and *office-by-office* procedures. The list system is employed by both dispersed and concentrated unions where the rank and file vote. With this method, the voters choose between entire lists of proposed officers. These lists (there are usually two or three) are drawn up in advance of the election by the candidates themselves; there are various subgroups each of which composes its own slate.

Two general considerations determine the formation of the proposed lists: policy or political orientation, and ability to attract votes. Leaders and supporters of each political tendency often draw up a slate composed of individuals of the same view. Usually the two currents in conflict are the extremist and APRA–moderate, but because of the wide variety of political tendencies found in worker organizations many other combinations are possible. In an organization where the APRA party is very weak one might find a list of extreme extremists opposing one of the moderate extremists. On the former list members of the Trotskyite and Rebel APRA parties would be found; on the latter, independents and members of opposition parties. The Communists would probably have their members on both lists. Or in organizations where extremists are very weak, the lists may reflect a division between militant Apristas and less devoted party members with some independents.

The second consideration, that of attracting votes, tends to lessen the ideological distance between the two or three lists. If a leader is popular with rank and file he may well appear on all lists, regardless of his politics. Duplication of parts of the lists is most likely to occur if political divisions are not acute. In some instances, even half of the proposed officers might appear on all slates. Apart from considerations of political orientation and popularity, those drawing up the lists attempt to represent the different sections of the working force. In a sugar workers' union, for example, candidates are drawn from the loading crews, the cane cutters, the crusher mill, and so on.

The office-by-office procedure is employed in practically all federations, most dispersed unions where elections are performed by delegates, and some unions where the rank and file vote. With this system, the officers are nominated and elected one by one in an assembly of the participants. Although the office-by-office procedure is more spontaneous than the list procedure, the political parties and groups within the organization do a great deal of maneuvering and deciding before the assembly is held.

A variation of the office-by-office system frequently used is a single list, multiple candidate procedure. It is used to avoid the long balloting process which, if a secret ballot is desired, the office-by-office system entails. All nominations are made in the assembly for each position and then voters construct their own list of preferences from the two or three candidates for each office. Each office is then awarded to the candidate who is mentioned the largest number of times for that office. This procedure has several disadvantages. There is no opportunity for a candidate defeated for one position to run for another since all nominations are closed before the vote is taken. Second, because nominations are limited—usually to three—alert, organized groups can get all their men nominated before other voters have had an opportunity to decide and attract the attention of the president of the electoral committee who receives the nominations.

Participation in elections is very high in unions of the concentrated type (the great majority of worker organizations). In these groups it seems that very close to 100 per cent of the eligible rank and file (dues-paying members) usually vote. If the list system is used the proportion tends to be higher than with the office-by-office procedure, since the lists can be distributed when workers leave the factory, an assembly not being necesssary. But with either system, participation is very good. This is a reflection of the small size of these organizations and their importance in the lives of the members.

In unions of the dispersed type where elections are performed by the rank and file, the proportion of participating members is somewhat lower. For example, in the elections for 1960 officers of the Lima Union of Trolley Operators, 634, or about 70 per cent, of the 900 eligible members voted.[1] This organization, while physically dispersed, is composed of workers all employed by the same company. Other dispersed organizations have much lower participation. In the elections for the 1960 officers' board of the Lima Union of Taxi Drivers, 1165 of the 8,000 members voted—about 15 per cent. The winning list of three received 616 votes, or about 7.7 per cent, of the total possible number of votes.[2] In the Lima unions of construction workers, pastry workers, and printing workers, a similar low proportion of the rank

1. *Norte Sindical* (Lima, January 1960), p. 6.
2. *La Tribuna* (Lima, December 29, 1959), p. 5.

and file—between 10 and 30 per cent—participated in elections.

In the unions of the dispersed type where delegates instead of rank and file vote, and in the federations, both regional and industrial, elections are well attended. The outcome of elections in these organizations depends on who the delegates are and which are the member organizations. The rank and file are removed from the electoral scene in all these organizations (as well as the CSEPP and the CTP) and delegates, most of whom are union leaders, effect the elections.

Regardless of the organization or the procedure used, elections themselves are almost always quite fair. They are arranged and executed by an electoral committee of three to five men who are nominated and elected in a previous assembly. The men chosen to serve on the electoral committee are either from different factions or are individuals with no apparent partisan ties. Leaders usually recognize that this must be so, for if any substantial sector of the membership were to feel that it was being cheated, division and noncooperation would probably be the result.

Closely related to membership participation in elections and the fairness of these processes is the rate of leadership turnover. As can be seen from Table 20, the proportion of individuals remaining on the officers' board year after year is relatively low. After one election only 40 to 60 per cent of the officers will remain on the new board. In the following years, the percentage of old officers (with respect to the base year) continues to decline, gradually reaching a constant figure in the established, stable organizations (Lima Union of Bus Workers, Federation of Textile Workers) or tending to reach the point of complete turnover in the newer organizations (Union of Paramonga Sugar Workers). Especially in organizations where there are sharp political divisions and an even balance between the forces, the turnover in leadership is high. This mobility, however, must not be confused with changes in political orientation, although leadership turnover can reflect such a change. There are many other factors that contribute to such changes, and within an organization

TABLE 20

Leadership Continuity in Selected Organizations

	Proportion of holdovers on the officers' board in the base years below					
Organization	1956	1957	1958	1959	1960	1961
Lima Union of Bus Workers	14/14ᵃ (100%)	7/14 (50%)	5/13 (38%)	4/13 (31%)	na	6/13 (46%)
Union of Paramonga Sugar Workers			30/30 (100%)	20/32 (63%)	2/28 (7%)	na
Lima Union of Taxi Drivers				13/13 (100%)	na	6/13 (46%)
National Union of Bank Clerks					12/12 (100%)	5/13 (38%)
Lima Union of Trolley Operators					13/13 (100%)	5/14 (36%)
Federation of Printing Workers	16/16 (100%)	*	7/16 (44%)	*	4/16 (25%)	*
Federation of Textile Workers				40/40 (100%)	22/34 (65%)	19/34 (56%)
Chimbote Regional Federation					24/24 (100%)	8/14 (57%)
Confederation of White-Collar Workers				13/13 (100%)	8/24 (33%)	*

Key: * = elections not held;
     na = not available.
a. The denominator represents the number of positions on the officers' board for that year (excluding delegate positions). As the reader will note, the number of positions may change from year to year.

which maintains the same general policy orientation, leadership will pass through many hands.

The low—or nonexistent—remuneration given to officers tends to make leaders themselves less anxious to return to their posts than they would be if trade unionism were a "plush" business. In recent years the continuous process of creation of new secondary organizations has given leadership considerable upward mobility, thus leaving openings in the unions. Finally, the small size of most of the organizations and the consequent daily, personal contact makes it impossible for officers to develop an aura of untouchability. Personal contact maintains both rank and file and officers as just men; nobody is famous.[3]

Understanding that leadership can and does change, the question arises as to what criteria the rank and file use to select their leaders. That is, in the constant process of leadership examination and turnover, what kind of men tend to remain on the officers' board as stabilization occurs? Although individual members may have a number of criteria for supporting certain leaders, the tendency over a period of time seems to be to choose those individuals who are successful in obtaining the largest gains for the workers with a minimum of sacrifice. These gains include not only wages and working conditions, but also intangibles such as the feelings of belonging, contributing, and achieving. They do not include, however, gains for other sectors of society, or larger efforts in national and world politics.

This conclusion does not apply either to most dispersed unions or to regional federations where, for reasons that have been discussed, degeneration rather than change in officers is the result of politically oriented or inactive leadership. But these organizations are of relatively little importance; in the overwhelming majority of the labor organizations leadership must satisfy the immediate, pragmatic demands of the membership. The leaders who fulfill rank and file expectations tend to be re-elected; those who fail, either by a too extreme, too irresponsible policy or overly conservative, inactive behavior are less likely to return to office.[4]

3. For a detailed analysis of the relationship of union size and other variables to participation and leadership turnover in the American International Typographical Workers Union see: Seymour Martin Lipset, Martin Trow, and James Coleman, *Union Democracy* (New York, Anchor Books, 1962).

4. Students of labor movements in other countries have observed this same tendency toward elimination or moderation of leaders urging sweeping political changes. Perhaps the most incisive statement of this phenomenon was given by Selig Perlman who noted that "There is a natural divergence in labor ideology between the 'mentality' of the trade unions and the 'mentality' of the intellectuals; and that, given the opportunity to exist legally and to develop a leadership from its own ranks, the trade union's mentality will eventually come to dominate." *A Theory of the Labor Movement* (New York, A. M. Kelly, 1949), p. ix.

It can be seen, for example, that within the older, established organizations, turnover is not even as great as the statistical method used for Table 20 would indicate. The experienced leaders having the confidence of the rank and file tend to re-appear on the officers' board, although not in a continuous fashion. For example, an individual may be secretary-general one year, grievance chairman the next, have no office the third, and then be secretary-general the next year. Over a period of many years, this process of selection will produce a group of experienced leaders with a rank and file orientation. Of course, one should not expect miracles. Insofar as rank and file expecta-tions are unreasonable, leadership may be forced to act on un-realistic demands. In fact, extremists occasionally came to power capitalizing on what they presented as leadership treason, but which was actually an attempt of the officers to temper rank and file demands to reality. A certain amount of demagoguery must be practiced by any successful labor leader.

It is difficult to prove conclusively the validity of this generali-zation about leadership selection. However, a close look at the events of the past five years reveals two marked tendencies which seem to substantiate this analysis: the failure of extremist labor leaders to maintain themselves in power (see Chapter 5) and the diminishing number of conservative, employer-influenced unions, of both obreros and empleados. The extremists, as suggested earlier, were too aggressive and demanded excessive rank and file sacrifices. The conservative "yellow" leaders have been rejected because they refused to fight at all.

In addition to the general process of selection that seems to be producing experienced, worker-oriented leaders, several or-ganizations have undertaken the task of orienting and training labor leaders. Among the groups operating schools for labor lead-ers are the CTP and the APRA party, the international trade secre-tariats, the Catholic Trade Union Movement, and the United States government under the Point Four program. All these groups, it will be noticed, are moderate forces.

It does appear that it is the labor leaders themselves who must be trained. Although many of them lack the basic skills in public speaking, negotiation, newspaper writing, accounting, and so on, neither officers nor rank and file are willing to trust others to carry out these tasks for them. There is good reason for this lack of trust. It frequently happened in the past that when an outsider came to advise or was elected an officer, he would use his position to guide the organization into action on extra-worker issues. Very rarely did an individual of a higher social and intellectual background come among the workers unless he had a grand dream or personal design of his own in which the day-to-day problems of the worker were seldom significant.

Today the only worker organizations where nonworkers still play a significant role are those of farm laborers and construction workers. The very low educational level of these workers (few can read or write) forces them to turn to more capable persons for guidance, invariably members of the APRA or extremist parties. Clearly these parties have other motives than the desire to help the workers to fulfill their immediate demands, but in the process of gaining control of these groups, a certain amount of productive activity takes place—activity which the workers themselves would have been unable to perform.

All other labor organizations are run by the workers themselves. Some organizations have clauses stating that only bona fide workers may hold office; all are very reluctant to give outsiders any position of authority, either formally or informally. It is significant to note in this regard that the former alliance between university students and workers is today largely ignored by labor leaders. This alliance was born in the early days of the labor movement (1915–30) when most labor leaders did not know what to do or how to do it. In those times it appears that many leaders were even unable to read or write—something which is quite rare today. Consequently, the students had an important, if not dominant, role in the labor movement. The general strikes of 1919, for example, were initiated and led by students. The two outstanding figures of the labor movement in the period 1919–30 were Victor Raúl Haya de la Torre and José Carlos Mariátegui, both men of university background.

Today the scene has changed. The university students frequently strike and demonstrate in support of a labor organization on strike, but worker organizations have not made any strenuous efforts in support of the students. Certainly a sympathy strike seems out of the question. Labor leaders have apparently gained enough confidence and experience to be able to handle their own problems in their own way. And although in many cases their ability falls short of what might be necessary for optimum effectiveness, their leadership is, in this writer's opinion, superior to the guidance which the university students have to offer.

Basic Leadership Attitudes

In the preceding chapters the behavior of labor leaders in many different areas has been explored. An attempt has been made to identify the specific environmental factors which shape their attitudes toward particular problems, such as strike policy, strike tactics, and structural alternatives. In addition to these more specific attitudes, it seems that many labor leaders possess certain basic "ideological" perspectives which would influence (albeit slightly in many cases) their behavior and therefore merit attention. In the following paragraphs some of the more salient ideological attitudes will be noted.

In their public pronouncements, the extremists are ambiguous in stating their position toward the employers and the existing political system. The old Fourth International faction of the Trotskyite party was the only extremist group publicly upholding a militant revolutionary position:

> The class of workers, peasants and exploited masses in general is stronger today than ever. Imperialism continues, year by year, day by day, to lose ground before the advancing revolutionary process which cannot be contained,

even by atomic war. The era of capitalist society is reaching its end, the hour of liberation from patterns of exploitation of man by man can already be seen. The comparison of the forces of the capitalist society and the world proletariat grows each day more favorable to our class.[5]

The other parties (Socialists, APRA Rebelde, the Pablo faction of the Trotskyite party, and the Progressive Socialists) remained silent on the issue of capitalism and "bourgeois democracy." The Communist party, following a bold national liberation front strategy, publicly desired to unite with the capitalists:

> The FRENTE [national liberation front] hopes to mobilize the proletariat, the peasants, the urban midle class, the intellectuals, and the local employers (burguesía nacional). That is, [the front] hopes to unite all the social classes against the policy of submission to North American imperialism, even when the consequences to the different allies in the anti-imperialist struggle cannot be the same and in spite of the diverse and even contradictory interests of the different allies.[6]

There is little doubt, however, that privately the members of all extremist parties take the position that capitalism and the existing political system must be destroyed. Conversations with many extremists reveal their deep hostility toward employers in particular and capitalists in general. Extremist labor leaders viewed the "bourgeois regime" with similar antipathy. Conscious of their underdog position for many years, the extremists seem particularly anxious to grind these enemies underfoot.

The moderates—Apristas and non-Apristas alike—while not doctrinaire, are quite hostile to employers. They view the capitalist as generally greedy, shortsighted, and lacking in consideration for the worker. But there is one important element in

5. *Voz Obrera* (organ of the Trotskyite party, old Fourth International faction) (Lima, May 1961), p. 1

6. *Unidad* (organ of the Communist party) (Lima, December 30, 1961), p. 1.

moderate thought which is lacking in the extremist viewpoint: moderates hold that the employer can be responsive to the needs of the worker. While capitalists are black, they are not beyond redemption. The moderates believe that ownership needs to be educated, forcefully if necessary, to consider worker welfare. The moderate view of ownership is well summed up in this paragraph of the New Year editorial in *El Chocolatero,* organ of the moderate-led Union of D'Onofrio Workers:

> Let us hope that in this year 1962 the capitalists will be broad-minded. Let us hope that the violence which drowns the just demands of the workers will be avoided, that the misery of the workers will be ended. Let us hope that many of those idle rich will come to understand that we workers are not destined to live in degradation and misery.[7]

The moderate attitude toward the government is again one of mistrust leavened with a note of hope. Moderates view the government as generally representing an oligarchy of capitalists and landowners. But, on the other hand, they see that in certain cases the government does act in their favor, and they tend to adopt an attitude of condescension and patience toward the government. They see themselves as holding back the justified wrath of the workers while the government fumbles toward an adequate solution. In the newspaper of the APRA-controlled Federation of Textile Workers this attitude of impatience was summed up in a rather interesting way: "How right were the old anarcho-syndicalists. Their criticisms about the social inertia of the state still have validity." [8]

Of course, as noted in Chapters 5 and 6, the behavior of labor leaders allied with a political party is largely determined by their party position with respect to the existing government. If, for example, an extremist party finds it desirable to support a

7. *El Chocolatero* (organ of the Union of D'Onofrio Workers) (Lima, December 30, 1961), p. 1.
8. *Obrero Textil* (organ of the Federation of Textile Workers) (Lima, January 1959), p. 3.

particular president, its labor leaders will adopt a more concilia-
tory posture. Thus, an extremist, while personally holding that
both capitalism and the political system should be ultimately
destroyed, may act in support of these institutions. Consequently
the degree of aggressiveness or moderation of either extremist or
moderate leaders will vary quite widely within the broad ideological perspectives presented above.

Closely related to the labor leaders' view of the employer and
the political system is their position on the economic organization of the country. There seem to be no defenders of the free
market in the Peruvian labor movement. All the arguments that
one might adduce in favor of economic competition are swept
aside by labor leaders with the categorical affirmation that competition between firms does not exist. Both moderates and extremists are convinced that, in the absence of government intervention, prices are fixed by "trusts," "monopolies," and "oli-
garchies." It follows, by their reasoning, that the free market
should be done away with, and supplanted by government control. In 1961, when Prime Minister Pedro Beltran lifted government controls on rice, the CTP made an official denunciation of
this action: "We wish that the ministries responsible appreciate
the constructive nature of this denunciation and adopt methods
to avoid what is called a 'free economy' but which saddles us
with the free enrichment, without controls, of the special few
who have the ability to control prices." [9] At the heart of labor's
case against the free market is the fact that without controls
prices will rise. Attributing price increases to the avarice of a
handful of producers, leaders have taken the position of insisting
that no price should ever rise. The pressure from organized
workers is one of the reasons why the government regulates the
prices of so many commodities. In the last few years worker
organizations have made major issues of opposing rises in the
prices of gasoline, meat, bus fares, and cement.

That price control frequently leads to subsidies, a black

9. Press release of the CTP published in *La Tribuna* (Lima, May 24, 1961),
p. 1.

market, favoritism, declining investment, and rising imports has not been fully appreciated by labor leaders. Not trusting the claims of either management or the government and without experts of their own, the leaders of worker organizations blindly follow their personal conviction that when a price goes up, the rich get richer and the workers get poorer. Even if a price increase is the direct result of the government levying a tax on a commodity, labor leaders will oppose such an increase. For this reason, taxation of consumer goods must be handled gingerly by an executive interested in surviving.

We might note in conclusion that few labor leaders are intensely concerned about nationalization of private industry. Most are aware that nationalized industries in Peru today offer some of the poorest working conditions in the country. While the Apristas have a vague hope that all industry will be state-run in the distant future, they do not expend energy supporting nationalization today. Though the extremists and opposition parties supported the proposal to nationalize the petroleum industry (largely American-owned), this particular issue centered on questions of national pride and "anti-imperialism"; there appears to be no thoroughgoing program of nationalization for its own sake.

4 POLITICAL BARGAINING IN PERSPECTIVE

11

THREE GROUPS OF SPECIAL IMPORTANCE

In the preceding chapters attention has been focused on the activity of private industrial employees. For most of these workers, political bargaining stands as an efficacious method for obtaining a wide range of worker objectives. In some cases, notably organizations of white-collar workers, this method is of limited utility, given the small size of organizations and cultural restraints upon the use of violence. The expectation was that such organizations might tend to lean more heavily on legal enactment in the future.

Three additional groups of workers will be considered here: workers in agriculture, bureaucrats, and public school teachers. Each group is closely connected with a major national problem: the agrarian situation which involves the Indians, agricultural production, land distribution, and rural living conditions; the inefficient and ineffective national bureaucracy; and the quantitative and qualitative deficiencies of the educational system. Most observers agree that reforms in these three areas are highly desirable. It is our view that if genuine transformations are to occur the workers involved must themselves generate the demands and power which would produce reforms. It seems unrealistic to expect benefits to rain down from the government or the Alliance for Progress while the employees involved remain inactive. We see the formation and activity of worker organizations as an essential process in reform.

The following discussion will elaborate upon this point. We shall explore the actual and potential problems involved in worker organization formation and discuss the role of these groups in generating and articulating specific solutions. The limits of political bargaining as a means of coercion will be examined, as well as the potential of legal enactment for those groups unable to employ violence.

Agricultural Workers

The problem of the land, the Indian, and agricultural production encompasses perhaps hundreds of distinct problems.[1] These brief remarks will outline only certain aspects of the situation relevant to group activity.

Along the coastal region of Peru agricultural production takes three principal forms: small ownership, sharecropping, and industrial farming. Although the first two types are not uncommon, the last is especially well developed in this region. In these industrial-type enterprises, the workers—who may number as many as 8,000—are employed as simple laborers. Ownership of both the means of production and the crop is entirely in the hands of the employer.

Under this arrangement, the formation of an industrial type of worker organization is possible and on many large plantations this has already taken place. Workers on the sugar haciendas were the first to organize themselves (in the period 1910–20) and now have considerable trade union experience. The 13 unions of the Federation of Sugar Workers operate like any other organization of industrial workers, and most have obtained for their workers wage and conditions benefits comparable to

1. The complexity of the agrarian problem in Peru has been explored by Thomas R. Ford in his work *Man and Land in Peru* (Gainesville, University of Florida Press, 1955). For purposes of discussion Ford uses 18 categories of land tenure and management systems (p. 76 passim).

those of urban workers. On the other haciendas worker organizations are less well developed, but progress is being made. On some of the large cotton plantations unions have been established and are becoming strong enough to present and enforce demands for better living conditions, school facilities, and occasionally, higher wages.

The impediments to organized activity in the coastal region are many. Ownership usually opposes the formation of a union, and often effects reprisals on workers who lead organization attempts. Being far removed from the urban labor movement, organizations of farm laborers receive very little assistance from more powerful worker groups. For example, if a union officer were discharged from a textile mill or a brewery, the CTP would immediately threaten a general strike; this would not occur in support of a discharged officer of a union of farm laborers. Also, the lower cultural level of workers on such haciendas makes it difficult to take collective decisions, to collect dues, and carry on sustained, coordinated activity. Most of the leaders themselves are ill-prepared for worker organization activities.

Despite these weaknesses, the outlook is favorable for successful group activity on the coastal plantations. Table 21 shows that the process of forming and establishing farm laborers' or-

TABLE 21

Recognition of Farm Laborers' Organizations by the Ministry of Labor, in Four-year Periods, 1941–1960

	1941–44	1945–48	1949–52	1953–56	1957–60
Number of farm workers' organizations recognized	1	36	1	3	33
Farm laborers' organizations as proportion of all worker organizations recognized	1%	13%	3%	4%	14%

Source: Information compiled from files of the *Dirección General de Trabajo* of the Ministry of Labor. Recognition of the Indigenous Communities does not come from this office and hence these organizations are not included in the table.

ganizations is well under way. And although these groups are very weak in any economic struggle with management, it appears that they will receive the assistance of the Ministry of Labor. The Cuban experience, rightly or wrongly, has taught government officials to look to the fields; when a union of agricultural workers engages in a strike, the ministry is expected to keep the situation under control by siding with the workers.

For example, in September 1961, the owner of the hacienda Chiu Chiu in the Barranca Valley discharged the secretary-general and grievance chairman of the union. The Ministry of Labor ordered reinstatement of the two men, the owner disregarded the order, and, with the guidance of APRA leaders of the moderate Federation of Farm Laborers and Peasants (see below), the union went on strike. After several weeks, the ministry saw that the situation could become serious and imposed a 10,000 sol ($370) fine on the owner and again ordered compliance. When the owner refused to take notice, the police were notified to arrest him. Brought before the minister, the owner was ordered: (1) to reinstate the discharged leaders; (2) to pay the fine; (3) to pay the wages which the workers would have earned during the 31-day strike; (4) to raise the daily wages for men from 5 sols (19¢) to 25 sols (95¢), and for women and children from 3 sols (11¢) to 12 sols (44¢). He complied.[2]

In the central mountainous section of the country, the sierra, the problem is more complicated and any solution more distant. At the center of the difficulty is the Indian, who, whatever his condition may have been during the Inca empire, has not succeeded in making himself a successful or productive part of modern society. Many Indians are found in communities of 200 to 2,000 persons, groups that vary widely in cohesion and development. The Department of Indigenous Affairs, now located in the Ministry of Labor, began a process of official recognition

2. Interview with Raúl Carrasco, secretary of external affairs of the moderate Federation of Farm Laborers and Peasants, in Lima, December 29, 1961.

of these communities in 1926. By June 1961, 1,586 communities with a total population of 1,367,093 had been recognized.[3] In many cases these communities or their members individually own the lands which they farm; in other cases sharecropping, leasing and subleasing, squatting, and other forms of land control are practiced. More common today than twenty years ago are industrial-type farms, but these are still small in number. It seems that the solution to the problems in the sierra lies in the development of two patterns of production: efficient, organized communal units of production, and the industrial agricultural enterprise.

The development of producers' cooperatives on the communal base will require a very high level of group life. Individuals with tiny plots of land must each agree to pool their resources—something that today they are reluctant to do. Collective investments, technical assistance, transportation and marketing facilities, housing, schooling, bookkeeping; all are aspects of cooperative life which must be handled collectively. Expropriation itself, in cases where it is necessary, will require sustained political activity.

At present the barriers to productive collective action include the illiteracy of the Indian, his suspicion of the new and his reluctance to change his established pattern of existence on one hand, and the inability of the government to render more than token assistance on the other. Nevertheless, certain progress has been made. Several communities have received aid from Point Four, UNESCO, the International Labor Organization, the Ministry of Agriculture, and the Ministry of Labor. The work of Cornell University specialists with the Vicos community is perhaps the best example of the creation of productive group life where it did not exist before. At this indigenous community in Ancash, social scientists since 1954 have worked with the Indians, guiding them to act collectively on problems of produc-

3. *Padrón General de Comunidades Indígenas Reconocidas Oficialmente al 30 de Junio de 1961* (Lima, 1961)

tion, education, and welfare.[4] In certain areas where a number
of cohesive communities exist, they have formed federations.
In the department (state) of Junín where community life is
best developed, the APRA party has been instrumental in joining
communities into federations, the first being formed in 1939.[5]

The strategic method the communities are tending to adopt
is legal enactment, lobbying for favorable legislative action and
administrative implementation of laws. Political bargaining does
not present itself as a successful tactic in most cases. The Indians
are not inclined to travel great distances (50–150 miles) to
larger towns where they might employ demonstrations with
success. Most of them are apathetic and not easily aroused to
sustained, violent activity; their organizations tend to be much
less cohesive than those of sugar workers, for example.

The small number of young men (between 18 and 35 years)
who live in the communities also inhibits the effectiveness of
political bargaining. Younger men are best suited, physically,
culturally, and emotionally, to engage in mass demonstrations,
parades, and attacks. Children, women, and older men do not
constitute a firm base for concerted violent activity. The average
size of a community is a little over 900 members (computed
from the figures given above). From this number one would
expect to find only about 100 to 150 men in the 18 to 25 age
group if the population were distributed normally. But it happens that it is precisely this age group which is most likely to
desert the community to work in the cities or at mining establishments or to join the armed forces. Consequently, the number of
young men who remain in the average community might be
as low as 20 or 30. This number contrasts sharply with the membership of the unions of workers on the coastal plantations where
400 to 4,000 young men are available.

4. For an account of this project see Allan R. Holmberg, "Changing Com-
munity Attitudes and Values in Peru: A Case Study in Guided Change," in
Richard N. Adams et al., *Social Change in Latin American Today* (New
York, Vintage Books, 1960), pp. 63–107.

5. Interview with Hipólito Mejía, secretary-general of the Federation of
Indigenous Communities of Yauli, in La Oroya, April 29, 1961.

Legal enactment, then, seems to be the only method left to the communities. It is a tactic that requires sustained activity on the part of only a few individuals. The remaining members of the community may go about their usual tasks while one or two energetic leaders scurry around Lima, begging to be heard. Although the communities are attempting to employ legal enactment, this is not to say they are highly successful. The same difficulties which discourage use of this method by industrial workers are present for the indigenous communities as well. First, the chaotic history of elections as well as restrictions on rural voting have prevented the communities from exercising power through the ballot. Secondly, the bureaucracy is not sufficiently developed to be able to carry out many of the laws that might apply to the communities. The scarce resources of the administration for such services as technical assistance and education have been placed in areas of higher political priority. Allocating some of these resources to the communities will require, in most cases, more than a soft word to the Minister of Agriculture or the Director of Indian Affairs.

Small owners and renters on the coast, in the sierra, and in the jungle region have also formed organizations which are beginning to handle collective problems such as irrigation, pest control, and marketing. The small size of these groups, the geographical dispersion of their members, and their isolation from larger towns and cities place the method of political bargaining outside their reach. As in the case of the indigenous communities, these organizations of small owners are attempting to employ legal enactment, but with only occasional success. In several cases they have asked the government for credit and technical facilities. Perhaps the formation and expansion of the *Banco de Fomento Agropecuario* (Bank for Agricultural Development) was, in part, the result of the influence of these organizations of small owners.

There are two organizations of farm laborers and peasants which have national scope: the extremist-operated Federation of Peasants and Farm Laborers (*Confederación de Campesinos del*

Perú—CCP) and the APRA-controlled *Federación Nacional de Campesinos del Perú* (FENCAP). The extremist CCP is not an organization in the sense that it has its own finances, an organic structure, or a coherent, representative decision-making process. It lacks all three. Rather it is a group of agitators in Lima and in certain agricultural areas, and includes members of all the extremist parties as well as members of opposition parties.

Important elements in both the CCP and the local centers of agitation (Cuzco, Chancay, Huancayo) are the Rebel APRA and Trotskyite parties. These two parties uphold the "pitchfork" doctrine; that is, power must be won by a full-scale revolution of farm laborers and workers, effected as soon as possible. Other sectors, including Communists, Progressive Socialists, and opposition parties, hold that in the present context such a revolution is neither possible nor desirable, but all are grateful for the negative propaganda which agitation and violence provide.

That violence is the objective of the CCP can be seen in an extremist account of the incident at Torreblanca (which leaders of the CCP provoked), when two workers were killed in a clash with the police:

> Since the problem was getting worse, the workers from the haciendas [a list of 10 plantations follows] . . . spontaneously decided to go to the hacienda Torreblanca on December 15, 1960, in order to hold an assembly with the purpose of contemplating the existing problem.[6]

This excerpt came from an article entitled "Repression is intensified in Chancay" (the valley where Torreblanca is located), published in the paper of the extremist-led National Union of Bank Clerks. The reporting of the event was designed to lead the public to believe that the government was a coldly calculating instrument of oppression, controlled by owners who would, if necessary, murder workers who attempted to better their condition.

However, a thoughtful reading of this extremist account gives

6. *FEB* (Lima, April 15, 1961), p. 12.

a picture of what really happened. Why did the "workers decide" to hold an assembly on the one hacienda where the problem existed? What decision were they going to take that had to be made at the hacienda itself? How do isolated groups of farm laborers "spontaneously decide?" Who owned or rented the trucks needed to transport the workers to Torreblanca? It seems clear that the extremist organizers were, to put it discreetly, looking for trouble.

It must not be overlooked, however, that violence in rural areas does tend to shape governmental policy in favor of the farm laborers. It may be true that extremists and opposition forces were relatively unconcerned about the demands of the workers involved. It may be that their object was to shake the Prado government. But, at the same time, the interests of the workers were advanced as extremist leaders taught them the elements of political bargaining. As much as one might wish to deplore agitation and violence, it must be recognized that such action does enhance the workers' position.

Simply because violence takes place in rural areas it must not be concluded that Peru, as the journalists put it, "is on the brink of revolution." Peru has seen rural violence for at least half a century. As early as 1906, the sugar workers employed violence and through its use have elevated their political and economic position. There is no reason to suppose that other rural workers will not do the same. The really important fact about violence in Peru is that it represents power and success. This is in direct contrast to the situation in the United States where violence has usually signified despair and defeat. That some Peruvian farm workers have advanced to the point where they may take concerted, violent action is probably a hopeful sign. For it is through the use of violence that these workers may, within the existing system of political bargaining, improve their socioeconomic position.

The APRA-operated FENCAP is a rather interesting combination of politics, altruism, and chaos. FENCAP was formed in January 1960, by enlarging the scope of a previously existing organization of another name. It is a heterogeneous collection of all types of agricultural workers' organizations. At the first national congress, held January 16–20, 1960, there were 29 organizations of indigenous communities, 8 of renters, 6 of sharecroppers, 11 of day laborers, and 5 organizations of small owners.[7] These 59 organizations that sent representatives to the congress represent only a small part of the total number of groups with which FENCAP has contact.

Since each of these many types of agricultural workers' organizations needs a staff of perhaps 100 full-time specialists to organize, advise, and develop the groups into effective worker organizations, the positive role which FENCAP can play is clearly limited. In general, the 10 or 12 active leaders of FENCAP have concentrated on the political aspects of these groups, organizing regional congresses and assisting in the resolution of known collective conflicts. The chaotic organic structure and the division of effort into dozens of distinct, unrelated problems are two of the effects of FENCAP's political orientation.

But in addition to gaining support for the APRA party, FENCAP has at least begun to serve as a productive national lobby for agricultural workers. Its leaders have met with officials of the Department of Indigenous Affairs and members of Congress and have, on occasion, employed this access to defend the interests of the peasants. For example, in March 1961, FENCAP, through a sympathetic congressman, publicly denounced the owner of the plantation "Sinto," a senator himself, in the Senate chamber.[8] Later, in May, the grievance chairman of FENCAP (Nicolás Benitez) made a trip to "Sinto" with an official of the Department of Indigenous Affairs to investigate the complaint of the sharecroppers.[9]

In the future, as the group life of agricultural workers develops, distinct types will probably form their own specialized,

7. *El Segundo Congreso de Yanaconas y Campesinos* (Lima, January 1960).
8. *La Tribuna* (Lima, March 20, 1961), p. 5.
9. Ibid. (May 18, 1961), p. 5.

national organizations. If these groups can mobilize votes and popular sentiment, and also win supporters in the centers of power, agricultural workers will begin to have a significant political impact. The Indian and other farm workers have considerable public sympathy in Peru. Few politicians would dare attack these "noble, but oppressed, descendants of the Incas." But on the other hand, few really know exactly what these workers want in the thousands of specific cases, and few will spend time defending peasant interests unless agricultural workers can present themselves as a political force.

The National Bureaucracy

The problem of building an efficient, effective bureaucracy is also directly related to the formation and operation of worker groups. Contrary to what some might believe, a large part of the Peruvian bureaucracy is not corrupt and inefficient because of the climate or Latin genes. Rather, there are specific analyzable causes of the existing situation; the most important is, perhaps, the set of norms that govern employment and promotion.

Patronage is entrenched from top to bottom. It works something like this: public figure (A) recommends close personal friend (B) to head a department. (B) makes his cousin (C) section head. Nephews (D) and (E) obtain jobs through (C). (F) owns a small factory which owes back taxes. (F) is a close friend of (A), and (G) who is second manager of the factory is the brother-in-law of (B). Will (E) collect the back taxes? Not if he is a normal human being.

It is interesting to watch this system in operation. Whether the issue be a parking ticket, a building code, a passport, or a condemnation notice, the matter is handled along the lines of personal access and patronage. If a conflict is generated between two individuals or groups over some legal disposition the bureaucracy must act upon, a fascinating struggle takes place. Each side amasses, through personal friendships and relatives, the maximum of influence: deputies, senators, subministers, or relatives of the president. Any public servant in the middle must know where his bread comes from and respond accordingly.

Patronage usually determines the outcome of appointments, promotions, and the many other favors which can be distributed to public servants. And the simple fact that most public employees do not receive—above the table—wages comparable to those of many industrial laborers is another objective feature which encourages corruption. The reader ought not to suppose that these brief remarks describe the bureaucracy in its totality. There are several quite effective, progressive branches of the administration and many sincere, efficient public servants. But in general, the bureaucracy does not function as impartially as it might. Being constructed on a personal basis, the Peruvian public administration tends to function along personal lines.

It appears that the only real hope for an improvement in the existing situation lies in the future action of organizations of public servants. The vast majority of public servants are dissatisfied with the patronage system. Although certain higher officials reap important benefits from the system, the ordinary employees and honest individuals experience only the negative aspects. They get no friends into office, and are themselves denied promotion when vacancies are filled by outside appointees; they must participate in corruption and inefficiency but lack the influence to make others return the favor. If they attempt to ignore personal pressures they may lose their jobs, or at least be assured that raises and promotions will never come to them. An individual may work 25 years in the hope that he might one day head the office and enjoy the higher pay, prestige, and the opportunity to employ his own ideas which would come with such a position. Then, when the opening is finally created, a stranger walks into the office with a letter of appointment signed by the president. Such defeat is frustrating not only for that individual but for all the other workers in the department who likewise lose promotions.

The pressure for improvement will have to come from the employees themselves. They have both the reasons and, if properly mobilized, the power to institutionalize an impersonal system of wage scales, promotions, and discharge. In addition, they would probably find it to their advantage to establish a system of qualification examinations for new employees. One of the frequent complaints of the civil servants is the incompetence of new appointees. And, of course, organizations of public employees would be important instruments for achieving economic gains. Such organizations have existed for perhaps 30 or 40 years but only recently have some begun to expand their scope beyond mutual aid activities. In understanding the problems of these groups one must first realize that public employees are forbidden by law to strike. Like any other law, this disposition has force only insofar as the government is willing to enforce it. The workers of the state-owned tobacco monopoly and the public school teachers are permitted to strike in spite of the illegality of such action. But in the case of employees of the ministries, the government is firmer. For in addition to considerations of stability and discipline, organizations of public employees do not count on as much popular support as do, for example, the government teachers. Militant leaders may be discharged by the government without risking severe repercussions.

Nevertheless, a few organizations have challenged the government by calling strikes. The telegraph and postal workers had, by 1959, created a national federation strong enough to sustain a strike. The dismissal of all leaders connected with the walkout of October 1959 (see below) left this organization incapacitated, in which condition it remained in 1961. The Association of Customs Agents is perhaps the only other public servants' organization with an active, militant orientation.

But other associations, formerly devoted exclusively to holding dances, are beginning to take up fundamental issues. The association of employees of the Ministry of Education, for example, protested in October 1961 that the reorganization of that ministry, which they had demanded, was not being carried out. In an open letter to Congress they denounced the unregulated promotions and other abuses, the mishandling of funds which went unnoticed, the creation of jobs for political appointees "without taking into account the large number of outstanding civil servants who have worked efficiently for many years . . . nominating, instead, people from the street, thus not providing the opportunity for developing an administrative career." [10]

Dissatisfaction exists. The problem is to mold this dissatisfaction into power—power which probably will not lie in the ability to strike. However, in the case of public employees, striking may not be necessary, for these groups, above all others, have excellent access. Ministers and department heads, as well as congressmen, must maintain cordial relations with the bureaucracy. If the public employees themselves could unite behind a series of specific demands, they might well obtain the support of many government leaders.

It is encouraging to note that a confederation of public employees has recently (1959) been established. The *Asociación Nacional de Servidores Civiles del Estado* (ANSCE) groups 21 organizations of public servants of the various ministries and other governmental agencies. The organization received a severe blow in October 1959, shortly after it was founded, when its president, Victor Checa C., attempted to call a total strike of all public employees in support of the postal workers on strike. The postal strike itself had been practically settled when the president, without the authority of the assembly of delegates, decreed a strike of the entire organization. The government reacted quickly and discharged 74 leaders of the few organizations which had obeyed the strike order.

It appears that the action of the president of ANSCE was a political maneuver designed to weaken the government. As an active sympathizer with an opposition party, he understandably sought a total strike of all public employees.[11] The government

10. Open letter to the presidents of the House of Deputies and the Senate, published in *El Comercio* (Lima, October 26, 1961).

11. Interview with Luis Núñez C., president of ANSCE in Lima, April 4, 1961.

was not seriously weakened, but ANSCE was practically destroyed.

A year later ANSCE was reconsolidated with a different officers' board and received official recognition from the Ministry of Justice (the Ministry of Labor does not handle recognition of public employees' organizations). ANSCE has not yet attacked basic issues, but remains in a state of relative inactivity, confining its attention to occasional attempts to modify the operation of the public employees' pension system.

In the future ANSCE may expand its scope of action. Even today classification examinations are occasionally mentioned, and on paper there exists a civil service statute which would partially regulate promotions. It seems that in the case of the public employees legal enactment offers considerable promise. The bureaucrats have excellent access and need not rely only on the electoral system. Most of the objectives of this group would not demand reallocation of scarce administrative resources, but simply require a change in existing norms. Civil service reform, then, apparently awaits the development of ANSCE into a cohesive, energetic lobby.

Public School Teachers

Education is perhaps the best example of a major problem which is being solved today by the activity of the worker organizations involved. In their short period of active existence, the organizations of public school teachers have already had a profound positive effect on the Peruvian educational system. Like the other organizations of public employees, the associations of public school teachers were first oriented toward social and mutual services. By the middle 1950s, the four types of public school teachers—primary, secondary, physical education, and manual training—had formed a national mutual society, the *Asociación Mutualista Magisterial* (AMM).

Even before the Odría dictatorship ended in 1956, the AMM had begun to concern itself with more fundamental issues, showing signs of a more militant orientation. Such an orientation was not convenient for Odría. He considered that "the purposes of the AMM ought to be exclusively those of social welfare," and decreed that "the AMM be reorganized so that its operation will correspond to only those ends." [12] One of Odría's officials from the Ministry of Education, José Rubio, was appointed to head the reorganized officers' board.[13] It is evident how very simple the process of worker organization control is under a dictatorship.

In the atmosphere of freedom that followed the change in government the teachers quickly drew their organization together. By 1960 the four national unions (all but the primary teachers' organization are called *asociación*) had developed a tightly knit structure and a militant orientation. Having very similar problems and the same employer, the different groups realized the importance of a federation. The AMM was converted into the *Federación Nacional de Educadores del Perú* (FENEP) —National Federation of Public School Teachers—with the four national teachers' unions as members. These four organizations have the following membership: National Union of Primary Teachers, 30,000; National Union of Secondary School Teachers, 7,000; National Union of Physical Education Teachers, 3,000; National Union of Manual Arts Instructors, 3,000. The total membership of FENEP is, therefore, about 43,000. Representation in the general assembly is proportioned 3:2:1:1, respectively; the primary teachers are consequently underrepresented.

Financially, the teachers' organizations are well established. The National Union of Primary Teachers receives about 30,000 sols ($1,100) monthly from the obligatory check-off made by the Ministry of Education. Committees have independent finances based on voluntary contributions of five or ten sols monthly from each member. FENEP itself receives only about 2,900 sols ($110) monthly from the unions, but extraordinary levies and other sources augment this sum considerably.

Many of the problems faced by public school teachers are similar to those of other public employees. For example, it used to be a common practice in some areas for political bosses to

12. *Decreto Supremo* No. 10, July 7, 1955.
13. *Magisterio* (organ of the AMM) (Lima, January 1956), p. 40.

utilize the district school for patronage. Political favors and friendships would be rewarded by appointment to a teaching post. Experience or training were irrelevant. So was the fact that experienced, trained teachers would then lose their jobs or be reduced to part-time work. Today, patronage of this sort has been almost eliminated. The local committee of teachers at the school, usually with the cooperation of the superintendent, would firmly oppose the displacement of experienced teachers for political reasons, backing up their position with a strike if necessary. If satisfactory results were not obtained at the local level, the national organization would take up the problem in Lima with the Ministry of Education.

Through group activity the teachers have also obtained the establishment of several favorable norms: (1) Teachers with full normal school preparation are given priority in the allotment of teaching hours so that these individuals will teach full schedules. (2) Normal school graduates are accepted over less well-prepared individuals for new positions. (3) Wages in the provinces have been raised to Lima standards; thus qualified personnel are attracted to positions previously filled by untrained individuals. (4) A master job–wage classification has been established, and although the teachers are not fully satisfied the system is shaped to reward those with more training and experience. All these changes, besides being beneficial to the teachers themselves, are having a significant impact on the quality of the Peruvian educational system. And quality itself is one of the objectives of these organizations, for the teachers are anxious to improve public education. For example, their pressure was instrumental in establishing the program of special summer courses for the many teachers without normal school preparation. The antiquated orientation and methods which have for so long debilitated the Peruvian educational system are under rigorous examination by the public school teachers. In professional journals and at symposia organized by the unions and their regional committees, the teachers discuss and debate new ideas, gradually adopting more productive approaches.

The basic method which the teachers employ to achieve their goals is political bargaining. In both 1960 and 1961 they struck for higher wages and were quite successful in winning increases from the executive (see Chapter 12). Examination of the strategic variables reveals why this method is so effective for the teachers. First, their organizations are large and cohesive. Their many members are able and disposed to use the tactics of political bargaining. Second, the teachers are located primarily in the larger cities, particularly Lima, where their impact on the government is most felt. Lastly, the teachers have enormous public sympathy in Peru and they receive support from many other groups, particularly industrial workers and students. With this firm base of power the teachers' organizations are rapidly correcting many deficiencies of the educational system. Their continued efforts in diverse areas seem certain to result in educational reform of the first magnitude.

Our exploration of these three problem areas seems to indicate that there are limits to the utility of political bargaining for certain groups of workers. We noted that the public school teachers and some groups of agricultural laborers can and do employ this method with success. But other agricultural workers, members of indigenous communities, small owners, and bureaucrats are not well situated to employ strikes, mass demonstrations, and violence effectively. These latter groups may employ legal enactment, but with relatively little success since the requisites for effective use of this method are, at present, not generally met.

12

THE OCTOBER 1961 STRIKE

OF THE PUBLIC SCHOOL TEACHERS

To put the preceding discussions into perspective it may be helpful to have an account of what happened in the case of one worker organization that presented a demand. Observing the conflict from a comprehensive viewpoint affords the reader a working understanding of the dynamic behavior of labor groups within the political context. The 1961 strike of the public school teachers has been chosen because it involved more sectors of society than any other labor conflict of the year.

The strike itself began on October 5, 1961, called by the National Federation of Public School Teachers (FENEP).[1] The cause of the strike was the unfulfilled demand for higher wages, a demand which had been presented many months before but on which the government had not acted. Following is the sequence of events leading up to the strike. On February 19, 1961, the National Union of Primary School Teachers had held a general meeting in the City Theater in Lima which was attended by 2,000 teachers.[2] The purpose of this meeting was not to transact

1. The reader may refer to the latter part of Chapter 11 for details on the structure of FENEP.

2. *Maestros Primarios* (organ of the National Union of Primary School Teachers) (Lima, March, 1961), p. 8.

business (the regular Assembly of Delegates performs this function) but to generate rank and file support for a wage demand.
The teachers first turned to the Congress.

On March 6, 1961, the National Federation of Public School
Teachers held a meeting in the Plaza Bolívar (in front of the
Congressional building) to urge the Congress to act favorably
on teachers' pay appropriations. There were two separate bills
which the teachers were supporting: one giving the teachers a
flat 8 to 12 per cent raise (depending on the category), which
had been passed by the Chamber of Deputies but was held up
in the Senate budget committee; the other awarding generous
increases to teachers on the basis of seniority, which the Minister
of Education, Alfonso Villanueva, had not submitted to the
budget committee of the Chamber of Deputies.[3] Largely because of executive opposition to generous salary increases, the
teachers were not successful in Congress. Consequently they
turned to more direct action.

Before the strike materialized, numerous meetings of the
federation's four member unions and their many respective committees were held to determine the sentiment of the rank and
file and, in the process, to develop the unity and enthusiasm of
the entire membership. By the end of September there was sufficient feeling in favor of a strike for the FENEP to announce the
customary three-working-day warning period. This warning
period gives the organization three days of pressure without
sacrifice; it was as if the leaders had said, "We have declared
a strike, but it will not begin for three working days." Declared
on Saturday, September 30, the warning period gave the government until Wednesday night, October 4, to accede to the demands of the teachers before a strike would materialize.

It must be noted that the teachers' strike was out of the ordinary in two respects. First, being public employees, the teachers did not have recourse to the Ministry of Labor; the issue
was before the Ministry of Education and Congress. Second, an
increase in teachers' salaries would represent a very sizable in-

3. Ibid., p. 1.

crease in public expenditures. It is one thing to raise the salaries of all mayors or all department heads, but quite another to do the same for the 50,000 public school teachers. The former raises could be worked into the budget easily, but the latter would require substantial tax increases or deficit spending. The government was anxious to avoid both. For these reasons no immediate moves were made to prevent the strike. The executive was here not balancing the interests of labor and management, but was itself the employer—with no surplus earnings to distribute. The warning period lapsed with little more than mention in Congress that something ought to be done.

During the first few days of the strike, FENEP was occupied with making the stoppage complete. Strike committees visited the few state schools which had continued to function and, without violence, saw that these schools were closed. By October 9 the strike was consolidated and the first public demonstration was held. It followed the usual pattern: heated oratory and a march to the Congressional Square. FENEP also set up a "permanent guard" of 10 to 20 members which remained in front of the Congressional building 24 hours a day with the banners and placards of the organization. The purpose of the demonstration and the "permanent guard" was to make the teachers' problem known and to gain popular support.

The issue began to build into an attack on the government. Members of extremist and opposition parties in Congress made long diatribes which centered on the harshness and inhumanity of the government. Opposition and extremist newspapers carried the same line, producing a continuous stream of vilification. Many moderate groups, while not drawing conclusions about the merits of the government, also supported the teachers' demands. Table 22 gives a rough picture of the support FENEP received from other groups. It is interesting to note that the extremist-led organizations immediately supported the strike. This rapid action was a manifestation of the extremist tendency to add to unrest whenever possible, regardless of the issue. Other groups also supported the teachers, and although no solidarity strikes

TABLE 22

Chronological Account of the Formal Declarations in Support of the Public School Teachers by Various Organizations during the Teachers' Strike of 1961

October 5	Strike Begins
	National Federation of Parents' Associations
October 8	Callao Regional Federation (E)[a]
	Cuzco Regional Federation (E)
	Students of San Marcos University, committees of the Department of Law (E), of Letters (E), of Economics, and of Education
	Student Association of the Normal School, La Cantuta
October 11	National Union of Bank Clerks (E)
	Federation of Taxi Drivers (E)
	Federation of Construction Workers (E)
	Federation of Farm Laborers and Peasants (E)
October 17	Federation of Mine Workers (Center)
	Lima Union of Bus Workers
	Union of Railroad Workers (Center)
October 21	Student Association of the School of Fine Arts
	Federation of Market Vendors
	Lima Union of Printing Workers (M)
	Federation of Bakery Workers
October 23	Violence at the Congressional Building, certain constitutional guarantees suspended
October 24	Students of San Marcos University, committee of the Department of Chemistry
	Students of the Catholic University, committee of the Department of Education
	Lima Committee of the National Front for the Nationalization of Petroleum (E)
October 25	Student Association of the National School of Engineering
October 26	Students of the Catholic University, committee of the Department of Letters
	Bloc for the Defense of Maritime Workers (E)
	Union of Government Maritime Officials in Callao
	Student Association of the National School of Agriculture
October 27	Lima Union of Printing Workers (E)

a. (E) denotes extremist control, (M) moderate.

materialized, that was the possible implication of these moves of support.[4]

The parents' associations were groups immediately involved in the conflict. In general, these organizations, closely identified with the Catholic church, remain aloof from major political struggles, confining their activities to film censorship and similar issues. On this occasion they pressured for a quick end of the strike so the children might return to school. They tended to support the teachers' demand, but made no explicit attacks on the government.

The executive was in a difficult situation. No one had any objection to paying the teachers more, but the problem, which all but a few officials seemed to ignore, was to find the money. The executive resolved the problem quite deftly by proposing an increase in the tax on cigarettes. This solution, which in normal circumstances would have created a storm of protest, was quietly accepted, for those groups and sectors already supporting the teachers could hardly, at the same time, protest a measure which was being enacted for the teachers' benefit. Congress immediately considered the measure, and following its usual custom, offered no substantial opposition to the executive proposal.

While the new wage scale was being worked out, the teachers, aided by opposition and extremist elements (mostly university students) continued to build up tension. There were several incidents of minor proportions on October 16, when belligerent students clashed with newspaper reporters and photographers. The aggression brought a protest from the Lima Association of Journalists.[5] On October 17 there were two public demonstrations, and on the same day hunger strikes began in Lima and in some of the provincial cities. The salary increase was promulgated on October 20. The leaders of FENEP had discussed the wage scale with the Minister of Education, but had not been satisfied. Nevertheless, the executive issued the decree in the hope that it would have an effect on the rank and file. Al-

4. Several of the groups of university students effected strikes of 24 and 48 hours but these went largely unnoticed.
5. La Prensa (Lima, October 17, 1961), p. 1.

though no mention of the actual increase was made, it seems that the figure was between 10 and 15 per cent, depending on the classification of the teacher.

However, the four unions and, subsequently, FENEP rejected the ministerial resolution establishing a new wage scale. The reason for objection was not clear, for it was impossible to determine the exact amount of the increase, distributed as it was in the many wage classifications. And certainly the leaders made no attempt to do so. It seemed that no one, including perhaps the leaders of FENEP, knew whether the distribution, the increase itself, or both were unsatisfactory. In fact, it appears that no one particularly cared at the moment. After only 15 days of a strike which had received considerable publicity, the teachers were still in a fighting mood. Although the government had delayed the emission of the decree for four days,[6] it appeared that the teachers still had not been out of work long enough to lower their minimum demands (which seemed to be in the range of 25 to 30 per cent increase) to a figure which the government was willing to consider.

The leaders of FENEP continued to discuss the proposed wage increase with the Minister of Education, but they were aware that, for the moment, further improvement would not be forthcoming without additional pressure. For additional influence, FENEP turned to the Confederation of Peruvian Workers (CTP). Although FENEP was not (and is not) a member of the CTP, the importance of the strike had drawn that organization into the battle. CTP officers had already been working with the leaders of FENEP, sitting in on interviews with the Minister of Education and familiarizing themselves with the issue. On October 17 the CTP held a general assembly at which the teachers presented their problem. In view of the importance of the issue and the wide popular appeal which the teachers' demand had, the

6. The Ministry of Education had prepared the new wage scale by October 16 or 17 but delayed making it public until October 20. The delay was probably intentionally designed to take the "fighting edge" off the teachers' demands, thus making it more likely that they would accept the decree.

CTP found itself obligated to consider seriously the demand of FENEP leaders that a general strike be called.

The first assembly had decided to postpone decision on the strike until October 20. In the meantime, the delegates of the CTP were to determine the position of their own organizations, and the leaders of the CTP would continue to work with the leaders of FENEP toward a satisfactory solution. The second assembly was held, as scheduled, on the night of the 20th. The atmosphere was tense—a distinct change from the usual drowsiness of CTP meetings. FENEP leaders did their best to convince the delegates that a strike should be called. They minimized the gains offered in the resolution which had been promulgated that day; they spoke of the sacrifice of their members, of the importance of the teaching profession, of the harsh treatment which they claimed the police had dealt some of their demonstrators; they offered to suspend the hunger strike if the CTP would issue the three-day warning notice for a strike. This last point had little effect: hunger strikes almost never result in injury. As happened in this case, those participating usually consent to be taken to the hospital after six or eight days.

The delegates, however, did not want to call a strike. That they were against such action was clear even before the meeting began. The informal processes of communication and coordination, discussed in Chapter 8, had already established a negative decision. The reason which the delegates gave publicly at the meeting for not supporting a strike was that they had not been notified by their organizations. To a certain extent this was true. Sufficient sentiment for a successful general strike takes time to build up, and although the teachers' strike had received good publicity, perhaps after only 15 days of strike the workers around the country had not been sufficiently aroused to be willing to sacrifice their own wages.

But this publicly given reason was only a part of the background. The leaders of the CTP were not convinced that the increase offered in the resolution was unsatisfactory. Some categories had received substantial increases and even the leaders of FENEP had not made it clear whether they were objecting to the distribution of the raise or the amount itself. The APRA leaders of the CTP felt a certain hesitancy in using a general strike against the government. As members of a government-supporting party, they held the position that a general strike must be used sparingly and only when the government had displayed intransigence, which it had not.

After three hours of debate, the delegates voted 49 to 2 (the two votes were those of extremists) to postpone action until another assembly to be held on October 24. Extremist and opposition leaders immediately attacked the leaders of the CTP as traitors and charged them with obeying the dictates of the APRA party. From the extremist point of view a strike was desirable because it would have shaken or even destroyed the Prado government which they opposed so bitterly. It was quite possible that the CTP would have supported the teachers at the next assembly if the leaders of FENEP had remained unsatisfied and the government had made no other offer. The CTP had deeply committed itself to assisting the teachers, and rank and file pressure to do something was beginning to build. However, there was a turn of events.

On the night of October 23, the teachers staged a large, energetic public demonstration. The demonstration itself, while noisy and impressive, was not violent and was not broken up by the special assault troops. About 30 minutes after the teachers' demonstration had terminated, a group of about 300 university students made a rapid, organized march to the Congressional building and attempted to force their entry. Normally all disturbances of this type are handled by the specially trained assault troops whose job it is to contain or dissolve demonstrations of a violent nature without causing injury. For this purpose they employ tear gas, mounted troops, and specially designed anti-demonstration trucks—armored vehicles which mount a water turret over the cab. However, when the attack on the Congressional building was made, these troops were in the part of the city where the teachers had held their demonstration (the

Parque Universitario). Only six or eight Congressional guards were present to repel the onrush. They did the only thing they could—fire their heavy field rifles. The students fled in stampede, leaving one demonstrator fallen dead.

A few of the leaders of the demonstration, experienced in the business of such actions and aware of the value of a corpse, immediately returned and carried the body first to an opposition newspaper building (*El Comercio*) and later to a school building where the extremist-leaning Lima Committee of Primary School Teachers was meeting during the strike.

All is not clear about this event, but a few points can be made. First, the Congressional guards did not fire at the mob, but in the air. If they had fired at the students, their several volleys would have left, at point blank range, perhaps a dozen dead. Second, the demonstrator was killed, as the post-mortem showed, by a bullet from a small calibre weapon which entered at the back of the head. Hence it seems unlikely that the guards fired the fatal bullet. It also seems doubtful that a loyal government police officer with a hand arm killed the demonstrator since all police are instructed not to cause injury and certainly not death in disturbances of a political nature. The police, like the guards, would have fired in the air. The only remaining possibility is that an extremist, either in uniform or as a demonstrator, actually fired the shot. But, on the other hand, the police did not produce the culprit; the government's case would have been bolstered had it been able to prove the culpability of the extremists.

Regardless of what actually happened, the event had two effects. First, the government decreed the suspension of guarantees. Theoretically prohibiting all meetings in the country for one month, it meant in practice that the government would not tolerate further disturbances connected with the teachers' strike. The "permanent guard" of teachers at the Congressional building had to be removed, and the leaders of FENEP had the assurance that further public demonstrations would be broken up by the assault troops.

The second effect was an intensification of extremist and opposition attacks on the government. The fallen demonstrator was
hailed as a martyr, the government held responsible. For example, *El Comercio* of Lima, perhaps the most vociferous opposition paper, began its account of the event as follows:

> Yesterday's bloody episode, which took place in Bolívar
> Square, shows how far the unjustified action of the authori-
> ties can go. . . . It is the tragic result of the government's
> lack of responsibility and the unrestrained aggression of the
> public forces.[7]

Distorted as this interpretation of the facts may be, it was the
opposition and extremist line at the moment. A very large sector
of society, composed of persons who had no better information,
accepted without question both the interpretation and its implications. On October 25, in spite of the suspension of guarantees, a large mourning ceremony for the dead student was held.
It was a restrained affair and the assault troops, while present,
did not interfere. The situation was very delicate, and the government judged it best to handle things gently.

The role of the extremists in this event should be appreciated,
for it was a role which they are free to play whenever a major
political conflict arises. The demonstrators who attacked the
Congressional building were not teachers, but university and
high school students of a muddled Marxist orientation led by a
few experienced extremists. If the same attack had occurred when
no conflict was before the government, it probably would have
received general repudiation. But coinciding with the demands
of a worker organization, it was hailed by both the leaders of
the teachers' organizations (who needed all the agitation and
popular support they could get) and opposition political parties
(whose desire to weaken the government is intense) as an act of
heroism. Thus, by timing their attacks on the government to
coincide with the specialized demands of worker organizations,

7. *El Comercio* (Lima, October 24, 1961), p. 1.

extremists achieved an impact far out of proportion to their tiny numbers.

The leaders of FENEP, while they publicly went through the motions of attacking the government and hailing the "martyr," gradually realized that the extremists had done them more harm than good. No more demonstrations were likely to be permitted, and sympathy strikes now seemed improbable. The CTP locked its doors, ostensibly in obedience to the suspension of guarantees. Of course, if the leaders of the CTP had greatly desired a general strike, they could have attempted it even in the face of the decree. But, as noted above, the APRA leaders of the CTP were not anxious for a strike. The suspension of guarantees provided a convenient excuse to retire from the scene.

In addition, the strike itself was beginning to get out of hand. Certain provincial organizations, satisfied by the raise already obtained and repelled by the thought of more violence, were threatening to go back to work. On the other hand, some of the Lima committees, headed by extremists and members of opposition parties, were expending energy and dissipating good will in attacking the government and demanding the resignation of the Prime Minister as well as of the Minister of Education. Such demands were, of course, only detrimental to the teachers' position, stiffening the government and compounding the demands, thus making a satisfactory solution more difficult.

Consequently, after October 25, the leaders of FENEP began to look for the best possible solution. They worked with the Congressional teachers' front (a group of teacher representatives and sympathizers which had been formed in the House of Deputies) and the House budget committee. They received promises of further increases to be worked out in the 1962 budget. From their negotiations with the Minister of Education they obtained the payment of salaries for the days not worked and the promise that the academic year would not be extended.[8]

With these concessions and the raise previously accorded, the

8. Later the teachers themselves, aware of the academic loss to their students, requested that the academic year be extended to make up for the lost days.

leaders judged that they could end the strike. Decision-making processes were put in motion about October 28. Opposition to ending the strike came partly from enthusiastic individuals unaware of the futility of continuing, but primarily from extremists and members of the opposition parties (Popular Action, Christian Democratic, and Odría parties) which were strong in the Lima Committees. These individuals were anxious to utilize the strike for its political value and were uninterested in the effect that extending the strike would have on the cohesion and utility of FENEP or the member unions.

On November 2, after several days of voting and revoting in the committees and member unions, the assembly of delegates of FENEP finally voted to end the strike. The decision was by no means unanimous in either the member unions or FENEP itself. But the decision was made and all members complied on November 3. Attacks still continued on the leaders of the CTP, on the government, and on the leaders of both the National Union of Primary School Teachers and FENEP, who defended their actions in the press. On November 9, the National Union of Primary School Teachers issued a press release which quoted telegrams of support and gratitude from seven of the member committees.[9] It seems that, on balance, the leadership of both the National Union of Primary School Teachers and FENEP, despite extremist attacks, retained the support of most of the rank and file.

Shortly after the strike ended, there was a reshuffling of the cabinet positions. Although not an effect of the strike, it is interesting to note that one of the posts which passed into new hands was Education. The ill will which had been generated during the strike made smooth, productive relations between the teachers and the incumbent minister impossible and it was considered advisable to appoint a replacement.

In December 1961, the House of Deputies levied new taxes on the petroleum, sugar, and fishmeal industries. Part of the income from these taxes would pay for further raises in teachers'

9. Printed in *El Comercio* (Lima, November 10, 1961).

salaries. The industrial producers fought these measures, without success, on the grounds that expansion and development would be curtailed. Although their arguments were perhaps exaggerated, they were not without truth. But it was the only course left to the government.

This brief account affords a certain understanding of the total context in which labor conflicts are settled and the role that various forces play. It is evident that, unlike the situation in the United States, where conflicts are partial and power dispersed, a major Peruvian labor issue involves virtually the entire society. For this reason the role of the government is a particularly delicate one. It must skillfully balance the considerations of fairness and stability in the short run with the conflicting long-range needs of economic development. And regardless of the course selected, the government will be mercilessly attacked by opposition forces.

13

THE FUTURE OF INDUSTRIAL STRIFE IN PERU

What is likely to be the future pattern of labor relations in Peru? In spite of certain hopes voiced in favor of collective bargaining, it seems doubtful that this system will be adopted. Only if the executive should achieve sufficient security to be able to refrain from intervening in labor disputes would collective bargaining be conceivable. But even then it would not be practicable for the workers. Because worker organizations cannot make successful use of the economic strike, collective bargaining would be a long hard winter for the labor movement. It would have to be imposed on the worker organizations for they would not willingly consent to it in practice.

The probable direction of evolution, assuming a free environment, seems to be the institutionalization of the existing system of political bargaining. The executive would continue to intervene in labor disputes and the power of worker organizations would remain in their threat to the security of the executive. But the change that can be expected is a substantial diminution of strife, or open warfare.[1] This expectation seems well-grounded

1. Throughout this chapter the term "strife" refers to actions which include a substantial element of waste or destruction: strikes, violent demonstrations, and destruction of property. The term "conflict" is used only to mean "disagreement." Conflict, then, is an unavoidable feature of any system, industrial or interpersonal, while strife is only one basis of conflict resolution and may be avoided.

in the experience of other countries. Students of industrial relations have recently devoted considerable attention to the problem of strife—particularly in the form of the strike.[2] The first
conclusion which has emerged from their studies is that there is
a long-term tendency for strike activity to diminish in industrializ-
ing countries.

Careful analysis has revealed that the reduction of strife cannot be attributed simply to the rise in the standard of living
and growing contentment of the workers. There appear to be
many institutional variables which determine the incidence of
industrial strife. In their work, *Changing Patterns of Industrial
Conflict*, Ross and Hartman have suggested ten institutional variables which they believe influence strike activity, variables that
may be applied to different countries in a comparative fashion.[3]
In this chapter we shall elaborate on their findings by discussing
some of the institutional factors that would affect the probable
future reduction of industrial strife in Peru. The findings of
this study point to three variables of critical importance in determining the amount of strife which accompanies the resolution
of labor conflicts:

1. The degree of cohesion and centralization of worker
   organizations.
2. The degree of specialization of worker organizations.
3. The condition of channels of access and communications
   between the workers, management, and government.

Each of these variables may be examined in the form of
generalized hypotheses.

1. *When worker organization structure is centralized and co-*

2. See Arthur M. Ross and Paul T. Hartman, *Changing Patterns of Industrial Conflict* (New York, Wiley, 1960); K. G. J. C. Knowles, *Strikes: A
Study in Industrial Conflict* (Oxford, B. Blackwell, 1952); Arthur M. Ross
and Donald Irwin, "Strike Experiences in Five Countries, 1927–1947," *Industrial and Labor Relations Review*, 4, (1951), 323–42; Arthur M. Ross,
"The Prospects for Industrial Conflict," *Industrial Relations*, 1, (October
1961), 57–74.
3. Ross and Hartman, pp. 63–64.

256 POLITICAL BARGAINING IN PERSPECTIVE

hesive, strife is less probable. As already shown, power in the
Peruvian labor movement is dispersed. While most of the small,
concentrated unions are relatively cohesive, the industrial and
regional federations to which they belong are not. While a few
dispersed unions are cohesive and centralized (the National
Union of Bank Clerks, for example), in most of these organizations power is dispersed as well. The low cohesion and decentralization can be identified as one cause of excessive strife, first, because they are conditions that contribute to the uncertainty of
decision-making. And uncertainty is itself a cause of strife. A
brief analysis of the elements of conflict resolution will show why
this is so. The contending parties in a conflict situation are dis-
puting a value desired by each. In order to win the disputed
value, each party must make sacrifices. A strike, for example, entails sacrifices for employees, employers and the government. The
only reason why rational participants endure these sacrifices is
because they judge that possession of the disputed value out-
weighs the sacrifices made in winning it. No rational party in
a conflict situation will struggle—that is, take actions which entail sacrifices—if it knows that it will be unsuccessful. When
defeat is certain one does not fight, for there would be no compensation for the sacrifices made in fighting. It follows, then,
that the only time strife will accompany the resolution of conflict (if the parties act rationally) is when one or more parties
are uncertain about the outcome. If the outcome is a foregone
conclusion then strife is an unnecessary waste for the losing
party.[4]

The outcome of a conflict will be determined, if strife is em-

4. The analysis being presented here is best applied to specialized "bread
and butter" issues. When the disputed values are of a more general, long-
term nature, uncertainty is practically impossible to overcome. If the issue
is, for example, the destruction of capitalism, it is unlikely that either side
would be convinced of defeat. Because the outcome is uncertain, extremists
continue to struggle in the expectation that one day they will be successful
and "capitalists," convinced that they will win, find the sacrifices of strife
well worth their expected victory. The effect of nonspecialized worker organization activity is discussed under the second hypothesis presented in this
chapter.

ployed to resolve the issue, by the actions each party takes and the effect of these actions on the power distribution. It must be kept in mind, however, that power itself cannot be estimated until it is known what actions the parties will take, that is, what sacrifices they are willing to make to win the particular value in dispute. There are, then, three variables which must be known for each party before the outcome of a particular conflict may be predicted: (1) the worth of the disputed value to each party in terms of (2) the sacrifices each party might make to win possession of the value; (3) the effect of these sacrifices (actions) on the relative power positions. If all parties know these variables for themselves and for the other parties, then strife becomes unnecessary. Instead of actually using weapons of coercion, the parties may resolve the conflict on the basis of the predicted outcome. If the outcome is uncertain, if the parties cannot predict, then a conflict must be resolved on the basis of an actual struggle.

Uncertainty will characterize situations of industrial conflict when worker organizations are noncohesive and decentralized. The worth of the disputed value to the workers cannot be known if the rank and file are broken up into many autonomous units, each with a different evaluation of the respective values and sacrifices. One group may feel that an issue merits an indefinite strike while another sector judges that a strike is not worth a successful outcome. With the workers broken down into separate opinion groups which act independently, no one will know how powerful the workers might be when they go into battle.

Strikes threatened by officers may not materialize. A demonstration called by one organization may be unbelievably successful or a complete failure. Once underway a strike may collapse in spite of the urgings of some officers. A solidarity strike may not take place at all or it might be more extensive than labor leaders hoped. Given a decentralized, noncohesive worker organization structure the participants, including the workers themselves, cannot know who will do what, when.

In such an atmosphere of uncertainty the parties are constantly guessing and hoping instead of adjusting their differences on the basis of an established power relationship and secure threats. Because the employers and the executive are uncertain about the intentions and capabilities of the workers they must experiment, they must say in effect, "We don't believe it. We dare you." The labor leaders themselves seldom know the fidelity of the membership on each issue and are tempted to overestimate their power. The peaceable allocation of values on the basis of what would have been the result if battle took place is not possible when uncertainty prevails. Consequently strife remains the only alternative.

Second, the decentralized structure makes peaceable conflict resolution difficult by forcing worker organizations into rigid timing patterns. Time is extremely precious to Peruvian leaders presenting a demand, since it takes many weeks to build up rank and file sentiment for a strike. Once threatened, a strike is difficult to postpone; once called off, a strike cannot be repeated easily. In a very real sense a strike in Peru is a work of art. Rather than being the businesslike decision of a centralized executive, a strike is frequently a unique creation of circumstance and emotion. Virtually all of the processes of peaceable conflict resolution require flexible timing on the part of the worker organizations: people must be persuaded, facts collected, loopholes plugged, and bargains arranged. In their present decentralized condition many Peruvian worker organizations must fight when the fighting is good—even when success is possible, but not certain, though nonviolent channels.

Ross and Hartman have dealt with the general question of decentralization in connection with factional struggles and unstable membership, two of their variables.[5] When labor leaders are contending for control of the organization or for new members, they argue, militancy is increased. This competition is certainly one feature of excessive strike activity in Peru where moderates and extremists are continually contending for control of the labor movement.

5. Ross and Hartman, pp. 63–64.

Lastly, centralization enables conflicts to be handled by skilled and experienced bargainers, men who are detached from the immediate disputes and who view the conflict in a larger perspective.[6] In general the leaders of the unions will be deeply involved in disputes at their plant. Frequently they feel that their prestige as officers and their worth as human beings depend on toughness. The local owners and managers also tend to be impetuous and shortsighted. Because of these personal shortcomings at the union level, conflict is often compounded unnecessarily and strife breaks out at the slightest provocation. If the bargaining pattern is centralized so that industry leaders deal with federation officials who speak for and control the member unions, particular issues of conflict can be bargained with detachment. In working out industry-wide agreements, these higher officials can devise solutions tailored to the complexities of the particular industry. And, of course, if the bargaining units were expanded to the industry level the simple number of strikes and incidents of strife would be reduced. Today in Peru bargaining is done, with few exceptions, at the union–plant level. At each of these hundreds of points a strike may break out and precipitate solidarity strikes of parent federations.

The Federation of Textile Workers serves as an example of how strife can be reduced through a cohesive, centralized structure. The federation is one of the few secondary labor organizations (affiliating unions) in Peru which has a credible strike threat. When the leaders announce that a strike will materialize both ownership and the executive believe them. As a consequence, although the federation is constantly embroiled in the disputes of its member unions, in most cases these conflicts are settled before a federation strike. In the case of this federation the threat of a strike has become almost as coercive as the action itself.

The skilled federation officers have begun to usurp the function of union officers in bargaining. The bargaining unit is still the union, not the federation, but because the federation officers,

6. This point was similarly noted by Ross and Hartman, p. 68.

to a considerable degree, determine the strike policy, union leaders usually place their disputes in the hands of these officers. Detached from the specific conflicts and viewing the needs of the federation as a whole, the officers can frequently arrange peaceful settlements where lesser leaders could not.

Their most useful asset is a specific strike which can be postponed or executed as the leaders see fit. The integrated structure of the federation makes it possible for decisions to be taken rapidly and the cohesion of the organization insures the implementation of these decisions. The assembly of delegates still makes the final decisions but more and more the officers of the federation are shaping these decisions beforehand. It seems probable that in the near future the Federation of Textile Workers will be bargaining for the entire industry. Such industry-wide bargaining would resemble collective bargaining in the United States even to the point that the strike would have an element of coercion upon ownership—as it does, to a limited extent, today. But the threat of executive intervention will continue to be the salient variable affecting the distribution of power.[7]

2. *The specialization of worker organization objectives, by reducing the area of conflict, reduces strife.* A specialized objective, as the phrase is employed here, is one which directly concerns the membership of the organization. An example might be the demands of a particular organization for better wages, hours, and working conditions for its members. The opposite, a nonspecialized objective, is a goal which affects primarily other groups, including other workers. A nonspecialized demand would be one dealing with, for example, race relations or foreign policy.

Specialization of objectives is, of course, a relative concept. American worker organizations, which are perhaps the most specialized in the world, frequently voice demands which are of

7. It has been suggested that excessive centralization and bureaucratization of trade union structure may be in itself a cause of strife as workers come to resent their leaders. See Knowles, *Strikes*, pp. 28 ff. Even when true, however, this point does not contradict our hypothesis since resentments and feuds in fact signify actual decentralization regardless of the formal structure of the organization.

little direct consequence to their membership. But in practice these extra-membership positions are of secondary importance, seldom being considered significant enough to merit extensive, active support. It would be difficult to imagine an American labor organization calling a strike in favor of aid to Yugoslavia or recognition of Communist China. In Peru, however, worker organizations take positions on a wide range of issues, frequently backing up their stand with strikes or demonstrations. Nonspecialized activity in the Peruvian labor movement generally takes the form of subservience to a political party. The leaders of worker organizations are usually members of a party and espouse its partisan world view. They may urge that the organization they lead support the position of their political party. The result is that, in addition to the strife which takes place over specialized objectives, Peruvian worker organizations precipitate strife over many issues external to their membership.

Specialization of objectives seems to be the point which Ross and Hartman had in mind when they made "strength of Communism in labor unions" a factor determining the relative frequency of strikes.[8] They also noted that the behavior of the Communists would reflect party strategy. In applying their generalization to Peru it should be added that all parties, not just the Communists, are interested in strike activity and that the strategy of any opposition party, including the Communists, certainly does include militant strike activity.

One must not be too hasty in condemning nonspecialized activity. One could take the view that such behavior is unselfish, that worker organizations ought to be concerned with other groups and other societies regardless of the consequences to public order. Also the power of the worker organizations in Peru depends on certain types of nonspecialized behavior. The solidarity strike, for example, is not a specialized act, unless one considers the eventual reciprocity involved. Nevertheless, as has been seen, it enhances the power of the workers in many cases.

It seems, however, that the tendency in Peru is toward more

8. Ross and Hartman, p. 63.

specialized worker organizations. The defense of unions by solidarity strikes of parent federations will continue to be important but the haphazard one-day protest strikes, as well as longer stoppages in support of distant causes, will become less frequent. The reason for this shift lies in rank and file attitudes. Whether for good or evil, most Peruvian workers today are self-centered. They resent losing pay through strikes which bring no benefit to them. They also resent, when they are aware of it, being used as tools for a political party. This attitude, as mentioned earlier, has resulted in a tendency toward the elimination of labor leaders who urge action on nonmember issues (see Chapter 10).

  3. *Highly developed channels of communication serve to reduce strife.* If negotiation is to replace strife in the resolution of conflict, worker organizations must have channels through which to negotiate. The logic of bargaining on the basis of threats instead of actual strife demands that these threats be adequately communicated. If labor leaders cannot be heard and dealt with within the institutional framework, then they tend to seek expression outside established processes. Ross and Hartman alluded to channels of communication ("dispute-settlement policies and procedures") but did not discuss the point in detail.[9] It does seem, however, that communication itself is an important variable in determining strike activity—a variable which might be taken for granted in a well-developed industrial relations system.

  There are two aspects to the problem of access and communication. The first deals with the formal mechanisms. As a reflection of their power, worker organizations in Peru have today gained formal access to decision-makers. When a labor leader is presenting a demand both management and the executive will hear his case. Even in the provinces there are 22 regional offices of the Ministry of Labor to which local labor leaders may carry their complaints and conflicts. In the 1956–62 Congress workers had sufficient access to lobby successfully for two important pieces of legislation. Although worker representa-

9. Ibid., p. 64.

tion in that Congress was perhaps inadequate in view of the number of workers, it seems almost certain that future, freely elected legislatures will be more worker-oriented. Formal worker access to the centers of power is a relatively recent phenomenon. It was not until 1949 that the Ministry of Labor was created. In only the past 15 or 20 years management has generally recognized that worker organizations must be considered realities. In the past, an owner would pretend that a union of workers did not exist, taking instant reprisal against an "insubordinate" individual (union officer) who walked into his office with a demand. Leopoldo Pita, an old-time leader of the Federation of Sugar Workers, recollects a novel method which a union of sugar workers once employed to avoid the reprisal that would have been taken against the man who presented a wage demand. A long pole was procured and the demand tacked on one end. Then all of the officers of the union, each holding on to the pole, marched into the manager's office and pushed the slip of paper at him. Thus no individual leader could be singled out for reprisals.[10] Today most sugar plantations have a department of industrial relations with a staff of three or four men who meet continuously with union leaders.

The second aspect of communication concerns the ability of leadership to use available mechanisms for access. Because processes of institutional decision-making are complex, labor leaders are frequently unable to participate because they lack the necessary experience. Hence, although formal channels of access exist, leaders may be prevented by personal shortcomings from using them. For example, the Arequipa Union of Trolley Operators had been demanding for several years that the company agree to provide pensions for retired workers—a demand which the company rejected. Fortunately, in 1960, this problem was taken up in Lima by a skilled and tenacious leader of the Lima Union of Trolley Operators, Victor Zárate. After working for many months with officials in the Ministry of Finance, Zárate ob-

10. Interview with Leopolda Pita, past secretary-general of the Federation of Sugar Workers, Lima, September 27, 1961.

tained ministerial implementation of an existing law which required all companies with a capital of more than 500,000 sols to provide pensions for their workers.[11] If Zárate had not intervened to obtain implementation of an existing law, the Arequipa organization might have resorted to a strike.

A partial view of the state of the Peruvian industrial relations system can be had by studying the information on strikes presented in Tables 23 to 27. Although the classifications employed

TABLE 23

Strikes in Peru in 1960, by Cause

Cause of strike	Number	Proportion
Failure to comply with norms and contracts	79	28%
Poor worker–management relations	64	22%
Solidarity·with other organizations	46	16%
Wage demands	45	16%
Discharge of workers	43	15%
Miscellaneous	8	3%
TOTAL	285	100%

Source: Ministerio de Trabajo y Asuntos Indígenas, *Estadísticas de Trabajo*, Bulletin for the first quarter (Lima, 1961).

in Table 23 are somewhat imprecise, comparison of this table with Table 24 points up a difference between the American and Peruvian systems. In the United States industrial strife centers on sharply defined, pragmatic demands. In Peru, because of the deficiencies just discussed, strife takes place over poorly defined or spurious issues.

This difference is shown clearly by the fact that in Peru wage demands accounted for only 16 per cent of the total number of strikes in 1960. In the United States, wages, hours and supplementary benefits were the stated causes of 47.8 per cent of the

11. Interview with Victor Zárate, secretary of social security of the CTP and past officer of the Lima Union of Trolley Operators, September 28, 1961.

TABLE 24

Strikes in the United States in 1960, by Cause

Cause of strike	Per cent of all strikes
Wages, hours and supplementary benefits	47.8%
Job security	10.8%
Shop conditions	11.4%
Jurisdiction	7.4%
Union organization (recognition and security)	7.2%
Sympathy	1.0%
Other causes	14.4%
TOTAL	100.0% (3,333 strikes)

Source: United States Department of Labor, *Analysis of Work Stoppages 1960* (Washington, 1961), p. 9.

total number of strikes in 1960 (see Table 24). The solidarity strike, which in the United States was the cause of only 1 per cent of the strikes, was the reason for 16 per cent of the strikes in Peru. This difference is a reflection of two facts. First, members of extremist parties in the worker organizations make a conscious effort to compound conflict by effecting solidarity strikes of the organizations they control. Secondly, the solidarity strike is, in the Peruvian context of government intervention in labor conflicts, a successful and hence frequently used tactic.

Table 25 shows that the number of strikes in each year of the 1957–61 period increased steadily. Tables 26 and 27 present a comparative view of the duration of strikes in Peru and the United States, respectively. They show another dimension of the contrast between Peruvian and American patterns of labor

TABLE 25

Total Number of Strikes in Each Year, 1957–1961

	1957	1958	1959	1960	1961
Number of Strikes	161	213	233	285	339*

* Includes estimates for November and December.

TABLE 26

Duration of Strikes, in Peru, 1957–1958

Strike duration	Number	Proportion
One hour to one day	98	46%
Two days to three days	53	25%
Four days to ten days	37	18%
Eleven days or more	24	11%
TOTALS	212	100%

Source for Tables 25 and 26: Ministerio de Trabajo y Asuntos Indígenas, *Estadísticas de Trabajo* (Lima, 1959, 1960, 1961).

TABLE 27

Duration of Strikes in the United States in 1960

Length of strike	Per cent
One day	12.3%
Two days to less than four days	15.4%
Four to seven days	14.0%
7 to 15 days	21.3%
15 to 30 days	15.4%
30 to 60 days	11.8%
60 to 90 days	3.9%
Over 90 days	6.0%

Source: United States Department of Labor, *Analysis of Work Stoppages 1960* (Washington, 1961), p. 22.

relations. In Peru strikes are much shorter than in the United States. This difference is partly a result of the faulty communications network in the Peruvian system. It frequently happens that a partial strike erupts before anyone—management, government, or even union leaders—knows about it. But the difference in strike length is also a reflection of the differences in bargaining systems. Collective bargaining as practiced in the United States requires that the union coerce the firm by withholding the labor supply. The effects of a shutdown upon the employer are usually feeble until inventories have been depleted and new orders pile up. In the Peruvian pattern of political bargaining, the executive is coerced by popular agitation that begins immediately with a strike and quickly builds to a climax. For this reason a strike of over 30 days in Peru is extremely rare; as seen in Table 27, more than one quarter of the strikes in the United States lasted over 30 days.

Unfortunately, the Ministry of Labor has not collected statistics on the proportion of the working force involved in strikes. Since the labor force appears to have been growing at the rate of only about five per cent per year,[12] there is little doubt that the employee involvement ratio increased during this period. However, our expectation, based on the foregoing analysis, is that a turning point will be reached in the not too distant future after which strike activity should diminish.

12. The employment index compiled by the Ministry of Labor showed a 4.44 per cent increase in employment in the Lima area 1960–61. *Estadísticas de Trabajo* (Lima, bulletin for the second trimester, 1961), p. 4.

14

DEMOCRACY BY VIOLENCE

This study has presented the system of political bargaining and has explored its implications for the Peruvian labor movement. The first chapter treated trade union methods as dependent variables and suggested the independent variables which led the workers to select political bargaining as their major strategy. At the same time an attempt was made to show why other methods, namely legal enactment and collective bargaining, were largely rejected.

It was suggested that legal enactment was relatively ineffectual because (1) the chaotic, nonrepresentative condition of the electoral system prevented workers from using their votes in a concerted, meaningful fashion, and (2) the administration was unable to implement, autonomously, many of the laws that were passed or might be passed. In the case of collective bargaining, the depressed state of the labor market was seen as the fundamental variable discouraging the use of this method.

We concluded that political bargaining had been selected because, relative to other methods, it was most effective. The basic variable which determined the efficacy of this strategy was the insecurity of the president of a free regime in the face of civilian violence. This insecurity was traced back to other variables—the nature of political conflict and the role of the military—and then some underlying structural factors which contributed to the basic relationships involved were discussed. The connections between the variables are shown in Figure 12.

Once political bargaining was established as the product of these environmental factors, the analysis in the following chapters shifted to the labor movement itself. The trade union method was treated as the independent variable and the various features —political party relations, structure, finances, etc.—as dependent variables. As much as possible, these features were analyzed

FIGURE 12.

Schematic Representation of the Principal Variables in the Political Bargaining System

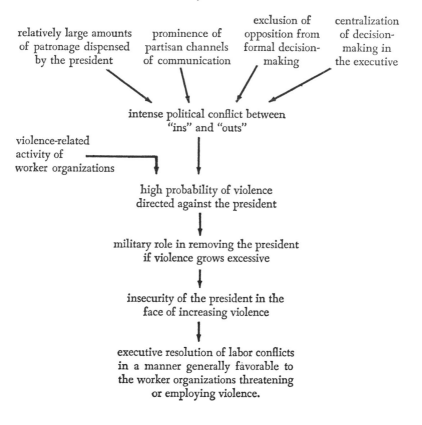

in their relationship to the bargaining pattern employed by the worker organizations.

In addition to being a trade union method, however, political bargaining represents at the same time a system of political interaction. In the following pages this pattern will be discussed from the perspective of the political scientist, making explicit some of the implications of our findings. Nothing said, however, should be taken to mean that political bargaining is considered the only pattern of decision-making in Peru. Other arenas, such as the electoral process, Congress, the courts, and lower administration, should not be disregarded if one seeks a complete picture of the political system. Political bargaining is designated as an important, even dominant, pattern, but not one which operates to the exclusion of all others.

In its broad outlines political bargaining has much in common with constitutional democracy as it is practiced in the United States. In both patterns the decision maker is responsive to citizens because they may threaten his tenure of office if they are dissatisfied with his policies. But the mechanisms whereby this responsiveness is achieved are quite different in the two systems. In a constitutional democracy the officeholder is made insecure through elections. He is prompted to respond to citizen demands because otherwise, he fears, votes will be mobilized against him.[1] In political bargaining it is the possibility of military intervention that the executive fears. And it is civilian violence which tends to provoke a coup against the incumbent president. Consequently the president seeks to reduce the probabilities of extensive civilian violence by satisfying the demands citizens make upon him. These two analogous patterns are diagramed in Figure 13.

In Peru, then, there exists an interesting reversal of the proverbial exchange of bullets for ballots. But the product of this

1. We are, of course, tracing only the broad outlines of the constitutional-democratic model. A full description of reality would require that this model be greatly elaborated and qualified. For an extensive development of the basic propositions given here see Anthony Downs, *An Economic Theory of Democracy* (New York, Harper, 1957).

FIGURE 13.

Political Bargaining and Constitutional Democracy: Basic Decision-making
Mechanisms

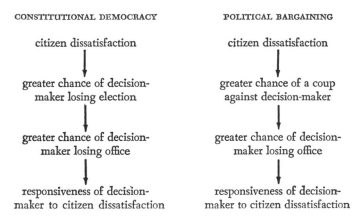

CONSTITUTIONAL DEMOCRACY	POLITICAL BARGAINING
citizen dissatisfaction	citizen dissatisfaction
greater chance of decision-maker losing election	greater chance of a coup against decision-maker
greater chance of decision-maker losing office	greater chance of decision-maker losing office
responsiveness of decision-maker to citizen dissatisfaction	responsiveness of decision-maker to citizen dissatisfaction

exchange is not the chaotic open warfare usually envisaged by
democratic theorists. The Peruvian pattern of political bargaining
is an intelligible system, a kind of "democracy by violence."
This possibility has been overlooked by many theorists who appear to see no middle ground between a peaceful constitutional
democracy and anarchy. The tendency has been to treat patterns
of violent interaction as "chaotic" (and therefore beyond analysis) or as the foreshadowing of a "revolution." Many scholars
have equated, usually implicitly, the persistent use of violence
with "the breakdown of the system." This view betrays an
undesirable element of ethnocentrism. As we have attempted
to show in the case of Peru, the persistent use of violence *is* the
system, or at least a very large part of it.

As one might expect, the general model given above for this
pattern of "democracy by violence" is not found in reality without imperfections. We have seen that organization is an important requisite for successful activity and that there are barriers of size and cohesion which must be overcome for effective
action. Also regional location (in Lima rather than in the provinces) and the disposition to employ violence (blue-collar work-

ers compared with white-collar workers, for example) affect outcomes. Hence, power is not evenly distributed. But similar imperfections are found in the distribution of power in a constitutional democracy: organization size and cohesion; disposition and ability of certain groups to turn out and vote; regional location. These factors greatly influence the outcomes of decisions in a constitutional democracy.

Of course, whether one wishes to call the Peruvian pattern a genuine "democracy" will depend upon the definition he selects for that word. We are not concerned with this semantic problem here. By employing the phrase "democracy by violence" we merely indicate that certain basic features usually associated with democracy are found in the Peruvian system of political bargaining. That the democratic norms of limited tenure of office and responsiveness of the officeholder to citizen demands should be achieved by the mechanisms of civilian violence and military intervention (two very "undemocratic" acts) poses an interesting problem for the political theorist.

Oligarchy

The suggestion that, on issues of political bargaining, large numbers of citizens have a voice in decision-making, goes against the popular notion that Peru is controlled by a small oligarchy. The exact nature and extent of the power of this group is never stated clearly, but most of the vague references to the "oligarchy" convey the impression of an extremely influential group. We are tempted to imagine, as one writer puts it, that (in Peru) "the politics have long been under the control of the landowning and commercial aristocracy, supported by officers of the army." [2]

One of the greatest difficulties encountered in dealing with the Peruvian oligarchy lies in determining who the oligarchs are. Although many writers—scholars and journalists alike—employ the word "oligarchy" without hesitation, an explicit operational

2. Preston E. James, *Latin America* (3d ed. New York, Odyssey Press, 1959), p. 202.

definition of this term is rarely found. The vagueness surrounding the concept has made it possible for writers to say anything they like about the oligarchy. As an undefined term it tends to be manipulated independently of any data. Follow, for example, these two somewhat contradictory conclusions about the oligarchy under Odría:

> Odría held power for eight years, during which the armed forces increased their customary lion's share of the national budget and the oligarchy was secure in its dominant economic position.[3]

> During most of his tenure in office, Odria had maintained a military dictatorship, cracking down on any and all dissidents. His regime handled certain elements of the oligarchy as cavalierly as it had treated the *apristas*.[4]

Was the oligarchy "secure" or was it "handled . . . cavalierly"? Unlike a scientific disagreement, this inconsistency cannot be resolved because neither writer provides an operational definition of oligarchy.

There are, of course, many possible definitions. One could employ income statistics, occupation, family background, or membership in social clubs. If it is suspected that 20, 40, or 60 families constitute an oligarchy, then a list of the names of these families or their distinguishing characteristics must be provided. It might be argued that some writers have employed the word "oligarchy" to refer to "upper classes" and have not meant to imply anything about political power. But oligarchy is a political term. It refers specifically to the rule of the few. Consequently, the search for an oligarchy is a search for a group that wields the preponderance of political power.

Once the proposed oligarchy has been identified there re-

3. Edwin Lieuwin, *Arms and Politics in Latin America* (rev. ed. New York, Frederick A. Praeger, 1961), p. 82.

4. Robert J. Alexander, "The Army in Politics" in Harold E. Davis, ed., *Government and Politics in Latin America* (New York, The Ronald Press, 1958), p. 159.

mains the more formidable problem: does this group rule? In order to be considered an oligarchy a group must be highly influential, controlling the outcomes of practically all important decisions. The methodological problems involved in determining the existence of an oligarchy or power elite which runs politics are impressive. The many logical and empirical problems which face the analyst cannot be dealt with here.[5] At a minimum, however, it appears that in order to test for the existence of an oligarchy we must know the answers to the following questions:

1. Who are the proposed oligarchs? How will they be identified?
2. Where are they influential? What issue-areas or key decisions are they supposed to control?
3. What is the position of this group on the specific subject under study *before* the matter is decided? If the proposed oligarchy is found to be divided or if many other groups support the same position taken by the proposed oligarchy, then the investigator faces serious problems in determining the power of this group.
4. What was the outcome of the particular decision, or collections of decisions studied? Did the proposed oligarchy win?

5. For an excellent discussion of the methodological problems involved in determining power distribution in political systems see Nelson W. Polsby, *Community Power and Political Theory* (New Haven, Yale University Press, 1963). See also John C. Harsanyi, "Measurement of Social Power, Opportunity Costs and the Theory of Two-Person Bargaining Games," *Behavioral Science*, 7 (1962), 67–80; Raymond E. Wolfinger, "Reputation and Reality in the Study of 'Community Power'," *American Sociological Review*, 25 (1960), 636–44; Peter H. Rossi, "Community Decision Making," *Administrative Science Quarterly*, 1 (1957), 415–43; Herbert Kaufman and Victor Jones, "The Mystery of Power," *Public Administration Review*, 14 (1954), 205–12; Daniel Bell, "The Power Elite—Reconsidered," *The American Journal of Sociology*, 64 (1958), 238–50; Talcott Parsons, "The Distribution of Power in American Society," *World Politics*, 10 (1957), 123–43; Nelson W. Polsby, "Three Problems in the Analysis of Community Power," *American Sociological Review*, 24 (1959), 795–803; Peter Bachrach and Morton S. Baratz, "Two Faces of Power," *American Political Science Review*, 56 (1962), 947–52. Also see next footnote.

5. What did the proposed oligarchy do to influence the outcome? What resources did it have at its disposal and which were employed? [6]

The data contained in this study make it possible to examine one possible oligarchy theory. Although other conceptions are available, the following definition seems to be one of the more credible alternatives.

1. The proposed oligarchy will be defined as the group of employers and top management personnel. This is a large group, to be sure, but easily identified and usually united on the issues to be considered. To restrict the definition to a smaller subgroup —large employers, for example—would obscure the fact that such a group is usually supported by many other individuals. In any case, it seems obvious that if this group as a whole does not prevail in the issue-area studied, then subgroups within it cannot be said to rule.

2. Expressed union–employer conflicts will be considered as our area of concern. This issue-area is important on two criteria: (A) the number of affected individuals is very large; (B) the outcomes are seen as highly significant by the participants.

3. We find that usually employers are united against the unions, opposing their specific demands on wages and working conditions. The employer position is ascertained from newspaper statements, from paid advertisements by the employers or their ownership federations, and from personal interviews with employers and their representatives.

4. The outcomes of these union–employer conflicts are by no means consistently favorable to employers. Many times (most of the time, in fact) the unions obtained far more than the

6. This list has been constructed from analyses and research proposals offered by the following writers: Robert A. Dahl, *Who Governs?* (New Haven, Yale University Press, 1961); Dahl, "A Critique of the Ruling Elite Model," *American Political Science Review*, 52 (1958), 463–69; Dahl, "The Concept of Power," *Behavioral Science*, 2 (1957), 201–15; Nelson W. Polsby, "How to Study Community Power: The Pluralist Alternative," *The Journal of Politics*, 22 (1960), 474–84.

employers wished to grant. One cannot say that employers were powerless, for sometimes the unions were clearly defeated. Also, the workers seldom obtained all of what they wanted. But the conclusion that employers always win or usually win these disputes is clearly untenable in the light of the data presented in this study.

5. An explanation of the outcomes of these conflicts must rest on an analysis of the resources available to and employed by each side. Employers have greater social standing and a superior cultural background which enables them to communicate more effectively with government officials. They are much more likely to be personal acquaintances of the Minister of Labor. They tend to be allied with consumers and taxpayers. They may present themselves as fundamental instruments of economic development. They may command publicity. They have money. But often these resources are not fully employed. Many employers may not be greatly concerned with a particular conflict and will remain inactive. Sometimes their arguments are weak or obviously false. Publicity may be denied by some newspapers (*La Tribuna,* for example).

The workers have resources on their side too. They may get free publicity from certain newspapers and from sympathetic congressmen. They may present themselves as underdogs, oppressed and miserable, and therefore worthy of special consideration. In addition to these weapons, the unions have a key resource not available to employers: violence. When this resource is properly mobilized it tends to outweigh any that employers might bring to bear. Arguments about inflation, invoking friendships, and perhaps even bribes would not prevent a substantial union victory when the executive is threatened by violence. Even the lowly agricultural laborers, when they are properly mobilized, win substantial gains using this resource. The ability to employ violence is the trump card in the Peruvian system of political bargaining and it is a card employers do not hold. It is this distribution of resources which explains why the business group does not regularly win conflicts with worker organizations.

Only one of the many possible definitions of oligarchy has been treated above. Given this conception, we conclude that there is no oligarchy in Peru. The group of employers and their immediate representatives, while exercising a modest degree of power in most union–employer conflicts, are by no means dominant. Moreover, since one major issue-area where lower-class groups have a significant impact upon decision-making has been identified, the idea that this oligarchy controls *all* political decisions must also be rejected.

Of course, anyone is free to propose alternative conceptions of oligarchy and different subject matters over which it is supposed to rule. But until systematic presentations exist, it would seem wise to avoid using "oligarchy" or similar "power elite" concepts. To a large extent the use of such terms has been a substitute for analysis. Politics, instead of being viewed as the product of complex patterns of interaction, is all too often dismissed as a struggle between the "oligarchy" and the "reformers." It is time that this caricature of Peruvian politics is consciously discarded.

The Structure of Decision-Making

The term oligarchy, then, would seem to be inapplicable to the issue-areas dealt with under political bargaining. Even if one proposes as oligarchs the large group of employers and their immediate managers (a somewhat unwieldy oligarchy, to be sure) it appears that this group does not win most of the conflicts. Nevertheless, it is on precisely the issues of political bargaining that Peruvians speak of the oligarchy most frequently. In the newspapers, at the rally or meeting, "oligarchy" is widely used. When Peruvians speak of the oligarchy they do not have in mind the modest conception suggested above. They see a very small group of nasty, selfish individuals who seem bent upon increasing the misery of the people. The self-interest of the oligarchy (which is allegedly followed with terrifying persistence) is held to be incompatible with everything good, including progress, happiness, and justice.

Everyone is against the oligarchy—even those who are supposed to be oligarchs. Luís Miró Quesada, for example, the publisher of *El Comercio*, often accused of being an oligarch, was a most vocal enemy of the oligarchy in the columns of his newspaper. It is perhaps understandable, therefore, that writers should have come to employ the term. How, they apparently reasoned, could millions of Peruvians be deceived? There is, perhaps, an explanation for the widespread use of the term, especially on issues of political bargaining. The explanation lies not in an actual description of the power structure but in the pattern of decision-making and the political phraseology appropriate to it.

In the United States the government is an arena of decision-making. The many diverse groups enter this arena and attempt to extract a favorable result. In Congress, regulatory commissions, the Supreme Court, or branches of the administration, various groups are seen battling each other: employers and workers, integrationists and segregationists, exporters and local industries, urban and rural groups, to name a few. The fragmented nature of the decision-making process provides a multiplicity of points of access so that virtually all groups and their representatives interact *within* the government.

In this inclusive structure of decision-making the diverse competing groups tend to confront their opposition directly. They are not encouraged to speak of an oligarchy because they (and their audience) perceive the size and diversity of the group or groups in opposition. Participants, naturally, seek to employ a political phraseology which is credible given this decision-making structure. They appeal to a higher standard to justify their demands: "the national interest"; "the national defense"; "constitutional rights." Opposing groups are labeled "selfish interests" or "lobbyists." Whenever possible an attempt is made to show that opponents are seeking "unconstitutional" objectives.

With political bargaining one does not find a symmetrical decision-making pattern where all groups confront each other within the structure of government. Instead the government is seen actively protecting one side and being assaulted by the other. The government's position of partisanship is a direct consequence of the extreme centralization of the system. The executive plays such a preponderant role in decision-making that he tends to *be* the government. As a single individual, the president can seldom present himself as a neutral participant. If violence occurs it is his job to react against it. In so doing he automatically allies himself with those groups that oppose or might oppose the demands of the attackers.

Thus the government protects those groups which are unable to employ violence on a particular issue. Usually these groups include employers, consumers, and taxpayers. The assaulting groups are usually workers or students. Professionals (doctors, lawyers) may be found on either side, depending on the issue. Sometimes consumers, represented by worker organizations, are on the assaulting side while retailers and some workers are being protected. The government, insofar as it repels the assaulting groups and resists their full demands, is a partisan. Consequently the attacking side does not confront its real opposition directly; instead it confronts the government.

The phraseology adopted by the participants reflects this arrangement. The attacking groups see the government as an opponent standing in the way of their demands. Their battle-cry is that the government (or more accurately, the executive) is protecting the "oligarchy." In this way they may justify their use of violence against the government itself. Also, by calling the protected groups the "oligarchy," the attackers further obscure the already unclear dimensions of their opposition. They obscure the fact that the groups defended by the executive may be large—often larger than they are. A widely-based attack on the government requires a strong rationale. If the government can be accused of defending the indefensible, of defending a monster-like oligarchy, broad support is more easily enlisted.

The opponents of the attackers, particularly the government officials themselves, attempt to undermine the assault by obscuring the real nature of the opposition forces on the issue. They accuse the assaulting groups of being "communists" or of being inspired by "agitators." Although there is often an element of truth in these charges, the fact remains that real citizen demands are imbedded in nearly all attacks. By labeling the assault as merely the work of agitators (and therefore devoid of real demands), the executive hopes to cut the attacking group away from possible allies.

The use of the terms "oligarchy" and "communist agitators" should therefore be interpreted in the light of the structure of decision-making. The observer will learn little about the existence of an oligarchy or the activities of the communists by listening to talk or reading newspapers. Both terms are political slogans, employed because they suit the needs of the participants.

The utility of viewing violence as a basic component of the Peruvian system of government has been demonstrated. The analyses of the mechanisms of leadership responsibility, of the power distribution, and of the decision-making structure were grounded in a descriptive model of political interaction. This model employed civilian violence and military intervention as central variables.

This study is not an attempt to explore political bargaining as applied to other countries. Our sole concern has been to unravel the elements of this pattern as it applied to the Peruvian labor movement. One does not need to look very deeply, however, to realize that the general pattern of political bargaining is an important system in many other Latin American countries. The literature on Latin American politics contains widespread awareness of the prominence of violence and military intervention. Explanations for this pattern abound, touching on a wide range of factors: Iberian or Latin personality,[7] economic underdevelopment and poverty,[8] illiteracy,[9] the weakness of the "middle sectors,"[10] the nature of the class system,[11] the "legitimacy vacuum,"[12] the lack of military "professionalism,"[13] and the role of the Catholic church.[14] This is by no means an exhaustive

7. See Lionel Cecil Jane, *Liberty and Despotism in Spanish America* (Oxford, The Clarendon Press, 1929). Jane spoke of a personality which contained the antithetical elements of "liberty" and "efficiency." Several writers have noted "Individualism," including Frederick B. Pike, "Sources of Revolution: Their Impact on Freedom and Reform in Latin America" in Pike, *Freedom and Reform in Latin America* (Notre Dame, University of Notre Dame Press, 1959), p. 43; W. Rex Crawford in "Pathology of Democracy in Latin America: A Symposium," W. Pierson, ed., *American Political Science Review*, 44 (1950), 145. See Arthur P. Whitaker, ibid., pp. 105–06 for a brief discussion of the theory of racial intermixing of Lucas Ayrragaray.

8. One of the earliest proponents of this view was James Bryce, *South America—Observations and Impressions* (New York, Macmillan, 1912), p. 546. See also Sanford A. Mosk, "Pathology . . . Symposium," pp. 129–42. Merle Kling points to economic development as operating through the mechanism of social mobility to produce violence in his article "Toward a Theory of Power and Political Instability in Latin America," *Western Political Quarterly*, 9 (1956), 21–35. For a discussion of the "rising expectations" theme see Karl M. Schmitt and David D. Burks, *Evolution or Chaos? Dynamics of Latin American Governments and Politics* (New York, Frederick A. Praeger, 1963), especially pp. 45, 241.

9. See, for example, Bryce, *South America—Observations and Impressions*, p. 546; and Russell H. Fitzgibbon, "Pathology . . . Symposium," p. 125.

10. John Johnson, *Political Change in Latin America* (Stanford, Stanford University Press, 1958), pp. 17–19, 92–93, 127, 179, 181.

11. See George I. Blanksten, *Ecuador: Constitutions and Caudillos* (Berkeley, University of California Press, 1951), especially pp. 169, 174; Blanksten, "Revolutions," in Davis, *Government and Politics in Latin America*, pp. 143, 145.

12. See Martin C. Needler, *Latin American Politics in Perspective* (Princeton, D. Van Nostrand, 1963), pp. 33–39. This same idea seems to be present in Kalman H. Silvert's discussion of "anti-nationalism" in "The Costs of Anti-Nationalism: Argentina" in Silvert, *Expectant Peoples* (New York, Random House, 1963), pp. 347–72. Fitzgibbon also speaks of the lack of "integration" in Latin American society: "Pathology . . . Symposium," pp. 120–22.

13. Lieuwin, *Arms and Politics in Latin America*, especially pp. 151–53.

14. Pike, *Freedom and Reform in Latin America*, p. 33.

list but it indicates the interest which scholars have in the problem.[15]

Several writers have suggested that military intervention ought to be treated as "normal," given the persistence of this pattern. Pike expresses this view:

> So much a permanent and integral part of Latin American politics is the revolution that to many it appears to be the only important political institution in the Southern Americas during nearly 150 years of independence.[16]

Silvert echos this position:

> If the normal way of rotating the executive in a given country is by revolution, and if there have been a hundred such changes in a century, then it is not being facetious to remark that revolutions are a sign of stability.[17]

In spite of the fact that violence is widely recognized as a prominent phenomenon, scholars have been reluctant to base their analyses upon it. The frequent use of terms such as "instability," "pathology," or "chaos" reveals a pervasive commitment to the American model of constitutional democracy. This bias has encouraged writers on Latin America to inject normative judgments into their discussions of behavior. As a result, we have a large body of opinion on the way people ought to act, but very little knowledge about why they behave as they do.

15. Specific discussions of violence in Latin American politics include William S. Stokes, "Violence as a Power Factor in Latin American Politics," *Western Political Quarterly,* 5 (1952), 445–68; Gino Germani and K. H. Silvert, "Politics, Social Structure and Military Intervention in Latin America," *European Journal of Sociology,* 2 (1961), 62–81; K. H. Silvert, *Reaction and Revolution in Latin America* (New Orleans, The Hauser Press, 1961), pp. 20–25; George I. Blanksten, "The Politics of Latin America" in Gabriel A. Almond and James S. Coleman, *The Politics of the Developing Areas* (Princeton, Princeton University Press, 1960), pp. 496–502; Russell H. Fitzgibbon, "Revolutions: Western Hemisphere," *The South Atlantic Quarterly,* 55 (1956), 263–79.

16. Pike, p. 28.

17. Silvert, *Reaction and Revolution,* p. 20.

Our argument, then, is for descriptive as opposed to normative models, for models that explain what does happen, not what ought to happen. This study attempts to construct such a model. There is no need to insist, however, that this construct must apply to all Latin American countries. Our particular conception of political bargaining was designed to explain one prominent pattern of interaction in Peru. It seems that many of the basic features of this system are duplicated in other Latin American countries, and that what has been said will be of some use in understanding political behavior elsewhere. Nevertheless, the wide diversity in political structures in Latin America leads to the belief that patterns of labor relations and political behavior vary considerably.[18] In dealing with any particular country, therefore, the investigator must be alert to this diversity and construct a model based on the reality which lies before him.

18. For accounts of some of these differences see Robert J. Alexander, *Labor Relations in Argentina, Brazil and Chile* (New York, McGraw-Hill, 1962); Charles A. Page, "Labor's Political Role in Latin America," *The Virginia Quarterly Review*, 28 (1952), 481–99.

INDEX

Italicized page numbers refer to tables and figures.